**Families in the Energy Crisis:
Impacts and Implications
for Theory and Policy**

Families in the Energy Crisis: Impacts and Implications for Theory and Policy

Robert Perlman
and
Roland L. Warren
Brandeis University

with the assistance of
Andrew B. Hahn and
Cecilia Rivera

Ballinger Publishing Company • Cambridge, Massachusetts
A Subsidiary of J.B. Lippincott Company

ST. PHILIPS COLLEGE LIBRARY

339.42
P451f

This book is printed on recycled paper.

Library of Congress Cataloging in Publication Data

Perlman, Robert and Roland L. Warren
  Families in the energy crisis.

  Includes bibliographical references.
  1. Cost and standard of living—United States. 2. Budgets, Personal. 3. Energy policy—United States. 4. Family—United States. I. Warren, Roland Leslie, 1915- joint author. II. Title.
HD6983.P47   339.4'2'0973   77-24314
ISBN 0-88410-068-5

Copyright © 1977 by Ballinger Publishing Company. All rights reserved. No part of this publication may be reproduced, stored in a retrieval system, or transmitted in any form or by any means, electronic mechanical photocopy, recording or otherwise, without the prior written consent of the publisher.

International Standard Book Number: 0-88410-068-5

Library of Congress Catalog Card Number: 77-24314

Printed in the United States of America

To all those who will bring about energy policies that are equitable effective, far-seeing and sensitive to other important human needs.

Contents

List of Figures	ix
List of Tables	xi
Acknowledgments	xv
Chapter One Introduction	1
Chapter Two An Analytical Model of Families and Crises	11
Chapter Three The Energy Crisis Unfolds in Hartford, Mobile, and Salem	41
Chapter Four 1,440 Families React	65
Chapter Five Family Adjustments	79
Chapter Six Attrition, Repercussions, and Energy Conservation	93

Chapter Seven
Different Families, Different Burdens 117

Chapter Eight
Three Years Later—Crisis II 143

Chapter Nine
Energy Conservation and Public Policy 169

Chapter Ten
Focus on Families 193

Appendixes

A. Survey Design and Implementation 207

B. Follow-Up Mail Survey in September 1975 213

C. The Validation Study 215

D. Socioeconomic Differences among Families in Brandeis Sample 219

Notes 225

List of Figures

6-1	Overall Changes in Driving 1973-74	100
6-2	Changes in Amount of Driving 1973-1975	101

List of Tables

1-1	Selected Characteristics of Hartford County, Mobile SMSA, and Salem SMSA, 1970	7
1-2	Sources of Energy—Three States and U.S.	8
2-1	Summary of Crisis Model	17
2-2	Classification of Stressor Events	19
2-3	The Crisis Model	38
4-1	Decisionmakers in Energy-Conserving Households	76
5-1	Differences in Mean Household Temperatures when People Were Home and Awake, Winter of 1972-73 and 1973-74	83
5-2	Percentage Increases in Residential Costs for Electricity and Natural Gas in Hartford, Mobile, and Salem, 1970-74	85
5-3	Proportion of Respondents Who Said They Reduced Use of Appliances Due to Price of Energy	86
5-4	Respondents Who Reported Less Time in Participatory Activities	87
5-5	Changes in Mode of Getting to Work	89
5-6	Alternatives to Driving Utilized by Respondents Who Reduced Driving	90
6-1	Comparison of Time Spent with the Family and Watching TV Before, During, and After the Peak of the Energy Crisis	96
6-2	Attrition in Electricity Conservation 1974-75	98

xii List of Tables

6-3	Changes in Heating Behavior 1973-75	99
6-4	Belief and Disbelief in the Energy Crisis 1974 and 1975	103
6-5	Percentage of Families in Sample Reducing Various Energy-Using Activities	109
6-6	Precrisis Energy Consumption per Household	111
6-7	Energy Savings per Household Resulting from Reported Changes in Behavior	112
6-8	Proportion of Energy Saved per Household 1972-73 to 1973-74	113
6-9	Actual and Estimated Savings in Heating 1972-73 and 1973-74	114
6-10	Actual and Estimated Savings in In-House Uses	115
6-11	Proportion of Heating Energy Saved by Various Methods by Households between Winters 1972-73 and 1973-74	115
7-1	Income Distribution of Study Sample and All U.S. Households	119
7-2	Percentage Reduction in Energy Use per Household by Income Groups between 1972-73 and 1973-74	126
7-3	Absolute Reduction in Energy Use per Household by Income Groups between 1972-73 and 1973-74	127
7-4	Ownership of Energy-Using Facilities and Appliances in Sample Households	130
A-1	Occupational Distribution, Brandeis Sample and National Data	208
A-2	Non-Agricultural Employees, Brandeis Sample and National Data	208
B-1	Characteristics of Mail Survey Respondents	214
C-1	Authorizations Sent and Returned in Validation Study	216
D-1	Income Distribution of Brandeis Sample by Metropolitan Area	219
D-2	Salient Characteristics of Households in the Sample	220
D-3	Work Status by Age of Household Head in Brandeis Sample	220
D-4	Household Income by Age of Household Head in Brandeis Sample	221
D-5	Incomes of Brandeis Households by Race	221
D-6	Responses by Income Groups to Selected Questions	221

| D-7 | Precrisis Typical Household Energy Expenditures | 223 |
| D-8 | Selected Responses of Black and White Respondents | 224 |

Acknowledgments

The four persons who enjoyed a remarkably close and pleasant association in this research effort want to recognize the assistance of many others.

Anita Fast contributed materially to the development of the analytical framework that is used in this study.

Walter Carrington did much of the work in devising and refining the Index that measures changes in the amount of energy used by households. Mary Hyde did the complex computer programming that was involved.

Fred Winkel and his coworkers at Audits and Surveys, Inc., which carried out the drawing of the sample, the actual interviewing, and the coding of the data, were interested and helpful well beyond the requirements of a formal agreement.

Professor A.K. Barakeh, Nancy A. Whitelaw, and Professor Seymour Warkov provided the basic background descriptions of the energy crisis of 1973-74 as it was experienced, respectively, in Mobile, Salem, and Hartford. Mark Stern, Lise Vogel, Scott Merlis, Mordean Moore, Mary Ann Jimenez, Joseph Regan, and Dan Perlman assisted with specific assignments during the project.

Professors Kenneth Jones and Norman Kurtz of the Heller School were generous in consulting with us on statistical methods for analyzing the data.

At various stages along the way, Anne Freeman, Viola Gonzalez,

---

This book is a product of research supported by the National Science Foundation, Division of Social Sciences, (Grant GS-43898X and Soc. 77-14956).

Linda de Luca, and Marianne Muscato labored long and hard on drafts, tables, and the final manuscript.

The project received the full cooperation of the gas and electric companies serving the three areas we studied. They are listed in Appendix C together with fuel oil and other suppliers who also furnished us with information on household consumption of energy. Many government officials and community leaders were generous in providing information on the local situations.

We are especially grateful to the hundreds of families who cooperated in the initial interviews in their homes and who subsequently provided additional information by mail and by phone.

With all this help, we are nevertheless responsible for the findings and conclusions of this study.

Chapter One

Introduction

When a crisis develops in American society there is a strong tendency to seek explanations and remedies at the higher reaches of the economy and the polity. Attention is seldom focused on the family. The energy crises of 1973-74 and 1976-77 illustrate the point. Public and scientific interest has been concentrated on technological, economic, and political issues but there has been far less concern about the effects of these crises on American families and much less interest in their responses.

This imbalance, this neglect of the family as a focal point of concern in the field of energy, is rather typical of the approach in this country to large-scale social and economic changes.[1] Moreover, the impact that family responses have on the unfolding of events is generally accorded far less attention than that devoted, for example, to corporations, legislatures, and interest groups.

These observations help to explain the purpose of this book, which is to propose a more systematic view of the dynamics that are set in motion when families are confronted by events that disrupt their accustomed patterns. The energy crisis is used here primarily to illustrate the ebb and flow of actions, reactions, and repercussions, with the family at the center of our field of vision.

This perspective assumes that the family is simultaneously the recipient of impacts from other institutions and the source of responses and adjustments that affect those institutions—as well as the family itself. In order to give this perspective greater coherence and hopefully to make it applicable to situations other than the energy crisis, a conceptual scheme was developed and is presented in Chapter Two. This framework or model is used in subsequent chapters to interpret what was learned from a study of 1,440 families during the energy crises of 1973-74 and 1976-77.

A parallel purpose of the study was to document the impact of the energy shortage on families, to analyze the adjustments they made, and to assess the meaning of the findings for public policies bearing on energy. Two issues in particular are addressed. One has to do with identifying effective and feasible conservation practices. The other concerns social justice or equity and what kinds of people sacrificed more than others in the course of the energy crisis.

Even at this more specific level, this book's purpose goes beyond the question of energy. In an era of decreasing natural resources and increasing costs, it is probably wise to assume that the shortages precipitated by the Arab oil embargo represent only one of a succession of disruptions that can be anticipated in the years ahead. The second crisis, for instance, involved severe weather, drought, and a natural gas shortage. A suitable framework for analyzing these disruptions should identify important dimensions on the basis of which different types of crisis can be described, compared, and better understood. Here again the framework should suggest ways of anticipating the role of the family in relation to crises, whether caused by shortages of natural resources and/or by deliberate policy decisions.

This emphasis on the family should require little justification. It is, after all, the family in which most people experience the exigencies of day-to-day living. Hill put it well:

> The modern family lives in a greater state of tension precisely because it is the great burden carrier of the social order ... Because the family is the bottleneck through which all troubles pass, no other association so reflects the strains and stresses of life.[2]

Those strains and stresses are, at least in part, the resultants of the policies and programs of governmental and nongovernmental organizations. Although there is now federal and state legislation regarding the impact of various policies and specific measures on the environment, characteristically the social environment has largely been ignored in these impact statements, especially the impact on families. One reason is the propensity in considering such questions to use economic analysis, which deals comfortably with problems that can be reduced to common denominators such as dollars or units of production, but has been less useful in calculating costs in other terms.

An additional reason, we believe, is the absence of a policy analysis framework which is sufficiently general to apply to the many different kinds of measures which affect family living—employment, price policy, housing policy, agricultural policy, transportation policy, foreign policy. As a result, policies in these areas are assessed in other terms. We believe that all these areas inevitably generate impacts on families, regardless of what their primary purpose may be. If the implications of any given proposal are to be assessed in terms of families, an analytical framework is needed to assess the impact of that proposal on families.

Much work needs to be done to produce the methodology for preparing "social impact statements" and for assessing the effects of policies on families. The aim of this study is more limited, taking as its subject the particular dynamics of families in crisis situations as illustrated in the energy shortages between 1973 and 1977. It is important at this point to say more about those shortages.

One of the richest sources of the continuous rise in the material standard of living in the United States has been the seemingly endless supply of natural resources from this land and elsewhere, particularly those that produce energy—oil, coal, water, and natural gas. Only in recent years has a shadow been cast over this flow of resources. Gradually there has emerged a recognition that natural resources for energy are not inexhaustible and that those that are controlled by the developing countries are no longer available to the United States at low prices.

Few people saw the shadow of the impending shortage. True, there had been power failures for a few summers and here and there shortages of heating oil, gasoline, and natural gas. But there was no widespread sense of urgency or even concern.

In the autumn of 1973 the Arab oil-producing states cut off shipments of petroleum to the United States to put pressure on this nation's policies in the Middle East. When they resumed shipments ten weeks later, they were joined by the other major oil producers in price increases that were double and ultimately five times the pre-embargo levels.

The reduced supplies of petroleum products and the subsequent cost increases produced a new situation, officially labeled an "energy crisis" by President Nixon. The shadow of scarcity and the fear of being deprived of resources that had long been taken for granted suddenly spread across the land. In fact, the actual shortages of gasoline and heating fuel were not long in duration nor were they severe in their effects on large numbers of people.

But what happened during that brief period—roughly from October 1973 through March 1974—suggests what may happen when the

United States and other industrial nations again experience rapid changes in the availability and cost of resources that are basic to their economies and living standards—water, clean air, minerals, and foodstuffs. The 1973-74 energy crisis and the one that followed three years later are very likely forerunners of more severe and far-reaching constrictions. Inherent in these are profound changes in the amount of goods and services and the patterns of living to which people in this country have become accustomed.

Consider the extent to which Americans are now dependent on "manufactured" energy. "As recently as 1850," Freeman observes, "people in the United States still obtained as much as two-thirds of their energy from human muscle-power and draft animals."[3] The phenomenal growth over the years in Americans' consumption of energy has made this country, more than any other industrialized nation and far more than the developing countries, profligate with nature's bounty. With only 6 percent of the world's population, the United States consumes 30 percent of the world's energy.

The steep rise in the use of energy in this country has an awesome set of accompaniments: the world's highest rates of production on farms and in factories and the highest per capita standard of living in history—as well as the fouling of air and water; the destruction and disfigurement of the environment; and prodigious waste, now glaringly in contrast to the poverty and hunger of billions of people in Africa, Asia, and Latin America. Moreover, reliance on foreign oil makes the United States economy vulnerable to both cut-offs and price increases.

The policy choices recently proposed by the Carter Administration to the American people are alien to them. Do Americans want a continually mounting standard of material comforts and conveniences—more and larger cars, more appliances in the home, more snowmobiles, and motorboats, the prospect of a quadraphonic radio in each car, a speaker installed in each door? Can they afford these in view of the human and ecological damage entailed? Will the American people be willing to pay the booming financial costs of such an energy-profligate society? Can they hope for an almost-magical solution through technology—improvements and innovations in nuclear, thermal, solar, and other kinds of energy—that will permit continuous economic expansion?

Or will the people of this country change their living standards out of concern for their environment, future generations, or the short-run effects on their pocketbooks? Will they accept a quality of life based on "declining expectations" in material terms, a simpler life-style with less high-speed travel, lower indoor temperatures in the winter, less artificial cooling in the summers, more dishwashing by hand rather than machine?

These choices bedevil not only the Western capitalist countries but the Communist nations and, increasingly, the developing countries. The hard facts of limited energy resources and the limits they place on production and consumption confront all types of economic organization. With this in mind, an official in the Allende government of Chile once remarked: "Socialism can arrive only on a bicycle."[4]

For the most part these issues are being debated in terms of national and international economics and politics. In the end, however, they are essentially human issues at the scale of the individual and the family. Their genesis and their resolution depend heavily on actions involving the household. This is not to say that by themselves the decisions and actions of American households will determine the demand for energy. Their preferences and choices in the design of homes and the means of transportation, in sports arenas, and in electric devices are subject to pressures and persuasion emanating from manufacturers, advertisers, and government itself. Despite their brush with two energy crises, Americans continue to be urged to buy devices that accelerate the consumption of energy.

The energy shortage of 1973-1974 was especially instructive. What can be learned from it? Was it a crisis at all? Or was it more like the first faint rumblings that sometimes precede an earthquake? Looking back on it may be like watching the earliest flickerings on a seismograph. Hopefully, however, something of value can be learned from addressing these questions:

1. Where did the first shock-waves appear? What was done, following the Arab oil embargo, by government and by profit and nonprofit organizations that first confronted families with new demands and constraints? How did this differ from one region of the country to another?
2. What aspects of living patterns and family welfare were affected? How did families of varying types and characteristics respond? What kinds of energy conservation did they adopt?
3. What were the variations in the degree of deprivation experienced by different kinds of families?
4. Viewing the family not only as a passive recipient of impacts but as an active generator of actions, what were the repercussions of family actions? What ripple effects moved outward from families to commercial establishments and employers?
5. How much did conserving behavior return to precrisis levels? And

how much of a "cushion" remained for further conservation of energy?
6. How well prepared were Americans to cope with the 1973-74 energy crisis and what did they learn from it?

These questions shaped the methodology for this study. Much of the information could only be obtained directly from households, and this led to primary reliance on a survey. However, the importance of capturing the interacting effects among families, profit and nonprofit enterprises, and governmental units precluded the use of a national sample which would have been too diffuse and thin to reflect this interplay.

Consequently it was decided to secure interview data from families and from enterprises or establishments in the same communities so as to chart their interactions. This was supplemented by individual and group meetings with knowledgeable individuals and with newspaper accounts. An additional requirement was to understand how the crisis was played out in areas of the country with disparate energy situations, social and economic characteristics, and climates. The use of metropolitan areas seemed advisable since they included urban, suburban and rural communities.

Within the resources of the project it was possible to conduct the study in only three areas. In the process of selection, only metropolitan areas with populations under one million and over 150,000 were considered since most Americans live in such areas. Data on metropolitan areas were examined for variations among these dimensions: (1) size of population; (2) median income; (3) percentage of black population; (4) percentage urban; (5) economic profile as reflected in manufacturing, government, and retail-wholesale types of employment; (6) temperature; and (7) principal types of energy used.

Using these criteria the decision was made to locate the study in Hartford County in Connecticut and in the Standard Metropolitan Statistical Areas (SMSA) surrounding Mobile, Alabama, and Salem, Oregon.[a]

---

[a]Among the 243 SMSAs listed by the U.S. Census in 1970, Hartford ranked 49 in population, Mobile ranked 78, and Salem 153. The selection of metropolitan areas with populations of different sizes and the inclusion of an area in Oregon were suggested to the study staff by the Federal Energy Agency.

Many analysts in the federal government and practically all outside the government use Hartford County rather than the Hartford SMSA for study purposes since the latter consists of parts of several counties, thus making calculations more cumbersome. Hartford County, which had a population of 816,737 in 1970, is used in this study rather than the SMSA, which had a population of 663,891.

Throughout the book we shall refer to the three areas as Hartford, Mobile, and Salem to avoid the repetition of "County" and "SMSA." When the reference is specifically to the city of Mobile, the city of Salem, or to the city of Hartford it will be clearly indicated.

Table 1-1 presents selected characteristics of the three areas with comparisons to the United States as a whole.

There are important differences among the three areas in the "mix" of types of energy consumed and in the energy price structure, as shown in Table 1-2. Since most data on energy are available only for States, the table uses those sources.

These differences in the "energy economy" of the three areas, together with differences due to climate, are partly reflected in the cost to the household consumer of the major end-uses of energy. The typical Hartford household paid $1,019 in 1972-73 before the crisis for heating, transportation, cooking, lighting, and other in-house uses, compared with $760 in Mobile and $742 in Salem, according to estimates made by our study staff. The latter two were close to the national average of $734.

The people of Hartford County live half-way between New York and Boston under energy conditions that are typical of the Northeast. New England's industry and commerce, and to some degree its residences, rely heavily on petroleum products that must be imported, mostly from abroad. Connecticut is "almost twice as dependent on petroleum as is the nation as a whole."[5] Energy prices there are substantially higher than in the other two areas.

Table 1-1. Selected Characteristics of Hartford County, Mobile SMSA, and Salem SMSA, 1970[1]

	Hartford County	Mobile SMSA	Salem SMSA	U.S.
Total population	816,737	376,690	186,658	203,166,000
% Urban	84.9	73.7	65.4	73.5
% Black	6.7	30.0	0.3	11.1
Median Income (1969)[2]	$12,057	$ 7,730	$ 8,992	$9,590
% Civilian labor force employed in:				
Manufacturing	33.0	22.7	17.1	25.9
Government	13.1	15.7	26.0	16.1
Wholesale, retail trade	18.6	21.5	19.9	20.1
Normal monthly average temperature[3]	49.8°	68.2°	52.7°	—
Estimated household energy expenditures 1972-73[4]	$ 1,019	$ 760	$ 742	$ 734

1. United States Bureau of the Census, *County and City Data Book, 1972.*
2. For income distribution and other socioeconomic characteristics of the Brandeis sample by metropolitan area, see Table D-1, Appendix D.
3. United States Bureau of the Census, *Statistical Abstract of the United States, 1973*, 94th edition (Washington, D.C., 1973), p. 181. The Salem temperature is taken from U.S. Weather Bureau Records.
4. For details, see Table D-7, Appendix D.

Table 1-2. Sources of Energy—Three States and U.S.
(in percentages—1975 data projected)

	Conn.[1] 1975	Ala.[2] 1971	Ore.[3] 1975	U.S.[4] 1975
Petroleum	81	23	41	45
Natural Gas	8	21	16	32
Coal	—	49	—	18
Hydro & Nuclear	12	7	41	5

1. Connecticut Energy Agency, *Executive Summary, Energy Emergency Plan for Connecticut,* January 15, 1975.
2. Southern Interstate Nuclear Board, *Evaluation of Fuels and Energy in the Southern States,* "Production, Consumption, Reserves," Report to Southern Governors' Conference, September 25, 1974, Atlanta, Georgia, p. 37.
3. Governor Tom McCall's Task Force on Energy, *Oregon's Energy Perspective,* May 31, 1973, p. 46.
4. Connecticut Energy Agency.

In Mobile, with its warmer climate, householders pay as much for air-conditioning as for heating, though, taken together, this is less in dollar terms than families pay for home heating in Hartford. Two features of the situation in Oregon differentiate Salem's experience from Hartford and Mobile. First is its heavy reliance on hydroelectric power at rates that are among the lowest in the country. Second, in part because of its vulnerability to power shortages in times of low rainfall and in part because of strong environmental interests, Oregon's state government has been vigorous in its conservation efforts.

A total of 1,440 households and 549 public and private establishments were interviewed in November 1974, with a follow-up mail questionnaire to the households in November 1975.[b] A rigorous multistage area probability sampling procedure was used in each area. While this study does not purport to be based on a national sample of households, by good chance the distribution of household incomes in the sample corresponds closely to the national distribution.

The terms "household" and "family" are used in this book interchangeably, a fact which requires both clarification and comment. In fact, respondents were chosen on the basis of households as the Census Bureau uses that term to mean all persons who occupy a house, apartment, or other dwelling that constitutes separate living quarters. This includes, but is obviously not synonymous with,

---
[b]The samples were drawn, the interviews conducted, and the schedules coded by Audits and Surveys, Inc., of New York City in collaboration with the study staff.

See Appendix A for description of additional data-collection during the summer of 1977.

"family," which refers to two or more persons "related by blood, marriage, or adoption and residing together in a household."

The distinction is important, empirically and conceptually. The traditional and popular image of a family as a full-time, wage-earning husband, a permanently out-of-the-labor-force housewife, and children is descriptive of only a minority of United States living arrangements—and a shrinking proportion of United States households. Households are decreasing in size and the number of single-parent families, unmarried couples, and persons living alone is increasing.

In our sample the two-parent-plus-child(ren) constellation accounted for 47 percent of the households. Husband and wife households were 26 percent of the total and single persons 12 percent, the remaining 15 percent consisting of other combinations. To have restricted this study to families would have meant the exclusion of many households that are significant social and economic units. The household sample for the study was drawn on the basis of census tracts in the Hartford, Mobile, and Salem areas.[c]

The screening procedure was designed to insure an interview with a well-informed respondent; it called for a maximum of three visits to a household to locate the female head of the house, the male head, or another adult, in that order of preference. A different

---

[c]See Appendix A for details on the survey design and implementation. The salient information is summarized below.

In the first stage a systematic sample of census tracts was selected in each metropolitan area with the probability of selection proportionate to the number of year-round housing units within each tract. In successive stages, a particular block and a specific housing unit within that block were selected at random. Interviewers were instructed to follow a prescribed path to the designated housing unit.

The results of the household interviewing were as follows:

Number of households contacted	1,913
No answer	301
No eligible respondent available	35
Screening refused	34
Respondent refused	80
Interviews completed	1,463
Interviews processed on tape	1,440

The research design made it possible to compare information obtained from the families with that obtained from profit and nonprofit enterprises. For the most part these sources were in agreement.

The sampling procedure for the establishments insured that the largest employers in each community would be well represented in order to capture the widespread effects of their actions. At the same time, a weighting system was used to reflect the contours of the local economy and the actual distribution of employees by size of enterprise. It is worth noting that approximately three-quarters of the establishments, after weighting, had 1-20 employees. Approximately eight out of ten served the public directly; this included governmental agencies in their service role, as distinguished from their regulatory role.

randomized procedure was used to identify the person who was to be interviewed on employment matters. Pretests of the household and establishment questionnaires were conducted first in the Boston area and subsequently in and around Paterson, New Jersey, before the instruments were put into final form.

One important limitation requires comment. The findings of this study are largely based on the statements of the respondents and are subject to the known limitations of self-reported data.[6] Wherever possible information from other sources in the three metropolitan areas and from other studies is reported in this book as a basis for comparison. We take some comfort from the fact that these sources have not revealed major divergences from our findings and interpretations.

This item, however, gives one pause about the validity of at least a small proportion of the self-reported behavior:

> Carburetor au gratin: After having conducted a telephone poll to find out whether Americans are really trying to conserve energy in the home, the Federal Energy Administration has concluded that five percent of the American public is lying. The last question of the poll—which included obvious queries such as "Do you use electrical appliances less?"—was "Have you installed a thermidor in your automobile?" Five percent answered yes. Thermidor is a way of preparing lobster.[7]

Validation of certain critical aspects of conservation behavior was sought from a sample of households originally interviewed (see Chapter Six for details). These respondents were asked to authorize their utility companies and suppliers of heating fuel to release to the study staff the amount and cost of the energy they consumed in 1973-74. This enabled the staff to compare their reported conservation behavior with whatever changes, if any, were made in their actual consumption.

A considerable amount of data was obtained from the survey, from local experts and informants, and by correspondence. The concrete and practical purpose of collecting this information was, to recapitulate, to add to knowledge about the energy crisis of 1973-74, with particular attention to the policy-relevant issues of *conservation* and *equity of sacrifice*.

The more basic goal of the study was to utilize this understanding of the energy crisis to develop a more general appreciation of how American families are affected by crises of this type, how they respond, and how their adjustments to crisis conditions give rise to further effects on the families themselves and on other institutions in society. In pursuit of this goal, the next chapter presents a general model of the processes and components involved in family responses to crisis conditions.

Chapter Two

An Analytical Model of Families and Crises

Our interest in the energy crisis and, indeed, in crises in general is related to a larger concern about the impacts of governmental and nongovernmental policies and programs on people as they live in families. What is lacking, among other things, is a type of policy analysis that can encompass many different kinds of measures that affect family living—regardless of the manifest or intended purpose of a particular policy—and that can trace through the effects on families and on other institutions.

This concern was enunciated by Vice President, then Senator, Walter Mondale as he opened a series of Senate hearings on American families. He said he was seeking "to explore how government policies in areas such as work, institutionalization, mobility, taxes, welfare, and housing influence the lives of American families," and he set as a goal helping to "make the question of how governmental policies affect families a larger part of the decisionmaking process."[1] Immediately after his nomination by the Democratic Party in 1976, President Carter made a major statement in a speech in Manchester, New Hampshire, that began with the statement "The American family is in trouble" and went on to emphasize the importance of reviewing national policies affecting the family.[2]

If the implications of any proposal or program are to be assessed in terms of the family, the analysis needs to give attention to four questions:

This chapter was written with the assistance of Anita Fast.

1. What are the probable impacts on families and how are they likely to adjust to such impacts? This deals with the *quality of living*.
2. To what extent and in what ways are different groups of families affected differentially, whether adversely or favorably? How are the costs and benefits distributed among families who differ on such characteristics as income, social class, race, and the age of their members? This concerns *equity*.
3. What effects are the adjustments made by families likely to have on other families and on various governmental and nongovernmental establishments? This deals with *repercussive effects*.
4. How lasting or transitory are the effects likely to be after the initial impact and adjustments? This concerns the *attrition* of the effects of the crisis.

These questions were considered both in the gathering of data for this study and in the development of a model which may be useful in assessing a broad array of measures and events. Reduced to its barest outline, the energy shortage involved a disrupting event, a series of impacts and adjustments, and a residue of changed behavior. These processes, involving *event/adjustment/residual effects*, are encountered in numerous human situations. Consequently there are several areas of research and conceptualization that are resources in devising an analytical framework for such situations.

In approaching this task, one is reminded, at a very general level, of John Dewey's early work on *How We Think*, in which he pointed out that most activity involves little conscious thought but follows the accustomed routines in habitual ways. It is only when for some reason there is an interruption in this routine, a situation for which habitual responses are not appropriate, that thinking, in any fundamental sense, takes place. One drives a car while talking or while deeply immersed in thought or revery, making the necessary activities almost mechanically. But let there be an obstruction on the road or the sudden motion of another vehicle or a loud noise from one's motor or the sight of a police car and one's attention is immediately focused on adjusting to the situation.[3] The energy shortage constituted such an interruption, or in some cases disruption, of customary activity, so attention was paid to it, adjustments were made, and life with all its complexities continued, though somewhat altered.

Of the various bodies of literature which address themselves to such situations, the literature on disaster affords a rich source for analytical concepts. Barton has identified five stages of disasters: (1) the predisaster period, (2) detection and warning of threat, (3) immediate response (relatively unorganized), (4) organized social response, and (5) long-run, post-disaster equilibrium.[4] One sees here a slight elaboration of the event/adjustment/residue pattern, applied to disaster situations. But disaster situations, though somewhat analogous, are not especially helpful, for they usually involve impacts which are much more intense than that of the energy shortage, much more disruptive. An early definition gives an indication of this greater intensity and disruption:

> [A disaster is] the impinging upon a structured community, or one of its sections, of an external force capable of destroying human life or its resources for survival, on a scale wide enough to excite public alarm, to disrupt normal patterns of behavior, and to impair or overload any of the central services necessary to the conduct of normal affairs or to the prevention or alleviation of suffering and loss.[5]

Barton places disasters in a larger category of "collective stress situations" in which "many members of a social system fail to receive expected conditions of life from the system."[6] This category, in its breadth, is somewhat more appropriate for the energy shortage. There is little doubt that thousands of people waiting in line for a small ration of gasoline at pumps throughout the country during the gas shortage would have wanted to be numbered among those who "fail to receive expected conditions of life from the system."

Another and perhaps richer source of analysis of the event/adjustment/residue processes is to be found in the literature on "crisis." The term has been applied in many contexts, to situations of minor as well as major intensity and at different system levels. It has been used frequently in the field of economics (monetary crisis, economic crisis) in international relations (the Cuban missile crisis, the Berlin crisis), and specifically at the family and individual level where crisis is associated with turning points in maturation,[7] or with the family cycle,[8] or with ad hoc situations like separation during war,[9] or bereavement.[10]

Although the literature on crisis is rewarding, a few reservations should be stated. First, the term "crisis" is usually thought of only within a specific, limited context (family or international relations or economy, etc.), so that although the same word is used, it is questionable how much correspondence in meaning exists in its use on different levels. This ambiguity is of course disadvantageous.

In the *Encyclopedia of the Social Sciences* article on crisis, Robinson is very blunt: "Because of its varied meanings the term 'crisis' has not been useful in building 'systematic knowledge' about social phenomena."[11] Although he mentions other fields in which the term has been employed, he concentrates on crises in international relations to such an extent that the article itself illustrates the one-sidedness with which the term is customarily employed, as well as the paucity of attempts to look for commonalities across the several meanings.

Another reservation about the use of the term has to do with intensity. How intense must the effects be before one can speak of a crisis? Behind this question are various nuances; for example, the same objective event (admonitions by government agencies to turn down one's thermostat or use public transportation more or turn off unused lights) may be perceived differently by different families. For some it may constitute a dramatic event, occasioning major readjustments. For others, it may be tossed off with a shrug. These different definitions of impact may occur even where the objective situation is similar.

But in a situation such as the energy shortage, the impact may not be similar for all families. Those who heat with electricity may be affected differently from those who heat with fuel oil. Those who already utilize public transportation may be affected differently from those who rely exclusively on their cars. Those who need their cars to get to work may be affected differently than those who use them only for other purposes.

Despite these reservations, it may be useful to illustrate from the literature on different contexts the extent of similarity and of differences in their conception of crisis.

Working in a context of international crises, Wiener and Kahn enumerated twelve generic dimensions:

1. a turning point
2. high requirement for action
3. a threat to goals and objectives
4. an important outcome
5. convergence of events to a new set of circumstance
6. uncertainties as to how to respond
7. reduction of control over events and their effects
8. heightened urgency, stress, and anxiety
9. inadequate information
10. strong time pressures
11. changes in relations
12. raised tensions.[12]

Lipman-Blumen has developed a crisis framework specifically for the analysis of macrosociological changes in the family.[13] Her paper begins by differentiating among three types of research on the effects of crisis on family structure: (1) studies of microstructural changes within the family in the face of individual or small-group crises, such as death, illness, poverty, and natural disaster; (2) research on large-scale societal crises and the impact on a limited population of families or family members, such as concentration camp internees in Germany during World War II or wartime separations and reunions of families; and (3) investigations of changes in macro-aspects of family structure stemming from large-scale societal changes (e.g. the business cycle and war conditions) and expressed for example in divorce, marriage, and remarriage rates.

Lipman-Blumen's paper focuses on role changes in the family during World War II. She begins with the premise that the nature of the role changes depends on the "relationship between two major factors: (1) the nature of the crisis, and (2) the state of the social system at the time of crisis." The paper goes on to define ten dimensions of crisis and seven aspects of the social system. There is a considerable area of similarity but also some significant differences between the Lipman-Blumen framework and the model that has been developed in this project.

One major difference between the two approaches is that the model in this book places more emphasis on crisis as a process involving successive stages and repercussive developments. Lipman-Blumen speaks of a crisis as a situation and tends to concentrate more on the characteristics and impact of the initial crisis events. Several minor differences will be pointed out as we set forth our model in the following pages.

Lipman-Blumen's definition of crisis is shown below, along with others drawn from the literature and reflecting in different ways the dimensions of crisis touched upon above:

> By crisis we mean any situation which the participants of the social system recognize as posing a threat to the status quo, well-being, or survival of the system or any of its parts, whose ordinary coping mechanisms and resources are stressed or inadequate for meeting the threat.[14]

> A crisis is defined as a critical moment, or any sudden or decisive change in the unraveling of life; an often painful shock or jolt whose solution is urgently needed. Crises usually exist outside the ordinary pattern of life, and often create a deep sense of insecurity or helplessness, blocking the customary "modus operandi" and calling for a new plan of action.[15]

> A crisis implies a limited period in which an individual or group is exposed to threats and demands which are at or near the limits of their resources to cope.[16]

16 Families in the Energy Crisis

> Any major interruption in the usual routine of need fulfillment.[17]

> Any interruption of the regular and expected succession of events; a disturbance of habit or custom which requires conscious attention on the part of the individual or the group in order either to reestablish the disturbed equilibrium or to establish new and more adequate habits or customs.[18]

> Any event which disrupts an established way of behaving on the part of a person or group of people, and which points up a conflict which the person or group is not prepared to meet.[19]

These definitions are of obvious relevance to the energy shortage, but they also are broad enough to cover many other types of situations. In fact, none of them was formulated in the context of the energy shortage. From them, one can conclude that the crisis rubric may be sufficiently comprehensive to be applied to different system levels and to different national situations, such as those brought about by depletion of resources, environmental hazards, blockages in access to necessary raw materials, war mobilizations and hardships, and so on.

In the construction of our own analytic model we have drawn freely, though not exclusively, on the crisis literature. Before presenting that analytic model, it may be well to disassociate our model from some of the more particularistic meanings sometimes attributed to the concept.

First, the term "crisis" is frequently applied to situations implying psychopathology, inability to cope, and other indications of high personality disturbance. Such attributes may or may not accompany crisis as we conceptualize it.

Second, the term is usually meant to apply to a situation which is threatening or injurious. We want to allow for situations which involve opportunities as well as threats.

Third, the term is often used to denote a turning point, as in the course of an illness.[20] In our view the notion of a turning point is too narrow. The entire illness, if it meets certain criteria, would constitute the crisis and the turning point would be only one stage in its development.

The notion of the turning point is employed perhaps because dictionary definitions of crisis feature the medical meaning of the term. Further, there is a certain correspondence—though by no means precise—between the notion of the turning point and the more widely held conception that a crisis does involve an adjustment of some type, and that "things are different" after that adjustment has been made. It is this "difference" to which we refer in our use of the term "residue."

Fourth, many crisis conceptualizations, particularly in the area of the family, focus on highly individual, idiosyncratic impacts such as death, separation, unemployment, mental illness, alcoholism, and so on. We hope that our model will be useful for analysis of such crises, but we are especially interested in its application to less idiosyncratic, more systematic crises which arise as a result of policies or events or measures taken (or not taken) at the national, state, or local level.

Fifth, and perhaps most important, the term "crisis" is usually employed to denote a situation which is more critical or desperate than that of most of the households in this study. To say that these households faced a crisis because of the energy shortage may give the impression that the impact was much stronger than was actually the case. For most people, it was a case of making minor adjustments or suffering minor inconveniences, rather than confronting a "crisis." But this is a distinction only of degree. Granted that the degree of impact was relatively moderate, the significant point is that the crisis literature has been found helpful in analyzing these more moderate impacts, as well.

Consequently, we shall employ the term "crisis" rather than the much more clumsy event/adjustment/residue term, but the reader is asked to bear in mind that although the configuration is similar to other types of crisis, the degree of intensity in the energy situation was *in most cases* on the mild side of the implications of the term.

The main elements of the model are identified here and are elaborated in the remainder of this chapter. Since the model is intended to be applicable to crisis situations in general, the illustrations that are used below are not limited to the energy crisis.

As can be seen, the model is largely sequential in nature. A major

Table 2-1. Summary of Crisis Model

1. The *stressor event*, which initiates or provokes the crisis.
2. The *initial impacts* on the family's capacities and task performance.
3. The *cognitive processes* by which the family perceives, evaluates, and decides how to respond to the stressor event and its first impacts.
4. The *adjustment* that a family makes, seen as a sequence of stages (exploration, change, stabilization/attrition) and as modes/mechanisms of adjustment involving capacities and tasks.
5. *Successive adjustments*, with impacts on the family and other systems.
6. *Residual effects*, including crisis-proneness and crisis-readiness.

exception is the system's cognitive processes, which operate at successive stages in the total process, as we shall see. In addition, it must be recognized that there may be overlapping in time between phases.

THE STRESSOR EVENT

Much of the family crisis literature emphasizes the point that the crisis is brought on by an event which precipitates or provokes it. We follow Hill in using the term "stressor event" for this crisis precipitant.[21] What are the characteristics of these events?

Some stressor events are internal to the family (death, separation) and others are external (loss of employment, a fire which destroys the home). Clearly, the energy shortage is of the external type.

Another distinction to be made is whether the crisis arises in connection with the family's stage in the family life cycle (childless couple, couple with children, children leaving home, etc.), or whether the crisis, even though internally induced, is independent of that cycle. Writers such as Erikson[22] have indicated the importance of identity crises associated with the physical-social maturation process. Schneidman relates crises to life stages and talks about intratemporal crises, occurring during a life stage; intertemporal crises, occurring at a transitional period; and extratemporal crises, occurring independent of the life stage.[23]

With regard to personal and family crises, Taplin asserts that most of the literature indicates that "the onset of crisis usually involves identifiable precipitors or antecedents, generally of a situational or interpersonal nature.[24] This leaves open the question of whether these antecedents or precipitators are identifiable at the time. In their study of collective responses to disaster threats, Lang and Lang make the point that the precipitators of crisis may be either unanticipated or anticipated.[25] Barton similarly classifies disasters according to whether their onset was sudden or gradual, and whether warning was possible or not, and if possible, whether it was given.[26] The distinction regarding warning seems appropriate for most if not all crisis situations.

Many writers emphasize that the event must be of such a nature that it is in some way disruptive. Thus, Lang and Halpern write that the usual coping methods are not effective;[27,28] Parad and Caplan speak of "a problem which ... cannot be solved quickly by means of his normal range of problem-solving mechanisms."[29] Quite clearly, events which fall in this category may be extremely severe or quite moderate. Hill lists a number of categories of precipitants which indicate greater intensity of impact, such as loss of a child, widowhood, hospitalization, unwanted pregnancy, nonsupport, infidelity, illegitimacy, desertion, imprisonment, and suicide or homicide.[30]

In her discussion of dimensions of crises, Lipman-Blumen poses two characteristics that further define the extent of impact.[31] One of these is called "pervasiveness versus boundedness" and refers "to the degree to which the crisis affects the entire system or only a limited part." The time perspective is the basis for the second dimension, "transitoriness versus chronicity," which she describes as "the degree to which the crisis represents a short- or long-term problem."

In their analysis of culture and stress, Spradley and Phillips point out a number of implicit assumptions which are often made concerning stressor events and indicate their questionability. They indicate that researchers tend to project their own ideas of what would cause stress onto objective situations which may or may not actually cause stress. Sometimes they do the reverse, inferring from what they consider a stress response that stress has actually occurred. Observers tend to think of stress as only negative, whereas it may occur in potentially beneficial situations as well. Finally, they seem to assume implicitly that a stressful event affects all families or individuals with equal intensity.[32]

Much of the literature reinforces this last point that the same objective event may affect different individuals or families with different degrees of intensity. In summing up the study on family adjustments to the crises of war separation and reunion, Hill writes: "If this study makes no contribution other than to point out the variability of the crisis as it impinges on different families, it will have been justified."[33]

Various types of classification of precipant events have been given. Hill employed the categories of dismemberment, accession, demoralization, and combinations of these.[34] He cites Burgess' classification as: (1) change in status, (2) role conflict among family members, and (3) loss of family members (departure, desertion, divorce, death).[35]

From the foregoing discussion of relevant literature, a set of categorizations of stressor events can be summarized:

Table 2-2. Classification of Stressor Events

Source	Internal-External
Relation to family cycle	Strong relationship-Weak relationship
Nature of warning	Diffuse-Clear; Extensive-Little
Disruptive effect	Intense-Moderate
Consistency	Similar for all-Differing
Quality	Harmful-Beneficial

Anticipating some of our findings, the energy shortage under consideration in this book can be characterized as a crisis event whose source was external to the family; moderately related to the family cycle; with extensive but highly diffuse long-run warning of eventual shortage but little clear short-run warning of the oil embargo and its effects on the family. The "crisis" had a moderate impact, though affecting different families with different intensities; and though moderate, almost exclusively harmful. Other types of crisis might be distributed differently along these six dimensions.

INITIAL IMPACTS

Perhaps the most significant characteristic of stressor events is that they disrupt, disturb, dislocate the family. But in what terms can one usefully conceive of this disruptive process and its effects? What aspects of the family's accustomed patterns are affected? What, in short, is disrupted?

The model assumes that stressor events have initial impacts on a family's capacities and resources and that these impacts in turn alter the performance of certain essential tasks and functions. We are beginning here to draw on conceptualizations of the family as a social system with specific internal components and processes and with significant relationships to other systems in the surrounding environment.

In this context, Parsons has written extensively of four "functional requirements" of all social systems: Adaptation, having to do with the system's capacity to apply resources to its task accomplishment; goal attainment, its ability to accomplish its goals; integration, its maintenance of a viable relationship among its parts; and latent pattern maintenance and tension management, having to do with maintaining stability of the system's value structure against possible external or internal pressure for change.[3,6]

On the more specific family level, Hill's categorization of the family suggests important structural components. It is "an arena of interacting personalities, intricately organized internally into positions, norms, and roles."[3,7] Presumably, any disturbance in these may affect its capacity. More specifically, referring to the family studies of Cavan and Ranck and of Earl L. Koos, he writes: "To these researchers a crisis-proof family must have agreement in its role structure, subordination of personal ambitions to family goals, satisfactions within the family obtained because it is successfully meeting the physical and emotional needs of its members, and goals toward which the family is moving collectively."[3,8]

Capacities

Building on this emphasis on capacity, we propose the following sixfold categorization of the capacities of families.

The first such capacity is that of *integration*—the system's ability to maintain a level and quality of relationships among its parts that determine the extent of commitment to the system as a social unit. In the case of the family, this involves the interpersonal relationships among the members. These relationships have utilitarian aspects, having to do with role allocation and the division of labor in task performance. They also have an expressive or affective side, having to do with the personal commitment of members to each other and to the family as a system. Hill alluded to this in the above quotation. Parsons uses the term "collectivity orientation"[39] to express the willingness of system members to be morally bound by the well-being of the system as such.

This collectivity orientation, we believe, is furthered by consensus on the norms governing interpersonal relations among family members. It is also enhanced by mutual agreement on reciprocal roles—that, for example, mother and son both see the appropriate role for mother in the same way and both see the appropriate role for son in the same way. Commitment to the family is also enhanced by relationships of mutual affectional support among the members.

Integration depends in part on satisfactory utilitarian need fulfillment, but also on the more expressive aspects of social systems. Participation in any social system must be at a sufficient level of member gratification and satisfaction so that the benefits of remaining in the system exceed the benefits of leaving it. As one can learn from many novels and from the experiences of many people, all utilitarian needs of members may be met and still the level of member gratification may be so low that separation, desertion, or divorce may occur, or children may run away from home. Thus, though there is overlapping, we consider member gratification sufficiently important to be treated separately.

To summarize, we see integration as a function of collectivity orientation, consensus on interpersonal norms, consensus on mutual role perceptions, affectional support among family members, and satisfaction of utilitarian and affectional needs of members.

A second capacity of the family as a system is that of *adaptability*. Both Hill and Angell have emphasized the importance of adaptability for families confronting crisis situations.[40] We define adaptability as the family's capacity to substitute one resource for another in meeting the demands placed upon it by its members or by external actors. Presently, we shall deal more specifically with the nature of these resources, and later, under adjustments, we shall treat the question of their substitutability. Still later, in Chapter Five, we shall indicate the extensive types of substitute resources that were employed in the process of adjustment to the energy shortage by the families under study.

A third type of system capacity is that of *cognitive competence*. By this term is meant the system's ability to obtain and process data and reach decisions which, given the nature of the situation, enhance the well-being of the system. This involves the family's access to information, its ability to search for relevant information and to scan it for its relevance and implications for family adjustments. It involves the ability to evaluate the importance of the information and to arrange it and process it in such a way as to make effective means-ends decisions—in other words the family's decision-making capacity. It is apparent that the interaction among family members in these processes may be of great importance.

A much more obvious type of system capacity is the possession of or access to *material resources*, such as housing, furniture, money, appliances, and assets of various types. In the present study such resources as automobiles, gasoline, heating systems, heating fuel, insulation, and various types of household appliances are highly pertinent. More generally, the family's material resource base constitutes a pool which can be drawn on in various ways in the process of adjustment.

Much the same can be said for the family's *nonmaterial resources*. Included in this category are knowledge and skills; information; human energy; support from external sources through kinship or friendship networks and organizational affiliation; the esteem enjoyed by the family; and time—the latter a valuable resource in the adjustment process, though often overlooked by investigators.

A final type of capacity is the system's ability to manage its *relationship to the environment*, especially those aspects which facilitate or enable it to perform external tasks and to acquire resources from the environment. A simple example is the performance of occupational tasks which bring income to the family. As we have mentioned, esteem is a resource; to receive esteem from "significant others" in the environment, the family members must behave in certain ways. The point is pertinent to energy conservation, where appeals to save energy out of a sense of civic duty are related to what kinds of behavior may cause the family to gain or lose the esteem of its neighbors.

It may be useful at this point to illustrate the kinds of events and initial impacts that can affect a family's capacities and performance.

The examples will be brief, but will not be confined to the energy shortage since the model is deliberately designed to accommodate other types of stressor events as well.

Various types of events may have a potential or actual impact on the family's *integration*. Quarreling over whether or not to take a job offer in another city (potentially a beneficial stressor) may weaken the husband-wife role relationship. A son or daughter flunking out of college may occasion strong strains on parent-child relationships which in turn may impair the son's or daughter's commitment to the family, thus threatening family solidarity.

A series of blows from the environment or within the family may impair the family's *ability to adapt* to new situations. It may develop a sense of despair and be unable to adapt. It is in this sense that Hiroto and Seligman refer to "learned helplessness."[4,1] Likewise, the aftermath of interpersonal wrangling over what can be done in response to the inability to get gasoline or the increased cost of heating fuel may impair the family's capacity to adapt to other stressor events as well.

The death or desertion of a member or the loss of employment by a wage earner may have a dazing effect on the family's *capacity to make decisions*. Several studies indicate that a stressor event may have the impact of numbing the family in such a way that pertinent facts are not considered, possible adjustments are not given attention; choice is narrowed, and decisions are made in erratic, impulsive fashion.

Much more obvious is the impact of a stressor event on the family's store of *material resources*. The house burns down; the family car is destroyed in an accident; a wage earner is unemployed; a serious illness generates a huge medical bill—such events usually have a serious impact on the family's available material resources. Less serious, but of the same type, were some of the impacts of the energy shortage as they affected scarcity of gasoline, increased cost of fuel, and so on.

Some stressor events may have a special impact on the family's *nonmaterial resources*. The disgrace of one of the members may drain the family's esteem among friends, relatives, and neighbors. The illness of a member may drastically curtail needed energy and skills to perform household tasks. Moving to a new neighborhood may destroy the informal support system which the family earlier enjoyed among nearby relatives and friends.

Some stressor events may impair the viability of the *family's exchange relations with the environment*. The loss of employment cuts off a source of income and may be reflected in rapid depletion of the family's stock of material resources available for purchases. Discontinuance of the local bus line may create a host of problems connected with the journey to work, shopping, or the availability of schools and recreational facilities.

The above examples of impacts on family capacities include stressor events encroaching on the family from the environment, such as unemployment, the energy shortage, or a power failure. There are also those which were induced within the family, such as death or desertion of a member, illness, divorce, and so on. In many instances, it is not possible to classify an event as completely externally or internally induced, thus illustrating the "openness" of the family as a social system and the importance of its exchange relationships with its environment.

Task Performance

The six capacities discussed above represent properties or competences of the family as a system. Some of them can be thought of as a "stock" or "reserve" of a particular kind of resource; others are more in the nature of a skill which varies from family to family. By themselves these capacities do not represent behavior. They are translated into behavioral terms through the performance of the family's essential tasks. The performance of tasks represents, so to speak, the capacities in action. Our model suggests that events impinge on the family's capacities and therefore, inevitably, on the performance of its tasks.

Most treatments of family task functions recognize either implicitly or explicitly that families must perform tasks for their constituent members, and that they likewise perform tasks for the surrounding society. Also implicit in many treatments of the topic is a recognition that the families provide for their members not only the satisfaction of certain utilitarian needs, such as preparation of food, provision of domicile, etc., but also affective needs, such as for emotional support, a sense of being accepted as a person, a supportive "retreat" from the workaday world. There is no widely accepted list of the tasks that families are expected to perform, partly because of vast differences in family composition, especially in relation to stages in the family life cycle.

Brandwein and her associates developed a listing including economic functions, domestic responsibilities, and support activities.[42] Cogswell and Sussman list the following functions: physical and psychological sustenance; care of its members—including food, shelter, clothing, interpersonal relations; affection, happiness, financial support, and purchasing; procreation; the care and socialization of children; linkage of the family unit to other families and linkages to the organizations of society so that members receive health care, education, occupational training, leisure time, and recreational time; support of each other in individual or family crises.[4][3]

The following categories will serve our purpose.

Family Task Performance

A. *Internal tasks*
   1. *Utilitarian*
      a. Household maintenance tasks—provision of shelter, home repair, cleaning, laundry, etc.
      b. Personal caretaking tasks—meal preparation, cleanliness activities, health maintenance, putting children to bed, etc.
      c. Socialization of children—limit setting, discipline, growth stimulation, etc.
   2. *Affective*
      a. Nurturance tasks—affection, understanding, problem-solving, encouragement, support, etc.
      b. Member gratification—opportunity for individuation and self-actualization; favorable affect in utilitarian task performance; personal sense of security, safety; congruence between family goals and achievements, etc.
B. *External tasks*
   1. *Utilitarian*
      a. Occupational tasks—income-producing activity of various types
      b. Acquisition of goods and services from the environment
   2. *Participatory*
      a. Participation in kinship and friendship networks which exchange utilitarian and affectional support
      b. Conformity to social norms as a basis for degree of esteem accorded the family.

The reader's attention is called to a feedback loop of relevance to the present study, and, we believe, of general relevance in the application of the model to other crises and even to other system levels. A system's capacity is an important determinant of its task performance. But there is also a feedback from task performance to system capacity. The manner in which families perform their tasks may strengthen or weaken such capacities as adaptability, integration, or ability to relate to their environment.

THE COGNITIVE PROCESSES

Our model postulates that a family responds and adjusts to the initial impacts which stem from a stressor event and which affect its abilities to carry out its vital functions. But the process is not mechanical or deterministic. A series of cognitive activities intervene through which the family perceives the event and its first-round effects, weighs and judges the implications, and decides on a course of action or inaction.

Let us begin with the subjective definition which a family gives to the first signs of a crisis. W.I. Thomas pointed out decades ago that events must be perceived and defined in order to be responded to. "Preliminary to any self-determined act of behavior," he wrote, "there is always a stage of examination and deliberation which we may call *the definition of the situation.*"[44]

Earl L. Koos described in his book on *Families in Trouble* the impact on two families of the circumstance that their young son had contracted gonorrhea. In the one case, this event was a severe shock, causing the family to withdraw from social participation with a feeling of shame and disgrace. In the other family, the situation was taken most casually, as a modest, slightly bemusing annoyance.[45] Hill has put it succinctly: "Stressors become crises in line with the definition the family makes of the event."[46]

Lazarus has pointed out two important appraisals operating in a crisis. The first deals with the extent to which the event is defined as a threat. The second has to do with alternative ways of coping with the situation.[47] Taplin indicates that various homeostatic and psychoanalytic approaches to family crisis behavior have neglected the cognitive aspects.

> Organisms function in environments, and must be adaptable in several respects in order to survive a variety of situations. Consequently, there must be perceptual processes which will produce profoundly differing effects in differing situations, and also a memory process to carry over selectively some lessons from earlier situations.[48]

Many other writers emphasize the relativistic perception of crisis events by different families. Hill points out three different levels of definition of crisis events. One is the objective event, a second is the cultural definition formed by the community, and the third is the family's own subjective definition.[49] The third, he says, is most important in determining the family's response.

A family's definition of the event reflects partly the value system held by the family, partly its previous experience in meeting crises, and partly the mechanisms employed in previous definitions of events. This is the *meaning* aspect of the crisis, the interpretation made of it.[50]

It may be well to point out that in the process of assessment, cognitive processes are meant to include not only cognition, in the Parsonian sense, but also cathexis and evaluation.[51] In other words, we are talking not only of the family's access to relevant information, its scanning processes, and its data-processing; we are also talking about the meaning and feeling tone which these data have for the family and how they evaluate them from the standpoint of affect. And we also mean to include any normative, moral, ethical, or ideological interpretation which they give to the information that they receive.

It is misleading to think of "the cognitive process" in crisis situations as being limited to a single, specific definition and assessment of the stressor event, important as that initial definition may be. Cognitive activities antedate the stressor event and they are active at every stage of adjustment to it, as we shall see in subsequent sections of this chapter. They are included at this point because of their importance in filtering the impact of the stressor event on the family's capacities and thus in the process of determining the family's sequence of responses to it. Consideration was given earlier to cognitive competence as a capacity in which families may differ from one another. Here we are concerned with the actual application of that capacity in the process of assessing the nature and importance of the stressor event.

The stressor event—in this case, the energy shortage—is assessed by families as to its impact on them. What the model suggests is that this assessment of importance is a cognitive process carried out with some attention given to the possible relation of the energy shortage to one or more of the family's capacities and thus to its performance of its task functions. The extent that these are perceived to be affected in important ways constitutes the perceived impact of the shortage on the family and provides the basis for various types of adjustive behavior. Hence, the impact of the shortage, even on families with similar characteristics, is not automatically the same. It may differ depending on the importance which each family attributes to the impact of the shortage on its capacities and performance. These assessments influence the types of adjustments that will be made.

ADJUSTMENT

We come now to what families do by way of adjustment, based on their perceptions and evaluations of stressor events. Adjustment can mean either an adaptive process or a changed state. We are concerned here with both the process of change and the specific types of changes that are made and their effects. In fact, there are a number of dimensions and aspects of the adjustment process that are so closely interrelated that they can be separated only for purposes of analysis.

The process can be viewed as a sequence of actions or stages over time. These successive stages differ, however, in the nature and permanence of the adjustments that are made, from the early exploratory testings and responses to a new level of stabilization at the end of the adjustment process.

The process can also be seen as consisting of various types of compensating mechanisms or modes of response. These may draw on different capacities of the family and may affect the performance of one or another of the family's tasks, again taking into account the intensity and permanence of the several compensatory mechanisms.

An important distinction should be made here: Certain mechanisms lead to effects that remain substantially within the family. These can be looked upon as "absorbed impacts" in which the family "pays" most of the cost of adjusting. Other adaptations pass along the impacts beyond the family; these "transmitted impacts" have repercussive effects on other systems. Obviously many adjustments have both kinds of results.

Bearing in mind the wholeness of the phenomenon we are describing, for purposes of presentation and discussion this section is given over to (a) the sequence of stages, especially the early adjustments and (b) the types of compensatory mechanisms and responses that families can make. Though inevitably there is some overlap, the next sections of the model deal with second round adjustments and the effects they have on the family itself (absorbed) and those they transfer to other systems (transmitted impacts).

Sequence of Stages

First it is important to point out that how a stressor event is appraised and what is done about it are two aspects of the situation which occur in only approximate succession. In many instances exploratory behavior constitutes not only a beginning adjustment to a crisis event, but continues the process of defining that event. The event takes meaning as different exploratory attempts are made to respond to the impact it is having on the system's capacities and task performances. W.I. Thomas, cited above, also made the point that to define the situation is to know one's role in it. Behavior and definition are tightly intertwined, in other words.

Psychologists have long noted the tendency for an unaccustomed stimulus to produce various types of overt behavior that are not necessarily goal directed. The infant stuck by a diaper pin thrashes around in its crib. Even mature adults may respond to hunger pangs with general restlessness, rather than with a move to the kitchen.

Often confusion, paralysis, or ineffectiveness in actions and choice of actions characterize the initial part of this exploratory period. This may be attributable to the first dazing effect of the impact, where the impact is intense, or may be caused by lack of or confusion in, the information received. This confusion may be exacerbated by the need for prompt action in an uncertain situation. Wright points out that under the impact of such time pressure, decisionmakers may not even make sufficient use of such information as they do have, but rather limit their scope of scanning and attention.[52] Olson and Lubach have discussed the process of "floundering" in cases where more dissonant information is being received than can be sorted out and utilized as a basis for deliberate, planned action.[53]

In any case, tentative thrusts may be made in attempts to adjust to the crisis event. In the energy shortage, more attention may be paid to advertisements about home insulation; one may begin to explore the availability of public transportation; attention may be drawn to the wattage of light bulbs and frost-free refrigerators. Much of such activity may be sporadic, spur-of-the-moment, and highly preliminary. Many false starts may be made, some of them being actually tried, others being tested out only in conjecture.

As time goes on, these tentative, exploratory adjustments begin to go through a selective process. Some are discarded, others are further developed. It is important to recognize that in the process of adjustment, individual adjustive measures may succeed each other in time. Here, we point out two ways in which this adjustive succession may occur. Some adjustments may be tentatively tried, then discarded in favor of others which seem more effective or less costly. The other type arises from the circumstance that some adjustments, when made, make other adjustments necessary or desirable. In this case, the later adjustment, rather than being a replacement of the earlier adjustment, is a consequence of it. We shall treat these under the section dealing with "Secondary Adjustments."

In considering how to induce changes in individual and group behavior, Kurt Lewin, the social psychologist, developed a rather complex analysis which he summarized in three stages: unfreezing, change of level, and freezing on the new level.[54] This conceptualization is useful: the impact of a crisis event has an unfreezing effect, in Lewin's terms, and with the initial exploratory behavior, the second stage, change of level, has begun. Finally there is the question of whether and how the new level is stabilized or refrozen. Lewin described the steady state of a system as a quasi-stationary equilibrium. Any state of a system is such because of a set of opposing forces which pressure it to change in different ways. The system's state at any moment is at the point of equilibrium among these forces. But these forces are dynamic, and they may change in intensity or direction. The unfreezing stage is one in which a change is made in this counterpoised force field.

Movement or change in the system then takes place until the forces are once again in balance, perhaps at a different level. Unless the forces supporting and promoting this new level are sufficiently strong, or sufficiently bolstered by other forces, the system may continue to move—either away from the initial state or back towards it.[55] Thus, the New Year's resolution is broken because "it doesn't have enough going for it." Or, to take an example of attrition from the energy crisis, the family which sets its thermostat back four degrees gradually moves it up during the ensuing months until that adjustive behavior has been completely washed out.

On the other hand, the forces supporting an adjustment—the secondary adjustments—may be great enough to stabilize it at the new level. Obviously, the importance of this aspect of crisis-adjustment to energy conservation policy needs no underscoring. We are interested in the extent to which the adjustments to the energy shortage were short-lived and the extent to which they resulted in a new, more conservation-oriented level of adjustment.

Modes and Mechanisms of Adjustment

Much of the crisis literature understandably deals with the psychological aspects of adjustment to crisis events. Thus, Rapoport writes:

> In general, the patterns of responses for an individual or family necessary for healthy crisis resolution may be described as follows: (1) correct cognitive perception of the situation, which is furthered by seeking new knowledge and by keeping the problem in consciousness; (2) management of affect through awareness of feelings and appropriate verbalization leading toward tension discharge and mastery; (3) development of patterns of seeking and using help with actual tasks and feelings by using interpersonal and institutional resources.[56]

Rapoport is concerned with crises of the type which involve grave problems of emotional adjustment. In the present study, we are more concerned with the utilitarian steps taken in response to the crisis event, and the processes which led to and resulted from these steps. In this connection, Miller's observation with regard to stress is especially pertinent:

> A stress is any force that pushes the functioning of important subsystems beyond their ability to restore equilibrium through ordinary, nonemergency adjustment processes. . . . All adjustment processes have their costs. A person works to keep in equilibrium his most vital variables as ordered along a hierarchy of variables he may be quite unable to report.[5,7]

This insightful description, translated into economic terms, means that individuals and families in their adjustments to crises seek to keep gains and losses on a number of different preference dimensions equal at the margin, so that overall benefit is held as high as possible and overall cost is kept as low as possible. Whether or not empirical man, as distinct from rational or economic man, always applies such rationality to the adjustive process is questionable. But the notion is useful analytically in economic analysis, in organizational theory, and ultimately in the utilitarian ethics of Jeremy Bentham, and it deserves mention in this context.

The means by which families adjust to crises bring the analysis back to capacities. While the model does provide for increases in these, for the most part crises involve losses—diminutions in a family's capacities and reductions in its resources. But whether the change is a loss or an addition (such as an increase in income or an improvement in the family's feelings of solidarity), the family as a system finds itself engaged in compensating actions to achieve a new equilibrium.

Families redress these crisis-induced imbalances through several modes of adjustment. Some consist of *replenishments* of a decreased resource or capacity, as when a family makes efforts with friends and neighbors to replenish a loss of esteem and thereby to restore the family's reputation. Adjustment may also involve a *rearrangement* within the same capacity or resource, as when a family modifies the distribution of roles among its members.

A third mode of adjustment can be seen as the *conversion* of resources from one form to another. For example, families in this study drew upon savings to purchase storm windows or insulation. Akin to this is *substitution* of one resource for another, as when a family replaces the personal care provided to a member of the family with the paid-for services of an outside professional person in situations of serious or chronic illness.

Finally, a system's response to stressor events may take the form of *resistance*. It should be borne in mind that "adjustment" is not synonymous with submission or even with accommodation. The response is often an action designed to repel or ward off the impact of crisis events; this can entail protest or aggressive behavior toward the source of the stress. This recalls the distinction between "absorbed" and "transmitted" impacts. Resistance can be viewed as a system's self-protective mechanism, one which frequently has the effect of pushing off change and costs to other systems.

On the other hand, rearrangement of resources and some substitutions may mean that the family is absorbing most of the impact. Replenishment of resources and certain conversions and substitutions may throw more of the weight of the adjustment outside the family to other systems. One of the questions to which we shall return in the final chapter concerns the flexibility that it is possible for different kinds of families to call upon in making adjustments, thereby throwing off the burden of the crisis to be borne by others outside the family.

These modes of adjustment—replenishment, rearrangement, conversion-substitution and resistance—must also be seen in terms of the family's capacities and tasks. The following categories have been found useful.

Changes Within a Capacity. If a capacity such as integration or material or nonmaterial resources is diminished, the adjustment may take the form of restoring that capacity or making modifications within it.

A crisis may present a situation for which the usual pattern of reciprocal roles is no longer possible or appropriate. *The Admirable Crichton*, James Barrie's absorbing account of the transformation in roles which ensued when an English family was marooned with its servants on a desert island, is a fictitious but dramatic description of role change in time of crisis. In this crisis adjustment, the butler emerged as the absolute despot. In the realm of less idiosyncratic and more generalized types of crisis situations, the early studies of the impact of unemployment on families in the Great Depression likewise found severe role rearrangements taking place, especially with the unemployment of the head of the household.[5,8] Such readjustments may be major or minor.

Changes Between Capacities. The depletion or impairment of one capacity may be compensated for by a change in another capacity. A depletion of material resource level may be adjusted to by an increase in the use of nonmaterial resources. For example, unemployment may mean less income, but an adjustment may be made in part by the previous wage-earner's utilizing time and skills to perform repair tasks which would otherwise have been done by an outside, paid service man or contractor. In the same vein, the entrance of the wife into the labor market may occasion a readjustment of roles and role expectations thus reflecting itself in a different configuration of family integration.

Changes Between Capacities and Tasks. Changes in any of the family's capacities can be expected to reflect themselves in changes in the family's performance of its tasks. A family may decide to continue its level of task performance by maintaining its existing level of expenditures at a time when income has been curtailed. This will result in a depletion of material resource capacity. On the other hand, a family may curtail certain expenditures for task performance, thus reducing the satisfaction of members' utilitarian and/or affective needs. Thus, in order to maintain a capacity, it reduces its task performance. (This, in turn, may affect its integration, a secondary adjustment which will be considered below.)

Changes Within Tasks. A family may adjust to a situation concerning its task performance by making changes and adjustments in the performance of those specific tasks. Loss of a job may be adjusted to by finding another one. Inability to go long distances for recreation may occasion new recreational activities closer to home. An absent working mother may occasion the father's performing a larger number of household tasks.

Changes Between Tasks. A family may attempt to adjust to a diminution in performance of utilitarian tasks (poorer quality meals, less use of the family car) by increasing the expression of affection and emotional support. Expressing this poignant situation in our stilted, analytical terms, changes in performance of utilitarian tasks are compensated for by changes in performance of affective tasks. The opposite adjustment is interesting to contemplate: the alleged attempt by many parents to substitute utilitarian satisfactions for affective satisfactions of their children—spend lavishly for their clothing but short-change them on time and affection.

Compensatory Adjustments with Environment. In order to adjust to a crisis impact, a social system may have to change its input/output relations with its environment. Several of the foregoing types of adjustment have involved a change in input/output relationship, but the category probably deserves its own separate listing. These compensatory input/output adjustments are distinguished from adjustments which represent the absorption of the crisis impact by the family.

In considering changes in input/output relations in this study, we employ a distinction which is especially useful in tracing through the reciprocal adjustments of families and establishments. These two social systems are related to each other along two principal dimensions. One is the employment dimension; the other is the consumption dimension. Establishments need workers which households supply; they also provide goods and services which households consume.

There is one reservation in this otherwise neat double bipolar relationship. Although all establishments need household members as employees, they do not all need them as consumers, since many establishments produce goods or services that are not consumed directly by families. Examples of the latter would be wholesalers, engineering consulting firms, and others that have social systems other than families as their consumers.

The labor force line and the consumption line do not exhaust the possible relationships between households and establishments, though they are certainly the two most important ones. We shall nevertheless need an "Other" category to take care of protest behavior and other transactions which may link establishments and households in friendly, affect-free, or hostile relationships.

In closing this section on adjustment, we remind the reader that our model is purposely designed to be broad in scope, accommodating the data of our energy impact study, but also being employable in widely diverse types of crisis impacts. In the case of our energy study data, the impacts came to most families through directly affecting their store of and accessibility to energy-related material resources, and in some cases to employment. These impacts affected various aspects of utilitarian task performance—shopping, travel to work, etc. Adjustments to them were made largely in the areas of changes within and between family tasks, and these in turn reflected themselves in compensatory input/output adjustments, thus affecting shopping patterns and, to a lesser extent, work patterns.

SUCCESSIVE ADJUSTMENTS

The adjustments considered in the preceding section may have secondary consequences, both for the family and for other families and establishments. The former type we call primary adjustments, the latter successive adjustments.

Perhaps the best way to begin our consideration of second-round adjustments in the family system is to remind ourselves that the cognitive process is important in the process of adjustment to initial impacts. The preliminary scanning and testing out of adjustments, whether in actuality or in imagination, frequently involves an awareness of the possible consequences on the family itself of making any particular form of adjustment. What will be the implications of selling the second car? Of turning down the thermostat during waking hours? Of taking the bus rather than the family car? Of postponing the vacation automobile trip across the country?

Presumably, families differ in this aspect of their cognitive capacity, some families being better equipped than others to anticipate the possible consequences of one adjustment path rather than another. Such considerations constitute constraints on adjustment possibilities, to be sure, but they also constitute guides for avoiding successive adjustments of a type which would unnecessarily impair capacities.

The depletion of savings in order to maintain a given level of family task performance has the secondary effect of leaving the family with less capacity to make subsequent adjustments through drawing on savings. Types of adjustments which place strains on role relationships may leave the family with less integration, less capacity to "stick together" in the next crisis. We have already pointed out that a succession of adjustment processes may under certain circumstances lead the family to be less adaptable, less capable of withstanding new stresses. Families may draw on the help available to them through kinship and friendship network support systems in a way that makes it difficult to make a similar set of demands another time.

It is important to note that the adjustment process should not be considered solely as an initial impact and then a single secondary impact, but rather as a series of adjustments and readjustments which must work themselves out before a relatively stable state is once again achieved.

In this highly interrelated world, social systems can be treated in isolation only analytically. What they do often has impacts on other systems, sometimes deliberate, sometimes not. Since one system's adjustment may constitute another's impact, the importance for policy considerations of tracing through the adjustments as they impact other systems is obvious. A manufacturing company may solve its declining market problem by reducing employment, thus affecting families whose adjustment to unemployment may increase the financial burden on public welfare agencies. The fact that this procedure may constitute an infinite regression does not in any way detract from the importance of the impacts caused by different types of adjustment.

These "ripple effects" have implications for the earlier observation that crises are not always injurious, but can represent favorable opportunities as well. What begins apparently as a "benign crisis" may ultimately include results that are unfavorable from the point of view of the system involved. An apt illustration comes from one of the countries that initially benefited from the fivefold increase in petroleum products that Americans paid after the 1973 embargo. People in Saudi Arabia have begun to have second thoughts about their oil boom.[59] There are concerns expressed about its impact on the quality of life; about the influx of Western customs that threaten the traditional culture; complaints about sudden growth and inadequate planning for electricity, water, and sewage to cope with the rapid expansion of the population in the capital.

RESIDUAL EFFECTS

It will be recalled from our discussion of stages in the family's response to crisis that a point is reached at which the adjustments begin to stabilize. This is what Lewin called the "refreezing" stage. The family accustoms itself to shorter recreational trips by car. Changes take place in time allotments and in daily routines which accommodate adjustments made in the work and consumption situation, and in energy conservation measures. Where such stabilizing adjustments do not take place, the initial adjustments may prove temporary, and may wash away with time, since the system really never adapted itself to accommodate them.

At some point, however, the adjustment process subsides and one can say that the crisis is over. We are interested now in what residue the crisis has left. What is the state of the family with respect to its ability to adapt viably to new crises, whether of the same or of a different nature?

There are two analytically distinct components which may constitute the state of the system with respect to adaptability to future crises. One is that from the experience of coping with the crisis, the system has "learned" something over and above the immediate situation. It has learned a little about how to cope, in general, and this learning may stand it in good stead in the future. We considered this aspect under system resources. However, there is the possibility that instead of being strengthened by a crisis experience, a family may be weakened by it. Hiroto and Seligman go so far as to describe a situation of "learned helplessness," which may derive from the successive carry-over of unsuccessful coping experiences.[60] Hill sums up both sides of the equation: "Successful experience with crisis tests and strengthens a family but defeat in crisis is punitive on family structure and morale."[61]

The other aspect or component of the crisis-readiness/crisis-proneness state has to do with the extent to which the adjustment to crisis has depleted material or nonmaterial resources which consequently are no longer available in such magnitude. As mentioned above, a family may suffer a period of unemployment and adjust to it well by depleting its savings. But if unemployment hits it again before it has been able to replenish its savings, it will not be so well positioned with regard to the necessary material resources. Other things being equal, the second period of unemployment will make a greater impact.

We called attention earlier to Lipman-Blumen's premise that the role changes that can be expected in response to crisis depend on the relationship between the characteristics of the crisis and the state of the social system at the time of crisis. She points out that the following factors will affect the system's state: previous experience with similar crises and the development of coping mechanisms and strategies; the effectiveness of the system in resolving analogous crises; and the length of time since and the nature of the most recent crisis.[62]

In the present study, a question related to crisis-readiness/crisis-proneness is the extent to which certain conservation measures have been put into effect and continued in effect through stabilization, and thus are incorporated into the present state of the family system. These measures are hence no longer available as a means of conservation in response to a possible new energy shortage. They have already been "used up." If a family insulates its house and reduces its fuel consumption, it does not have these avenues of conservation the next time a fuel savings is called for. In this sense, these families are more vulnerable to another energy shortage because they have used up a large part of their "cushion" of potential adjustive actions.

With this final residual category of crisis-readiness and -proneness, the analytical model is complete. We have presented it in terms of the family because that unit is the focal point of this study. We want to say now, and emphasize the point, that the dynamics that have been used to describe families facing crisis situations are applicable to other social systems—establishments, states, the nation as a whole.

Obviously the model as presented above does not correspond in all its specifics with social systems at other levels. For example, the tasks performed by an establishment are different in content from those performed by a family, the former involving such tasks as providing goods and services to consumers, earning profits, and paying employees. But the main features of the model are applicable to systems other than the family. This holds for the main stages of crisis, the general effects on system capacities, and the processes of adjustment in terms of mechanisms and over time. Likewise, the model can be useful in studying the repercussive effects and the residual effects of a crisis in the case of a nation or local community.

In the next chapter we make frequent references to the model first in relation to the national situation and then in connection with the three metropolitan areas under study. It will also provide a basis for presentation and treatment of the data regarding establishment adjustments. Its principal use, however, will be in the presentation and analysis of the family data which constitute the core of the present study.

One final note of caution. The model developed in the preceding pages obviously does not fit any concrete situation perfectly, certainly not the energy crisis. Like a New Yorker's mental map of the United States, some parts of the model will not be found in our discussion of the energy crisis; other parts will be exaggerated or underdeveloped. Hopefully, the model will nonetheless serve as a useful guide in understanding the general dynamics of crises as they confront families and social systems at other levels.

Table 2-3. The Crisis Model

1. The stressor event
   - Source — Internal-external
   - Relation to family cycle — Strong-weak relationship
   - Nature of warning — Diffuse-clear; Extensive-little
   - Disruptive effect — Intense-moderate
   - Consistency — Similar for all-differing
   - Quality — Harmful-beneficial
2. Initial impacts
   - A. On the family's capacities
     - Integration
     - Adaptability
     - Cognitive competence
     - Material resources
     - Nonmaterial resources
     - Ability to manage environmental relationships

Table 2-3 (cont.)

    B. On task performance
       Internal tasks
          Utilitarian
          Affective
       External tasks
          Utilitarian
          Affective
3. The cognitive processes
4. Adjustment
    A. Sequence of stages
       Unfreezing/exploration
       Change level
       Stabilization/attrition/refreezing
    B. Modes and mechanisms of adjustment
       Replenishment
       Rearrangement
       Conversion/substitution
       Resistance
         a. Changes within a capacity
         b. Changes between capacities
         c. Changes between capacities and tasks
         d. Changes within tasks
         e. Changes between tasks
         f. Compensatory adjustments with environment
            Labor line
            Consumption line
5. Successive adjustments
       Impact on the family
       Impact on other systems
6. Attrition
7. Residual effects
       Crisis-readiness/crisis-proneness

❇︎ *Chapter Three*

The Energy Crisis Unfolds in Hartford, Mobile, and Salem

A crisis "begins," according to the model set forth in the previous chapter, when some event impinges on the capacities of a family and disrupts its accustomed behavior. There follows a succession of adjustments that produce impacts within the family and reverberations on other institutions. Clearly, in these interactions one system's adjustments to a stressor event may become the stressor events to which other systems must adjust.

In the energy crisis of 1973-74 the precipitating occurrence took place outside the United States. It affected national, state, and local government in this country and their reactions impinged on thousands of profit and nonprofit enterprises whose responses in turn became disruptive events for the families who were interviewed in Hartford, Mobile, and Salem. This chapter describes these initial interactions in the energy crisis, drawing upon the earlier discussion of stressor events (see Table 1-2). A brief contrast with the energy crisis of 1976-77 concludes the chapter.

There were warnings of an energy shortage well before the oil

---

Much of the information in this chapter was compiled by three local researchers: Professor A.K. Barakeh of the Department of Economics, University of South Alabama, collected the information on the Mobile SMSA; in addition, Prof. Barakeh advised on the collection of data on costs and consumption of energy in the Mobile area; Nancy A. Whitelaw of the Institute on Aging, Portland State University, collected the information on developments in the Salem area; Professor Seymour Warkov of the Sociology Department, University of Connecticut, in the Hartford area. In each area, additional information was obtained from interviews with local and state officials, the Chambers of Commerce, the utility companies and other sources, as well as from a reading of local newspapers.

embargo of October 1973. A stream of writings by experts on natural resources and actions by organizations dedicated to protecting the environment had been flowing for years. Immediately before the embargo there were stirrings. For example, the major petroleum companies had begun to ration their supplies by curtailing deliveries early in 1973. Amoco introduced a rationing program for its 31,000 dealerships that set deliveries at 75 percent of the 1972 level. Texaco announced an allocation program for several areas east of the Rockies. The principal feature of these allocation programs was the establishment of delivery levels set in relation to those of the previous year. The House and Senate in April of 1973 sought to empower the president to allocate crude and refined petroleum products, but the Nixon Administration was opposed and no bill was passed at that time. However, the president did warn of higher prices and shortages and did urge conservation in his Energy Message in April.

ADVANCE WARNINGS IN THE THREE AREAS

Advance notice of what lay ahead was also evident in the three metropolitan areas under study. In Hartford shortages of natural gas predated that area's difficulties with oil. In the winter of 1972-73 one of the two interstate suppliers of natural gas curtailed deliveries to its commercial and industrial customers; the other held the line by disallowing consumption increases. In September 1973 Connecticut's Public Utilities Commission was expressing cautious optimism about the electricity supply for the winter; despite record-breaking power usage, the summer electric supply had proved adequate. By October, however, the local newspapers began to predict a crisis and the Public Utilities Commission announced that available electricity might not meet demand.

As early as 1971 a tightening of natural gas supplies had occurred in Mobile when industrial users became subject to twenty-four-hour notice of interrupted service. The volume of natural gas sold by United Gas Pipe Line to industrial customers in Mobile dropped by nearly 50 percent from 1971 to 1973. Industries had been forewarned and had begun to convert to coal or fuel oil.

The next indication of an energy problem came in August of 1973 when the Alabama Liquid Petroleum Gas Board Administration in Foley (Baldwin County) reported that butane gas would no longer be available for home use. Residential users were urged to switch to propane gas, which was somewhat more hazardous in storage but was less scarce than butane gas. The Fairhope City Council, also in

Baldwin County, voted to refuse applications for gas service outside of the city limits after being notified by the United Gas Pipeline Service that natural gas supplies would be rationed to the city that winter. Such rationing was unprecedented in the city's history.

Even earlier in the summer, many of the major oil companies had begun to allocate gasoline to their service stations. Despite these warning signals in Alabama and Connecticut, no formal state or local government actions were taken until after the events of October.

Oregon experienced an energy shortage and the state government responded six months before the dramatic events in the fall of 1973. In May the governor announced the creation of a task force to recommend immediate and long-term solutions for the state's energy problems. The action was prompted by an imminent shortage of hydroelectric power resulting from low water levels behind power-generating dams, a light snowpack in the mountains, and shortages of fossil fuels, particularly diesel oil used to operate electricity-generating turbines.

The problems of the electricity shortage were compounded by curtailed gasoline supplies which compelled the governor to declare a limited emergency in Central Oregon in July and to direct the Oregon National Guard to lend 5,000 gallons of gasoline for agricultural use. The following month he responded to the deteriorating power situation by declaring a statewide energy emergency, by ordering drastic cutbacks in the use of energy in state buildings and grounds, and by asking Oregon's citizens to undertake voluntary conservation measures.

In September the governor established an Energy Council to develop a plan for mandatory reductions in energy use in the event of an emergency. A few days later he issued an executive order banning all outdoor lighting for commercial or display purposes, stating that previous requests for voluntary cutbacks had not produced savings of sufficient magnitude, adding that "We must save energy at the rate of 7½ percent of normal consumption each month and I fully expect we will have to raise our sights."

What can be said, then, about the warnings that preceded the energy crisis? There were indeed ample indications of a growing shortage of all forms of energy. And there were some early responses to the shortage, though not on a national scale and not by the federal government. At the state and local levels in the areas covered by this study, the response was partial and uneven; strong in Oregon, weaker in Connecticut and Alabama. For the most part, Americans did not heed the warnings.

The overt act that precipitated the energy crisis of 1973-74 came quite suddenly and with little advance notice. As an economic and political move to exert pressure on United States policy in the Middle East, the Organization of Arab Petroleum Exporting Countries on October 17, 1973 announced an embargo on oil sales and shipments to this country. This can be called the precipitating stressor event in this crisis as long as it is recognized that the shortages brought about by the Arabs' action came on top of energy problems that had been germinating for some time. Actually, the OAPEC move cut off less than 5 percent of the U.S. oil supply. By November 7 President Nixon was on television to tell the American people, officially, that there was an energy crisis.

If October 1973 can be considered roughly the beginning, the "end" of the crisis can be fixed, also in approximate terms, in mid-March 1974. Five months after their announcement of the embargo, the Arab governments lifted the prohibition on sales to the United States as a result of the latter's peace initiatives addressed to the Israeli-Arab confrontation.

Many of the responses and adjustments to be examined in this book were concentrated in those five months, though it can hardly be said that the situation had fully stabilized at the close of that period. In this study our interest and data were extended four years beyond the fall of 1973 in order to assess how much the energy-related behavior of the surveyed households had stabilized or how much attrition had occurred.

This discussion of the unfolding of the crisis begins with a summary of the main actions and reactions as seen from a national perspective. We then look at the development of the crisis in each of the three metropolitan areas.

THE NATIONAL PERSPECTIVE

Within a few weeks of the oil embargo, President Nixon responded with exhortation, urging the American people to reduce their temperatures at home and to cut down the use of their cars. One of his first acts was to request $10 billion for Project Independence, a program designed to make the United States independent of foreign energy sources by 1980. The program was never adopted and in time came to be looked upon as utterly unrealistic.

It is evidence of the complexity of American politics and policy-making and also typical of first responses to crises that the initial efforts to meet the 1973-74 energy crisis with a national energy policy thrashed around not for a short time but for years, stretching from President Nixon's April 1973 message to the comprehensive program presented by President Carter in April 1977.

The last weeks of 1973 saw the opening of congressional debate and conflict with the White House over energy policy that continued unabated until President Ford signed the Energy Policy and Conservation Act in December 1975. The policy differences revolved (and continue to revolve) around regional interests; differential impacts on various industries; decontrol of prices and/or rationing; taxation of windfall profits; the relaxation of environmental protections; the extent of government control of personal and corporate behavior; and the effect of continuing dependence on imported oil on this country's freedom of action in foreign affairs.

What did follow the embargo was considerable discussion of many possible measures to be taken and the actual adoption of a few of them. In his first statements President Nixon recommended staggered work hours; special bus lanes to speed the movement of large numbers of commuters; and the encouragement of car pools by providing preferential parking for car pool vehicles. And he announced his support of year-round Daylight Savings Time and of a 50 mph national speed limit. If these and similar measures failed to produce the necessary fuel savings, the president warned, gasoline rationing might be necessary.

Before the end of November the federal government's response to the oil embargo had moved from exhortation to compulsory regulation of some aspects of energy production, distribution, and consumption. As a result of the passage by the Congress of the Emergency Petroleum Act and its reluctant signing by President Nixon, the president was empowered to ban gasoline sales on Sundays and to set speed limits. And he was required to set up an allocation program for crude oil and all refinery products.

After long debate the Congress approved a 55 mph speed limit on the highways and enacted year-round Daylight Savings Time. Soon thereafter the White House announced a ban on Sunday sales of gasoline; cutbacks in deliveries of home heating oil; and a 15 percent reduction in the amount of gasoline to be refined.

In December the Federal Energy Administration developed a master plan for allocating gasoline and fuel supplies. Priorities were given to essential community services. Farming and manufacturing were assured adequate levels as were public transportation and mail delivery. But problems arose in the allocations program, as we shall see later in this chapter, particularly in terms of confusion and friction between the FEA and the state energy offices. The federal administration set overall priorities and specified amounts but the states then had to parcel out these allocations. In addition, deliveries were still controlled by the private companies.

In addition to exhortation and regulation, a major economic

impact confronted consumers of energy. The wholesale price index for fuels rose 65 percent during 1973 and retail prices reflected this increase on into 1974.

By and large then the first adjustments by the federal government to the embargo crisis were, as the model suggests, exploratory, tentative, and marked by much indecision.

By February of 1974 the role of the federal government in allocating petroleum products began to diminish. The administrator of the program said that since shortages existed for the most part only in certain areas of the country, the states should take charge of allocations. He thereupon released 84 million gallons of gasoline to twenty states that were experiencing shortages. Within a month there were increased allocations to both agriculture and industry and most restrictions on fuels soon came to an end without fanfare. The crisis that had dominated the headlines for five months quickly slipped to a lower priority on the nation's agenda.

The greatest impacts of the crisis came between mid-October when President Nixon announced the existence of an energy crisis and mid-February when he stated publicly that the crisis had passed, though an "energy problem" remained. Undoubtedly the most severe and widespread effects of the crisis were the direct and indirect consequences of the cutbacks in the production and distribution of gasoline and other petroleum products and the sharp rise in their cost.

One of the most immediate and dramatic responses was the truckers' strike in December 1973. The truckers, most of them owner-operators, called their strike to protest the bind in which they felt they were caught between a steep increase in the cost of diesel fuel and a freeze on the rates they were permitted to charge for hauling freight. Serious shortages of meat, steel, fruit, and other products developed as the strike went on amid growing violence in several states. It was estimated at the end of the eleven-day truckers' stoppage that 100,000 workers had been temporarily laid off in industries affected by the strike. In March the Labor Department revealed that 292,000 workers were receiving unemployment benefits as a result of the energy crisis, though not necessarily as a result of the truckers' action.

Probably the single most pervasive aspect of the crisis, not as dramatic as the strike nor as hard a blow as losing one's job, was the simple inability to get gasoline at pumps across the land. The further results of this drying-up of a resource that had long been taken for granted were felt across the country. There were of course other shortages—for example in petroleum-based plastic materials and in heating and industrial fuels here and there—but the most widespread result is captured in the now familiar picture of long lines of motorists waiting and fuming at gasoline stations.

The impact of the oil embargo and its initial reverberations brought about, in Lewin's terms an "unfreezing" of the situation (see Chapter Two). But just as the ensuing adjustments could be expected to differ from family to family, so too did they differ from one part of the country to another. We want now to examine how the crisis unfolded in Connecticut, Alabama, and Oregon and the three metropolitan areas of Hartford, Mobile, and Salem, looking first at the ways in which governmental systems responded and then at the adjustments made by establishments.

THE CRISIS IN CONNECTICUT

The period of exploration, experimentation, and indecision that characterized the national government scene in the early stages of the crisis had its counterpart in the states and localities. In Connecticut, two weeks after the announcement of the oil embargo but before it could have any direct effects, the governor called the situation a "calamity" and urged conservation and emergency planning. A fortnight later a legislative committee recommended emergency and long-range fuel-conservation measures, including granting the governor the powers he would possess during a national disaster or war—rationing of home heating oil; lowering the speed limit on highways; and banning outdoor advertising and ornamental decorations using electricity. The committee also recommended providing no-interest state loans to homeowners installing insulation and storm windows, establishing a state energy board to gather facts and recommend programs, and changing building codes to help fuel conservation. But no immediate action was taken.

Later in November, the governor requested that electric companies cut voltage 5 percent during the peak hours of 4 to 8 P.M.; the companies complied. He also asked for a voluntary 50 mph statewide speed limit—a request which met with mixed success according to the state police. By Thanksgiving, the governor had made the 55 mph speed limit mandatory to meet federal regulations. State offices were told in November to conserve energy, to lower thermostats, and to use fewer lights. The state was said to be considering a four-day week for its employees.

The State Commissioner of Consumer Protection launched an investigation into complaints of discrimination, price-gouging, and tie-in selling at gas stations, and promised that the state would prosecute price-gougers. The state was also reported to be considering a plan to increase the number of insulated homes and businesses in Connecticut. Many such energy-saving ideas, both state and local, never came to fruition. Fourteen antipoverty agencies asked for but did not receive $4 million to give loans and grants to poor people on fixed incomes facing hardships because of the rise in fuel prices. Early in January, Connecticut complied with federal regulations and returned to Daylight Savings Time.

In February the governor took a stand on gasoline rationing. He opposed coupon gas rationing and proposed a four-step voluntary plan instead: gas stations should be open on Sunday; they would give fillups; customers should be permitted to buy gas only if their tanks were less than half full; and towns should decide for themselves how to control gasoline buying and how to stagger station hours. These voluntary measures were not particularly effective.

In March and April, Connecticut along with New York and Massachusetts lobbied in Congress for relief from rising fuel prices. In May the governor signed a law banning contrived fuel shortages designed to raise prices and affect competition and in June he made recommendations on fuel conservation for the summer, urging that airconditioners be set no lower than 78° and that the energy agency request a relaxation of office dress codes for men. For the most part, however, after March the pace of activity at the state capitol decreased.

These actions at the state level became stressor events, pressing upon the municipalities within Connecticut. Faced with the continuing threat of gasoline and oil shortages, the immediate realities of the allocating system, and urgings by the governor to plan for approaching emergencies, the localities responded also somewhat tentatively with a mixture of planning, exhortations to households and establishments to conserve, and some resistance to pressures that seemed unreasonable and unfair.

Much of the effort of the cities and towns in Hartford County went into advocacy on behalf of gasoline retailers who were asking for higher monthly allotments than the authorities had granted. The allocations system worked out to be particularly severe on the city of Hartford, where one-third of the gasoline stations had had to close because of the shortage. Many of these were marginal enterprises which, once forced to close, were unlikely to survive long enough to re-open. Some were new, struggling, minority-owned businesses. If the allocations assigned to these closed stations were lost, the city's supply of gasoline would indeed be inadequate for the normal demand.

The city administration in Hartford took the protests about allocations to the state energy board and then to the federal office in Boston. The city won a few of these cases, but the processing of protests was so slow that many decisions came after the gasoline shortage had ended. As an interim measure, the city's energy officials tried to keep the public informed as to which gasoline stations were open at what times; this often meant warning motorists that gas was not really available in the city.

Another adjustment that took the form of resistance came in connection with the attempt of the State Board of Education to shorten school hours. The episode also illustrates the fact that some legal powers were not sufficiently defined to provide clear-cut answers to jurisdictional issues thrown up by the energy crisis.

The Connecticut State Board of Education ordered all public schools to add three days to the 1973 Christmas vacation and to close school buildings at 4 P.M. and on weekends from December 21 to April 15, thereby cutting down on sports, recreational, and social activities. In addition, it recommended such energy-saving measures as a ban on student parking and lower temperatures in school swimming pools and auditoriums.

A wave of protest followed the state board's ruling and many towns refused to comply. Coming to the support of the protesting school systems, the state attorney general maintained that the State Board of Education did not have the legal authority to close schools. The governor's position resembled his stance on other energy matters; crisis decisions, he said, should be left to local decision-makers for "maximum flexibility." In December the Board of Education reversed its earlier ruling, conceded it had overstepped its authority, and left the decision to close schools to local boards of education.

In Hartford County a number of town councils reacted to the crisis atmosphere by setting up energy commissions to take both long- and short-range actions. In Newington, for example, the commission was mandated "to study energy shortages and their impact on the town," to keep the council and the school board informed of developments, and to coordinate conservation policies. After-hours activities at Town Hall were curtailed and the town considered a four-day work week for its own employees. Bloomfield proposed a car pooling plan. The Glastonbury Emergency Energy Coordinating Council was authorized to keep a running inventory of the fuel of town suppliers; to declare energy emergencies if necessary; to ration energy supplies; to reduce lighting in schools and offices; and to consider the possibility of buying storm windows for all town structures.

By January most local energy committees had issued guidelines for energy conservation and had set goals of 10 percent to 15 percent fuel savings for the winter months. The proposals of the mayor of South Windsor were representative: he recommended the lowering of thermostats; no heat in unused rooms; regular servicing of oil burners; improved home insulation; and replacement of leaky hot water faucets.

Many towns drew up contingency plans for an energy emergency or blackout. In Newington an agreement was reached with gas dealers to provide fire and ambulance drivers with fuel in case of emergency. In South Windsor three oil dealers agreed to act in rotation to handle emergency cases of citizens running out of home heating oil. Builders in Windsor offered both expertise and large heating equipment in case of crisis. West Hartford purchased a second fuel tank in which to store fuel for town vehicles. Hartford made plans to use public schools as shelters for heatless residents. More than twenty towns in the Greater Hartford area opened energy crisis centers with phone lines and a variety of information: how to complain about price gouging; where to find emergency fuel; how to convert oil heat systems to wood. In most cases, these crisis centers were the only features of the emergency plans ever put into effect.

THE CRISIS IN ALABAMA

Alabama, in contrast with Connecticut, depends mostly on bituminous coal and natural gas for its energy. With gasoline relatively easy to obtain and with only a slight dependence on oil for its industry and its homes, state and local government in Alabama felt little need to take strong actions on the energy front. They were, of course, subject to some of the same stressor events coming from Washington and the day after President Nixon's energy crisis message to the Congress, the governor created the Alabama Energy Management Board to coordinate conservation planning.

In a November 8 message, Alabama's governor stated that he had no power to reduce speed limits without the consent of the legislature, which was not in session. Nevertheless, he urged motorists to lower their speed to a maximum of 50 mph and state employees to lower thermostats in state buildings. While the governor's appeal seemed to have an effect upon some drivers, Alabama State Troopers reported in November that compliance with the request was not general.

In January the federal law setting a 55 mph speed limit prompted the governor to issue an executive order (since the legislature was not in session) lowering the speed limits accordingly. A month later Alabama joined fifteen other coal-producing states in drawing up a national policy statement aimed at obtaining maximum coal production combined with the best possible land reclamation practices.

In immediate response to President Nixon's November 7 television address on energy, local government began to adopt conservation steps. Most of these were designed to conserve the municipalities' own energy supplies. On November 8, for example, the Mobile City Commissioners asked city employees not to exceed 50 mph. At the same time, temperatures in city buildings were lowered to 66-68° and much stricter methods to control the use of gasoline by city vehicles were adopted.

The city of Mobile eased its restrictions on the burning of leaves in order to conserve fuel and studied a proposal to cut back on garbage pickups from three to two weekly and to cut trash pickups to one per week. The Public Works Commissioner estimated that the city could save about 100,000 gallons of gasoline per year by these actions. This proposal was eventually adopted in the fall of 1974. The city adopted an ordinance to save gasoline by permitting drivers to turn right after stopping at red lights, rather than having their engines idle while they waited for the light to turn green.

The impact of the crisis on Alabama's capacities and resources was not serious and hence the adjustments made by state government and by Mobile were largely limited to urging fuel conservation on industry, commerce and motorists and to implementing the federal allocations program and the speed limit. Municipal government adjusted chiefly by reducing some operations so as to save energy.

THE CRISIS IN OREGON

In Oregon, as we pointed out above, energy shortages were experienced and confronted well before the October embargo. In September an Energy Information Center had been set up and the governor's office had initiated steps to monitor and develop alternative sources of energy. As the state began to adjust to the heightened sense of crisis brought on by the embargo and national reactions to it and as winter came to Oregon, measures were adopted that were in some respects similar to those in Connecticut, sometimes with the same result.

Priorities for fuel allocation were established, with residential users having top priority, followed by farmers, the food-processing industry and other agriculture-related concerns. In October the governor requested all elementary and secondary schools to close for a month starting December 14, asserting that the state school superintendent agreed with his proposal and would contact local school districts. On the following day, however, the superintendent stated his opposition to school closings and announced that he would not ask school districts to comply with the governor's request.

By mid-November, the short-term hydroelectric outlook was beginning to improve. The director of the Public Utilities Commission announced that heavy rains had filled all the reservoirs on the Snake, Willamette, and Columbia Rivers. He urged the continuation of consumer efforts to conserve energy but recommended the lifting of the outdoor lighting ban, which was removed shortly thereafter.

As the immediacy of the electricity crisis began to fade, Oregon felt the impact of the nation's oil crisis. In early December gasoline supplies were running low and stations were closing for many hours during the week. In early January, the governor proposed the voluntary rationing plan which was known as the "odd-even system." Emulated by other states as the "Oregon plan," it provided that cars whose license plates ended in an odd number would buy gasoline on odd-numbered days and even-numbered license plates would buy on even-numbered days.

Later in January the governor sought broad emergency powers and declared that he was willing to share these with the legislature or its representatives. Debate over the emergency bill continued for several weeks, culminating in a compromise which gave the governor thirty-day emergency power but required that funds for any emergency program be approved by a special board. By the time the legislature passed this bill, however, the energy crisis was already beginning to recede.

In late December, the governor had announced that he was certain Oregon was not getting its fair share of fuel and asked the Federal Energy Administrator for a full disclosure of inventories of oil companies. In early February, statistics were released showing that Oregon was receiving only 79 percent of its 1972 sales, ranking it forty-fourth in priority among the fifty states. This disclosure was followed by a request from the governor for a 9 percent increase in Oregon's fuel allocation. Two extra gasoline allotments were received at the end of February and were crucial in easing the energy situation.

On the local level, Salem-area governments played only a minor role in attempts to manage the energy shortage. As was the case with Hartford and Mobile, efforts focused on conservation programs within city agencies rather than on moves to rearrange fuel consumption patterns in the community.

Salem officials felt the energy crunch as early as August 1973, when they learned that the city would not be able to obtain another annual contract for gasoline and heating fuels. Henceforth, the oil companies could guarantee only month-to-month service. City department heads announced a program to cut city fuel consumption by 10 percent. The major item on the program was the reduced use of city cars through the increased use of bicycles, buses, and car-pooling. At City Hall, power cutbacks went into effect during the late summer and early fall. By the end of August, city officials reported that night lighting was cut back 69 percent at City Hall and 92 percent at the library. Janitorial schedules had been changed to daytime hours.

In mid-August the Salem School District could guarantee bus service only a few weeks into the future as gasoline allocations remained on a month-to-month basis. Suggestions from state officials that schools eliminate night football games met with stiff resistance and the Salem school board refused to discontinue the events. Because of their popularity night football games often generate funds that help to support the rest of a school's athletic program. School boards showed more enthusiasm for reducing energy consumption during the day. Salem schools succeeded in cutting electric power use for September 1973 to half of that of September 1972.

Overall, however, despite a strong state executive and a twofold energy crisis, the actual impact of government action does not appear to have been significantly greater in Salem than in Hartford or Mobile. Until the end of the crisis period in 1974, the governor did not possess the power to take comprehensive action. When he attempted to move beyond pleading for conservation or cutting back government energy use, as in the cases of the display advertising ban and the attempt to close schools, public resistance, including that of some government officials, was strong. At the local level, government action outside of the school system was minimal.

THE ESTABLISHMENTS RESPOND

Taken together, federal, state, and local governmental adjustments to the oil embargo did generate a set of pressure or stressor events on establishments in the form of urgings and outright controls. The remainder of this chapter addresses the question of how the establishments, defined here as both profit-making and nonprofit-making enterprises, responded to these events.[a] We begin with one type of response, *resistance*, which a social system utilizes when its viability seems threatened. This clinging to the status quo ante was noted in the model and was illustrated several times in the responses of state and local governments. The establishments were no exception.

A widespread reaction to the allocations system, for instance, came from the independent petroleum distributors who claimed that they were being forced out of business by the large companies. Similarly some businesses in Oregon, such as motels and restaurants, filed pleas that they would be compelled to close their doors permanently because of the ban on outdoor, illuminated signs. They were backed by many citizens who were dissatisfied with their darkened cities. On top of this, the attorney general's office questioned the governor's authority to issue such a proclamation. As a result of the counterpressure, a board was created to decide upon exceptions to the general ban.

In Connecticut, many organizations, hard hit by the gasoline allocations arrangements, mobilized to protect and preserve themselves. The list of special-interest groups that appealed to the Connecticut Energy Emergency Agency for high priority in gas allocations was long and varied. It included: senior citizens, the Connecticut Education Association, the Connecticut Nurses Association, the Connecticut Medical Association, the Red Cross, the United Cerebral Palsy Association, commuting college students, and clergymen. In the profit sector were associations of funeral directors,

---

[a]The selection of the 594 establishments surveyed in this study and the weighting system used in processing the data from the interviews are described in Appendix A. *After weighting*, the main characteristics of the establishments were as follows:

Economic Sector	Percent of Establishments
Wholesale trade, retail trade, finance, insurance, and real estate	63.8
Agriculture, mining, construction, manufacturing, transportation and public utilities	23.4
Medical and health, education, and all non-profit	12.8

Number of Employees	
1-20	72.2%
21-250	22%
Over 250	1%
Not known	4%

Seventy-nine percent of the establishments served the public; 21 percent did not.

newspaper distributors, plumbers and heaters, amusement park owners, traveling salesmen, trailer-drivers, and many self-designated "critical" industries.

In Alabama the state government had to confront the dissatisfactions of the independent truckers. The governor expressed sympathy with the strikers but declared himself unable to deal with their problems since they involved matters beyond state control, such as diesel fuel prices, speed limits, and ceilings on freight rates. The Alabama Energy Management Board took the major role in the negotiations between the truckers and the governor's office. On February 8, the governor called on the National Guard's military police to join forces with state troopers to guarantee the safety of trucks on the highway, the first time in five years that National Guard units had been called upon to keep the peace. Shortly thereafter, the strike ended.

A proposal by Mobile's mayor that shopping centers be closed at 6 P.M. to save energy met with objections from business and was abandoned. It also drew from the Alabama Power Company the response that no shortages of electricity were anticipated in the area, but the company encouraged customers to use energy wisely.

This pattern of reacting so as to maintain the status quo was not however the main kind of response that establishments made. Consider, for a moment, the characteristics of most, though not all, of the establishments in this study. They rely on a flow of materials, labor, and other resources as inputs. Their main tasks are to provide goods and services, primarily through the market, and they require a certain level of demand from buyers. They are, moreover, subject not only to legal regulation but must also be sensitive to nonmaterial pressures, such as appeals to their sense of civic responsibility.

In the adjustments described below it is apparent that many establishments, viewed as social systems, experienced incursions on their capacities and performance of tasks as a result of decreases in the flow of inputs; reductions in the demand for certain goods and services; and a strain on their adaptability. (In a minority of cases, these changes were increases not decreases and the crisis was experienced as beneficial rather than harmful.) These were in addition to exhortations to be "good corporate citizens" and cooperate in energy conservation. While it is difficult to attribute a particular adjustment to one or another of these pressures (more often several were probably involved), it is evident that the establishments made many adjustments, other than those of resistance.

The immediate, generalized responses of commercial, industrial, and nonprofit establishments to the oil embargo and the president's first call for conservation were much the same in the three areas under study. In Mobile, for example, a number of business and civic organizations quickly announced plans to conserve. In mid-November, Downtown Mobile Unlimited, an organization of merchants in the downtown area, voted to cut back 50 percent to 70 percent on lighted Christmas decorations. A bank declared that it would illuminate its sign only four hours a day, lower the temperature of its offices to 68°, and set a 50 mph speed limit for all its vehicles. A few days later, a steel company north of Mobile announced similar conservation measures and added that its work day would begin one hour earlier to take advantage of daylight. The response was very similar in Hartford and in Salem, where conservation steps were under way months earlier because of the electric power shortage.

But subsequent to these first, diffuse responses came more specific adjustments, especially to the shortage of petroleum products. Let us try to trace through and compare the responses to the reduced supply. In Salem on the first Saturday night in December 1973, "Sorry, no gasoline" signs went up as customers stocked up for Sunday closings. The next day one station was open. Dealers soon took off Saturdays, Sundays, and some afternoons during the week when supplies were exhausted. An informal survey on December 28 showed that three towns in the Salem metropolitan area were simply out of gas and three others were being serviced by only one or two stations.

Only in Mobile were there no long lines or waits at the pumps. Many stations closed on Sundays, but no limits were set on purchases except during the first quarter of 1974 when some stations set a ten-gallon limit toward the end of the month to conserve their allocation. Mobile drivers had to pay higher prices but were only mildly inconvenienced by restricted supplies.

However, a few companies in Mobile experienced operating difficulties because of shortages. As early as November 2, Southern Airlines announced that in response to the short supplies of aviation fuel and reduced passenger needs, the number of daily flights from Mobile would be cut from eighteen to seventeen. Soon thereafter, Mobile tugboats encountered problems in obtaining adequate oil supplies, although there was no serious interference with port operations. Tugboats were finally put on allocation by their suppliers. As a direct result of the increase in fuel prices, all shipping lines raised their freight rates to all destinations.

It was in Hartford, however, that the shortage hit the hardest. The newspapers reported that the federal authorities allocated to Connecticut in November and in January 10 percent less than the amounts of gasoline consumed a year earlier. In February the cut was 20 percent. By March it was back to 10 percent and by April the shortage was essentially a thing of the past. But while it lasted, it was severe.

By the end of November many Hartford stations were out of gas. Some, confronted with long lines of would-be buyers, limited their sales to one or two dollars' worth per customer. In December and January signs of consumer panic began to appear. Gas lines were twenty to thirty cars deep. In some towns police were assigned to maintain order among frustrated and angry customers. Fuel theft became a problem. Sunday driving decreased. At the end of March the Hartford *Courant* announced that one-third of Hartford's 163 gasoline stations had closed. Some of them never reopened. All stations kept short and irregular hours and it was reported that some were selling gas for only 20 minutes a day.

Some establishments in the Hartford area were concerned about their employees' getting to work in the face of the gasoline shortage. One-fifth of those interviewed said they encouraged car pooling among their employees. This was higher among enterprises serving the public and it reached 90 percent among the firms with more than 1,000 workers. An intensive effort was launched in December to promote car pooling, known as the Greater Hartford Computer Carpool. It involved the cooperation of the Automobile Legal Association, the Connecticut Motor Club, and the State Department of Transportation. Station WDRC and the Connecticut Public Television both aired carpool information.

Express commuter buses and carpool programs were credited with saving two million gallons of gasoline annually by the Connecticut Department of Transportation in October 1974. Of this projected savings, 94 percent was attributed to the system of commuter buses taking passengers into Hartford and other cities and 6 percent was attributed to the interchange carpool parking lots and special carpool parking lots and special carpool toll programs. The state-subsidized bus operation showed an increase of approximately 20 percent over the comparable period in 1973.

RIPPLE EFFECTS

The devices employed by the gas retailers to handle their reduced supplies were simultaneously adjustments to the allocations system and stressor events for the motorists. But short hours and limited sales were not the only response, nor the only inconvenience for the household sector. Prices were increased, particularly sharply in

Hartford. They rose there from the high 40s and low 50s in November to 67.7 cents a gallon at A-1 stations in February. In January, the Internal Revenue Service fined a local station for selling at 77.9 cents a gallon. Rumors of bootlegged gas circulated widely.

The providers of energy in all its forms increased their prices. The cost of electricity in the residential sector had already risen 30-45 percent in the three metropolitan areas between 1970 and 1973, and for the same period the price for natural gas rose 35-67 percent. But the prices charged for electricity went up farther and faster during the five months of the crisis. According to newspaper reports, the customers of the Hartford Electric Company experienced a 30 percent boost in rates. Within our sample in the three areas, 38 percent of the establishments said their electricity rates had gone up.

But the energy crisis had effects well beyond the price of energy itself. Among establishments directly serving the public, one-fourth reported that the energy situation accounted for most of the increase in the prices they charged and one-eighth said it accounted for part of the increase. Of those reporting energy-related price increases, 17 percent pointed to the rising cost of fuel oil as the main reason. Among renters in the survey, 11 percent said their landlords had given the energy problem as the reason for part or all of an increase in rent.

Except for gasoline, the availability of other forms of energy was not seriously affected during the crisis months. Only 4-5 percent of the establishments in this study reported, for example, having difficulty getting heating fuel; it was somewhat harder to come by in Salem where the figure was 12 percent. No major problems with electricity or natural gas were reported.

Even though supplies were available on the whole, establishments made many adjustments in their use of energy. It is not simple to determine which were adjustments to the steady, steep rise in prices, to the appeals by public figures to conserve energy, or to direct controls. With respect to the latter, only 18 percent of the establishments surveyed said their operations were directly affected by federal, state, or local energy regulations; this was highest in Salem with 38 percent, but only 13-17 percent in Hartford and Mobile. In any case many establishments took steps to decrease their consumption of energy—thereby frequently creating new conditions to which family members in their roles as consumers and as employees would be called upon to adjust, as we shall see in the following chapters.

Three-quarters of the Hartford establishments said they lowered their temperatures, including many who heated with natural gas. In

Mobile, 41 percent dropped the indoor temperatures. In both communities the decrease was 4° on the average. In Salem, however, where fuel was harder to obtain, there was an average decrease in temperature of only 3.4°. Normally, in all communities indoor temperatures during winter had been kept at about 70°.

Some clues as to the varied forces behind these adjustments in heating can be discerned in the experience of Hartford. Regardless of the kind of energy used for heating—67 percent used oil and 28 percent natural gas—three-quarters of the Hartford establishments said their heating costs had gone up during the crisis months. When asked for the most important reason they had lowered their temperatures, 36 percent of the Hartford respondents attributed their action to the price of fuel. Practically as many (34 percent) said they had "felt a duty to save energy" and 19 percent said they had reduced temperatures because of the lack of fuel, though only 12 percent said they were subject to heating fuel allocations.

During the summer of 1974, air-conditioning was reduced in all three areas, but not as much measured in degrees Fahrenheit as was the case with indoor heating during the winter of 1973-74. Virtually all Mobile establishments are air-conditioned at least in part. One-fourth of them reported cutbacks due to the crisis. On the average temperatures rose by 0.9°. In Salem also, one-quarter of the air-conditioned enterprises surveyed said they cut back, reportedly by 2.7°. In Hartford more establishments (one-third of those with air-conditioning) reported an average of 3.1° warmer temperatures as a result of using their air-conditioning less.

Considerable reductions were made in lighting. This was reported for 50-60 percent of the establishments in Hartford and Salem and 22-37 percent in Mobile. The savings were affected by turning off lights completely, using fewer lights or smaller-watt bulbs, and cutting down on display lighting. One-third of the surveyed enterprises had outdoor advertising signs and among these a high proportion (70 percent) cut back on their display lighting.

A smaller but still noticeable proportion of establishments of the kind that served the public reported changes in the hours they were open. In Salem this was 37 percent, in Hartford and Mobile only 11-12 percent. Most, though not all, of the change in hours was attributed to the energy crisis.

In their adjustments, some of the establishments took steps that directly affected their employees. Overall, 11 percent of the establishments spoke of a change in work schedules, usually a rearrangement of hours rather than an increase or decrease in working time. Differences in work assignments, reported by one-third of the establishments as a result of the energy situation, most often involved changes in the use of company vehicles and to a lesser extent machinery and other equipment.

The impact of the energy crisis compelled certain establishments to lay off workers. It will be recalled that nationally almost a quarter of a million people were reported out of work during the crisis months as a direct result of energy developments. In his study Early found that between November 1973 and March 1974 total unemployment in the country increased by 8.9 percent.[1] He said "we can be reasonably certain that most of the increase in unemployment" was the result of energy-related job cutbacks. "Most of the impact seems to be centered around shortages of gasoline for personal use with gasoline stations and automobile manufacturing and distribution showing the biggest losses."

Among the establishments contacted in our study, one out of five reported layoffs of workers due to the energy crisis. Most of these involved one to five employees and were heaviest in the establishments serving the public. Generally the reason given was "lack of business" due to the energy crisis. In Salem, where more than one-third of the enterprises reported layoffs, the main reason given was the cutback in heating fuel.

The actions taken by the establishments and described above affected families in many ways. The families' responses created pressures and opportunities to which the establishments, in turn, had to respond and adjust. A fuller picture of the reciprocal effects that were generated between establishments and households will emerge in the chapters that follow.

SUMMARY

We have described the energy crisis of 1973-74 from the perspectives of different levels of government and of the establishments in three metropolitan areas. Our account began by noting that an energy problem had been apparent to environmentalists and certain energy experts long before "the crisis." Their warnings had generally been ignored. Actual shortages and cutbacks in the delivery of energy had taken place, but these too failed to mobilize action on any broad scale. However, in Oregon the state government had responded to a hydroelectric power shortage that preceded the national petroleum crisis by half a year.

The concrete event that set off the crisis came with little advance notice when the Arab oil-producers cut off exports to the United States. In the short run, this country had to adjust to a sudden decrease in a vital resource.

The first responses came from the Nixon Administration primarily in the form of exhortations addressed to lower levels of government, to the private sector, and to the citizenry to save energy. The president projected a far-reaching proposal, which turned out to be unrealistic in every respect, to make the nation independent of foreign oil in less than a decade. The appeals to voluntary action were accompanied by warnings, echoed by State officials, that if voluntary cooperation were not forthcoming, the government would have to resort to controls.

Certain controls were in fact put into effect. They dealt with the most immediate aspects of the petroleum shortage principally by (1) allocating petroleum supplies and regulating the times at which gasoline could be sold, (2) making daylight savings time year-round to save electricity, and (3) limiting highway speeds to 55 mph.

It is worth noting here that while these short-term measures were adopted (somewhat reluctantly), more basic, long-term policies were discussed but not enacted into law despite the likelihood that the "crisis" was an expression of a chronic problem in the United States. In part the inability of the Congress and the Administration to adopt long-range policies was related to the pluralistic nature of American politics, nowhere more evident than in the pulling and hauling over costs and benefits in the energy field among regions, industries, and consumers. These conflicts also help to account for the reluctance to impose regulations and controls.

State and local governments also reacted for the most part by trying to cope with the most immediate, concrete problems cast up by the crisis. They resisted federal cutbacks in allocations of petroleum products and tried to get as much as they could for their industries and citizens. School boards resisted the attempts of state officials to change the hours that schools would be open.

But municipal and state governments also took steps to save energy, mostly through reductions in their own operations. With an eye to improved intelligence and decision-making, state and local governments set up planning and watchdog groups to collect data and draw up contingency plans in case the crisis would be prolonged and become more disruptive. This was, in effect, an effort to enhance their capacities to cope with energy-related problems, particularly by strengthening their cognitive competence.

The establishments confronted the crisis with a variety of adjustments and responses. A minority among them, apparently feeling that their viability was at stake, reacted with resistance to the changes they were being called upon to make. This was the case, for example, with gasoline stations that fought allocation decisions that threatened them with extinction. Resistance was most explicit and explosive in the truck drivers' strike.

The more typical reaction of establishments was to make adjustments to the new situations with which they were faced. Many of these were voluntary accommodations to the appeals to conserve energy. The lowering of temperatures in manufacturing, commercial, and office facilities, and the cutbacks in lighting illustrate these adjustments. Other responses, such as decreasing a store's hours of service because of a drop in sales and income, were less voluntary.

Who absorbed the costs and inconveniences of these adjustments by the establishments? Some were passed along to consumers in the form of price increases and reductions in service. Some costs were paid by employees, certainly those who were laid off. Some establishments incurred losses. The following chapters elaborate on the reciprocal effects that took place between the establishments and the households in Hartford, Mobile, and Salem.

Overall, the ways in which government, industry, and commerce reacted were not unlike the initial responses to crisis that were discussed in the development of the analytical model in Chapter Two. At all levels and in all systems uncertainty and hesitancy characterized the first reactions. The adjustments that were actually made were, in a sense, those that were unavoidable or that could be made at minimum cost in economic or political terms.

Thoroughgoing commitments to permanent and fundamental changes were avoided. Before it became necessary to consider such adjustments seriously, the pipelines from the Arabian oil fields were reopened to buyers in the United States and the "crisis" seemed to be a thing of the past.

CONTRAST WITH CRISIS OF 1976-77

When this chapter was written in the closing months of 1976, it was possible to speculate about what might happen the next time a crisis developed. Within a few months the "next time" had arrived and the country was in the midst of its second and more serious energy crisis.

Chapter Eight describes the 1976-77 crisis from the point of view of the national scene, the events in the three metropolitan areas covered by this study, and the actions and reactions of a sample of the households originally contacted in 1974. Here we want simply to draw some general comparisons between the two crisis periods.

In place of the oil embargo invoked by the Arab exporters, the country's second energy crisis was precipitated by internal factors acting together: record-breaking winter temperatures over much of the nation and a shortage of natural gas. Changes in long-established weather patterns not only plunged sections of the Northeast into the coldest January since 1870, but simultaneously brought unseasonably warm and dry weather to the West, raising the spectre of drought and energy shortages in places dependent on hydroelectric power. At the same time natural gas deliveries were suspended in large parts of the North, East, and South.

Within a few weeks the disruptions were more widespread and more critical than they had been three years earlier. The impact on thousands of families was far more harmful. Many families were forced to abandon unheated homes and seek communal refuges. The additional fuel required to heat homes, coupled with the ever-rising costs of fuel, meant that homeowners were paying far more for heating than they had the previous winter.

Thousands of schools and businesses closed. Unemployment due to the shortage reached almost two million for a short period of time, compared with hundreds of thousands in 1973-74.

Crisis I came toward the end of the Nixon Administration, already grievously wounded by the Watergate scandal and in poor condition to launch bold initiatives. Crisis II came within the first weeks of the Carter Administration, poised and eager to demonstrate its competence and effectiveness. Indeed, as *Time* magazine reported, President Carter met his first crisis by

> moving fast and forcefully. He dramatized the crisis—and the presidential role in it—by hastily convening a Cabinet meeting, then taking a quick trip to frozen Pittsburgh. He declared eleven states disaster areas because of snow or drought ... the President delivered his first fireside chat, calling upon both consumers and producers to join in an effort to deal with the energy crisis.[2]

The president proposed and the Congress immediately enacted a law giving the federal government the authority to transfer natural gas supplies from areas with a surplus to areas with shortages and permitting the price of interstate gas to rise, an action analogous to the speed limit, daylight savings, and allocation measures taken in the initial stage of Crisis I.

The following news items convey the sense that government at all levels, the general public, and the private economy were affected more directly and extensively and responded more sharply than had been the case three years before:

> In a state that is heavily dependent on natural gas for home-heating and for industry, the Governor of New Jersey invoked World War II emergency powers permitting him to order home thermostats to be set at no more

than 65°. Businesses were given a choice: operate at 65° for 40 hours a week or for unlimited hours at 50°. The Governor said the police would enforce the regulations.

In Georgia officials estimated that the natural gas shortage had forced some 75,000 persons off payrolls totaling $30 million a week. Apparently the necessary emergency legislation was still not in place, since the Governor said he would consider initiating legislation to deal with the crisis. Commercial consumers were asked to cut hours of operation and hospitals to lower thermostat settings.[3]

The Ohio Legislature was called into special session to deal with a state of emergency. Schools remained closed in much of Pennsylvania, Ohio and Tennessee and energy cutbacks left thousands of workers idle in Tennessee, Georgia and Mississippi. Power and gas reductions continued from Minnesota to New York despite milder temperatures.[4]

By any measure, the second energy disruption came closer to being a crisis than did the first. As the weather warmed up and the flow of energy was restored to those areas suffering an acute shortage, the atmosphere of crisis eased. But in the months following the peak of the crisis there was a major difference between the two periods. In mid-April, the Carter Administration proposed to the people and to the Congress a comprehensive, complex energy program.

The strategies for reaching the goals set forth by the Carter Administration—particularly the proposed tax on gasoline and on "gas-guzzling" cars—began to confront the American people with difficult choices. At this writing, the program is working its way through the Congress, having already encountered stiff resistance to some of its features and acceptance of others.

A detailed discussion of Crisis II and of effects on the behavior and attitudes of households in Hartford, Mobile, and Salem is presented in Chapter Eight.

Chapter Four

1,440 Families React

The adjustments that governments and establishments made to the oil embargo in late 1973 confronted America's families with a new set of circumstances. If the new conditions did not constitute a full-fledged, serious crisis for most families, they nonetheless required adjustments on the part of most households. The process that takes place between the emergence of such events and a family's response is neither mechanical nor uniform. A set of cognitive activities intervenes in which families perceive events in their environment, assess their meaning, and choose responses that seem appropriate and feasible.

The model presented in Chapter Two refers to the family's ability to perform these functions as its cognitive competence, with the recognition that this capacity differs from family to family. The competence consists of the ability to obtain and process information; to scan it for its implications for the family; and to assess potential adjustments so as to select those that protect the family's well-being. Based in part on their values, norms, and previous experience, families define stressor events differentially and employ different ways of reaching decisions.

Change in a social system, which is implicit in this process, is seen by Moss as essentially a processing of information.[1] This begins when the system encounters incongruities that invalidate a portion of its current information and perceptions (invalidation). That part of the system's "information repertoire" that has been invalidated is rejected and new information is sought and examined (exploration). As new information is accepted, new communication patterns are established (innovation) and finally routinized (habituation).

The dynamics of invalidation/exploration/innovation/habituation are reminiscent of Lewin's sequence of event/unfreezing/change/refreezing. But whether one uses these terms or speaks of perceptions/assessments/choices, the subprocesses are neither sequential, tidy, nor in any sense final. They criss-cross and double back; they are subject to continuing modification as new information is received from an ever-changing environment, internal and external. It is only for purposes of analysis that these components can be treated as discrete processes.

The process of evaluation requires a comment. In addition to weighing the possible effects of a stressor event on a family's capacities to perform its tasks, evaluation also engages the family's norms and values—its ideas of which responses will be desirable or good and which will be undesirable. At a less fundamental level, assessment of potentially (or actually) threatening events also depends on the attitudes and beliefs which may predispose a family to certain kinds of actions and not to others.

The data on the energy crisis from this and other studies permit a discussion of the cognitive process in terms of the processing of information, the meanings and definitions that were made of the situation, and the decision-making that took place. The respondents in Hartford, Mobile, and Salem were asked about these matters, as were Americans throughout the country who were interviewed in other surveys.[2,3]

The stressor events to which Americans were reacting were described in the preceding chapter—governmental announcements of an energy crisis; exhortations to conserve; and a few restrictions on behavior in the form of speed limits, year-round Daylight Savings Time, and allocations of gasoline and fuel oil. The impact of these events was filtered through public and private establishments and reached families as diminished supplies of gasoline, layoffs and other work-related changes, and price increases, along with other adjustments in consumer-related practices.

The climate in which American families had to interpret these events was unusual. In the fall of 1973 the credibility of the federal government was at very low ebb. The energy crisis came on top of this country's Vietnam and Watergate agonies. The rampant distrust of official pronouncements both from governmental and private sources undoubtedly affected the way in which many American families viewed the energy crisis.

WAS THE CRISIS "REAL" OR NOT?

The household respondents in the present study were asked whether, at the height of the energy shortage, they believed "there was a real shortage of energy at that time." The wording of the question was taken from an NORC survey in order to make the findings comparable with that survey. It is important, in understanding the replies, to call attention to some ambiguity in the question which may have colored the respondents' interpretation of the term "a real shortage."

One meaning of the term is: Do you believe that there was in fact a shortage in the availability of energy, regardless of how or why the shortage may have occurred? A different interpretation is: Do you think the shortage was contrived and in that sense the crisis was phoney? The evidence that many people placed this second interpretation on the question—and held the view that it was phoney—comes from their subsequent statements holding various actors responsible for "rigging" the crisis for their own benefit. We shall attempt to separate the responses along these lines in the following analysis, though it is not always possible to do so.

Across the three metropolitan areas covered by this study only one-third (36 percent) of the respondents said they considered the energy shortage to be real. There were regional variations in the size of this group of "believers" in comparison with the "nonbelievers" or skeptics. In Hartford 45 percent of the respondents said they considered the energy shortage to be real. It is difficult to avoid the conclusion that this was higher than it was in Mobile and Salem because people in Hartford were indeed experiencing the crisis more directly and keenly and therefore brought this meaning to the question. In Mobile, those who believed there was an energy shortage amounted to 34 percent and in Salem 27 percent, proportions that were closer to those in several other surveys.[4]

The respondents who said they did not consider the shortages to be real were asked to explain their position. Here there were no important differences among families in Hartford, Mobile, and Salem. The most frequent explanation was aimed directly at the energy producing companies: 27 percent said the shortage was contrived to increase profits; 12 percent felt consumers were manipulated by companies; 10 percent suggested the whole affair was "phoney, fishy . . . a rip-off." Nine percent said that tankers were not allowed to unload and 10 percent suggested that the energy shortage was part of some broader political strategy.

When the householders in the Brandeis study who considered the crisis rigged were asked which group they held to be most responsible for the energy shortage, 36 percent blamed the oil and gas companies; 12 percent mentioned "big business," and 27 percent pointed to the national government. Interestingly, the Arabs were blamed by only 7 percent of the households and the Israelis by 4 percent.

There is no doubt that there was a widespread conviction that the energy crisis was contrived. The *Harper and Atlantic* survey found that 86 percent of their respondents felt the fuel shortage "could have been avoided." The *New York Times* reported after a survey of ten cities and suburbs that many Americans were slowly coming to believe that the shortage existed but were confused about whom to blame.[5] They wondered whether shortages might not have been exaggerated by powerful interests for their own political or economic gain. National figures such as George McGovern and Ralph Nader continued to sound a skeptical note, maintaining that the shortage had been brought about by oil companies and their political allies.

A study in Texas found that half its respondents looked upon the energy crisis as a political contrivance and 43 percent of these called it a move to divert attention from Watergate.[6] As to the credibility of sources of information, the Texas interviewers asked which information source people found to be accurate and honest most of the time with respect to energy. Fifty-eight percent of their respondents said this applied to television; 36 percent said they believed their local newspaper; and 36 percent said this of their radio stations. But only 10 percent of the respondents found literature and announcements from any of the following sources accurate and honest most of the time: government, oil companies, natural gas companies, and electric power companies.

The Brandeis survey used the same wording for its question about the reality of the energy shortage that was used in a series of surveys by NORC. Those surveys concluded that "Agreement is widespread that responsibility for the energy crisis lies most heavily on the federal government and the oil companies, and there is little tendency to blame Arabs, Israelis, environmentalists, or individual consumers." Similar results were reported by Gallup nationally and in Los Angeles, Texas and Detroit.

Bartell reflects the climate of opinion in Los Angeles in this observation:

> In general, Los Angeles residents believed the oil companies were holding back oil in order to increase profits. Those who blamed the federal government generally did so because they felt the government should have anticipated the shortage, controlled the oil companies, and prevented or at

least ameliorated the crisis. The reasons for blaming President Nixon were of an entirely different quality and intensity. Respondents not only spoke of incompetence and lack of control, but also of a political payoff and possible fraud. An overwhelming number of those blaming the President viewed the energy crisis as the result of Nixon paying off a campaign debt to the oil companies. Comments such as "the oil companies donated so much money to his reelection that he has no control over them," "he had a price to pay the oil companies as they gave him millions of dollars for his campaign," and "he has money now because the oil companies have paid him off" were the norm.[7]

Within this generally skeptical cast of opinion about the energy crisis, the Brandeis study found only minor differences among income groups. There was a slightly greater tendency in Mobile and Salem for the highest income group to believe in the reality of the crisis than was the case with the lower income groups. The reverse was true in Hartford. In none of the cities were the differences marked.

More consistent and more substantial income-related differences were found with respect to the question "who is responsible." Overall, the higher the family's income the greater the tendency to blame the oil and gas companies for the energy shortage. Conversely, the lower the income the greater the likelihood that families blamed government in Washington. Whether these differences represent variations in the information flow to families in the several income groups or perhaps more deep-seated attitudes toward government in general is not clear.

These findings, however, are only partially in accord with a Gallup survey which showed that proportionately more of the higher income groups tended to hold the oil companies and the federal government responsible for the energy crisis than was the case with the lower income families. In that study, nearly one-third of all families with income over $20,000 blamed the federal government or oil companies compared to about one-fifth of all families earning under $5,000. Lower income people and non-whites were more likely to blame the Nixon Administration than were whites and people with incomes over $10,000.

It must now be apparent that many families in this study took a rather jaundiced view of the energy crisis in general and were none too trustful of either the information they received or the motives of the principal actors on the national scene. By no means, however, did all the families define the situation in the same terms. We distinguish below five different ways in which families assessed the events of the energy crisis.

FIVE DEFINITIONS OF THE ENERGY CRISIS

In an important sense it is not appropriate to speak of perceptions of "the energy crisis" as though the crisis were a single event impinging with a unitary force on all the families in this study. The energy-related developments of 1973-74 were undoubtedly perceived more in terms of what was happening to gasoline or to electricity or to fuel oil than in terms of energy as a whole. Hence it is clear—judging by the behavior that followed the families' cognitive processing of the information on the crisis—that, for example, certain families perceived the "gasoline crisis" in one way and the "electricity crisis" in quite a different way.

An additional qualification is in order before presenting a typology of perceptions of the energy crisis. Patently the same family could, and in many cases did, change its perceptions and behavior over time, an aspect of adjustment that is described at the end of the following chapter. Subject to these qualifications, the five views of the energy crisis discussed below represent various ways in which families interpreted the meaning of the crisis for them and for the response they would make. Clearly the five perceptions are not mutually exclusive.

1. *Perception of moderate or weak stressor event.* A substantial number of families, as will be evident in Chapter Five, did not in fact change their behavior or, more accurately, certain aspects of their behavior. It is reasonable to suppose that where this was the case, the family did not consider the crisis events as strong enough or threatening enough to require an adjustment. For example, an upper income family might well have found the increasing cost of electricity so marginal and inconsequential in the total scheme of their expenditures that the price increases were not seen as sufficient cause for conserving on lights and electric appliances.

2. *Perception of the stressor events as serious and threatening to vital capacities and functions.* This perception was reflected in many examples in the previous chapter, such as in energy-related layoffs. It is also directly linked to efforts to resist the impact of the crisis and to ward off impending changes. Most of these efforts involved concerted action through organizations. The truckers' strike is the most obvious example of interpreting the consequences of the energy shortage as so grave for the income of the independent truckers' families, that they decided to mount a counteroffensive against the threat. This same perception that the crisis might jeopardize important capacities and functions was seen in some of the protest actions of local and state government and business and consumer groups.

The two perceptions noted above were inferred from behavior. The three presented below are based on the answers of respondents to direct questions about the reasons why they took steps to conserve energy. They constitute therefore self-reported perceptions.

3. *Perception of a shrinking resource.* Family behaviors are contingent directly or indirectly on the continual flow of resources from the environment. When this flow is perceived as being in jeopardy or actually reduced, families may decide to compensate by changes in their activities. This partial or complete lack of a resource was really only a problem with gasoline. Approximately 80 percent of the respondents in Hartford and Salem said they found gasoline hard to come by; in Mobile this was 60 percent.

Among the households who reduced the use of their cars, approximately one-third attributed this to the fact that they had trouble getting gasoline or could not find it at all. The reduced driving that resulted can be related to the long lines at gas stations and the sometimes frantic shopping around for gas that have already been described.

Availability of heating energy was a minor reason for reducing home temperatures, since only 6 percent of the households—concentrated in Hartford—experienced difficulties buying fuel. Less than 2 percent reported problems obtaining electric power.

4. *Perception of the energy shortage as pressure on the family's financial resources.* It should come as no surprise that price emerged as the most important reason given by the households for the energy cutbacks they made. This was true overall for reduced driving, lowered temperatures, and air-conditioning cutbacks. The assessment that energy (in the form of electricity) was costing too much in relation to other family needs and its use must therefore be cut down is reflected most strongly in the fact that two-thirds of the households who decreased their use of appliances gave price as the most important reason.

5. *Perception of the crisis in normative terms.* Values, ideologies, and norms evidently played a part in the perceptions and responses of a not inconsiderable number of respondents.

A sense of duty was cited as the most important reason for conservation by 38 percent of the families in the study who reduced temperatures in their homes; by 24 percent of those who decreased their driving; and by 23 percent of those who cut down on the use of air-conditioning. Whether this was in response to the exhortations of political leaders; a result of convictions and beliefs about ecology and the environment; a desire to cooperate with and conform to the behavior of other families; or was done for other reasons, it is difficult to determine.

In the model it was pointed out that members of a family have more (or less) of a feeling of loyalty and commitment to the family as a unit. In the case of families who acted out of "civic responsibility" it may be their sense of identification with their community and/or the nation that is expressed in their behavior.

The influence of neighborhoods on family decision-making has been the subject of continuing study by Donald Warren and David Clifford, including a survey of responses to the energy crisis.[9] Reporting on their survey in eight neighborhoods in the Detroit metropolitan area, they argue that "norms of household energy usage are filtered through geographically based social units such as neighborhoods and local communities." They point out that activities involving energy consumption have high visibility and require recurring decision-making which is "subject to continual feedback from 'significant others' " in the environment. For example, keeping fewer lights on or even lowering the thermostat can come to the attention of neighbors.

Warren and Clifford argue that families are subject to what Merton and Blau have called "behavioral conformity," i.e., the roots of their behavior lie not in predispositions and basic attitudes but in the external constraints which group norms engender. They found differences in energy-related behavior that were associated with the typology of neighborhoods they had previously identified based on such factors as the degree of integration, the rate of turnover of families, the degree to which their activities are oriented inward or outward, and the extent of anomie.

We commented earlier that many research findings have found little or no direct connection between attitudes and opinions on one side—as distinct from strongly held norms—and action on the other. This proposition was reinforced by the findings of this study. Attitudes as to whether the energy shortage was real or not apparently made little difference in people's energy-related behavior.[10] One is tempted to think that people who were cynical about the crisis and/or had not experienced it palpably would not make much effort to conserve in comparison with those who either thought the crisis "genuine" or suffered some actual discomfort.

Whatever interpretation the respondents put on the question, the nonbelievers defined the situation in such a way that they responded as though it were real to the same extent as the believers did. One can examine the distribution of "believers" and "nonbelievers" with respect to reduced driving, lowering thermostats, and cutting electricity, lighting, and air-conditioning. The percentage of each group who made these changes is remarkably similar; the largest variation is

5 percent between the skeptics and the believers. During and after the crisis the nonbelievers reported keeping their homes only 0.2° to 0.6° warmer than the believers, and drove their cars only 1.0 to 1.2 mph faster on the highways.

Among those who reduced their energy use, there was practically no difference in the reason given (i.e., price, availability, or duty) by the believers and nonbelievers. For example, it might be expected that those who believed the crisis to be real would be more likely to be influenced by considerations of civic duty. In fact, only 26 percent of the believers cited duty as their most important reason for cutting down the use of their cars in comparison with 22 percent among the nonbelievers. Similarly, 39 percent of the believing group said they reduced their home temperatures because of a feeling of duty; 37 percent of the cynics or skeptics gave the same reason. By the same token, price and availability were cited in very much the same proportions by the two groups as their motivations for conserving.

To recapitulate, five differing perceptions of the meaning of the energy crisis have been discussed: (1) as a weak or "noncrisis"; (2) as a major threat that must be resisted; (3) as a diminution in the flow of a needed resource; (4) as pressure on financial resources; and (5) as a situation calling for action based on values and norms. Some comparisons of the relative strength of the last three perceptions can be made, taking into account regional differences.

The preeminence of price as the most compelling reason for altering consumption behavior needs some qualification. Price was only a few percentage points higher than the lack of availability of gasoline as the first reason for reduced use of the car. And price was just a few points higher than "a felt duty to save energy" in accounting for lower temperatures in the homes of the respondents. On the other hand, the price of electricity was given by two-thirds of the households who decreased their use of air-conditioning, in contrast to a sense of duty which was mentioned by less than one-fourth of these households. One-fourth cited duty as their first reason for cutting back on driving.

Another way of testing the possible association between belief and values on the one hand and behavior on the other is to focus attention on those respondents who said that their sense of duty motivated them to conserve energy. Did they act very differently from those who said that high prices or the sheer fact of a shortage was the major, impelling reason for conserving?

The respondents who stressed duty did reduce their highway speeds on the average more than the others, though the amount is not impressive. They dropped down 9.6 mph compared with 8.4 mph for the price-conscious and 8.3 mph for those who found gas hard to get. But those concerned with duty increased their highways speed in the year following the peak of the crisis more than the others. The averages were +2.6 mph for the duty-conscious; +1.3 mph for the price-conscious; and +1.7 mph for those hard hit by the shortage during the crisis.

As for specific kinds of driving that were cut back, there were no strong or consistent differences between the drivers who said they acted out of duty and the others. Thus, for shopping, recreation, chauffeuring children, and visiting, the proportion of duty-conscious drivers who cut back was in each instance within 5 or 6 percentage points of the other two groups. In other words, based on their responses about changes in driving behavior, we again find no startling differences based on convictions of a civic responsibility to conserve energy as opposed to the more pragmatic reasons of price increases and shortages of gasoline.

More can be learned about the relative significance of price, duty, and availability as factors leading to changed behavior if interregional differences are examined. The gasoline shortage was given as the major reason for cutting down on driving by a plurality (41-47 percent) of the households with cars in Hartford and Salem. Price and a sense of duty were considered most important by only one-quarter to one-third of the households who reduced their driving. Among those who lowered their home temperatures, a sense of civic responsibility ranked highest (40-41 percent) among the motivations expressed in Hartford and Salem.

By contrast it was price in Mobile that was articulated as the overwhelming reason (by 63-80 percent of the households) for using less energy for travel, heating, and air-conditioning. (However, in Hartford, cutbacks in air-conditioning were attributed to price by 55 percent of the eligible respondents.) Less than one-fifth of the Mobile household respondents referred either to duty or to shortages as their main reason for cutbacks. There is no clear explanation for this heavy emphasis on price in Mobile; it does not seem to be related to the higher proportion of low-income families in Mobile.

This inquiry into the perceptions and assessments that influenced energy-related behavior must also take cognizance of the part played in decision-making by expectations. There is evidence in studies by economists and social psychologists that families' expectations concerning the future figure prominently in their decision-making. The

NORC surveys looked for attitudes about the likely short-run (six months) and the long-term effects of the crisis (five years).

NORC reported that "most respondents perceive the short-term effects as more serious than the long-term effects (54 and 40 percent respectively)" and that "the public expects an absence of energy shortages before 1980." The researchers concluded that "there are two types of expectations. Short-term expectations are influenced by exposure to shortages, and themselves determine evaluations and conservation behaviors. Longer-term ones are insensitive to recent experiences of shortages, relatively stable over time, and unrelated to evaluations of the energy shortage and conservation behaviors."[11]

The force of expectations as an element in the cognitive process was confirmed by Bartell's analysis of four predictors of conservation behavior. He compared (1) social characteristics, (2) perceptions of the seriousness and duration of the crisis, (3) perceived reduction by others, and (4) expected effect on employment. Only the last of these showed a consistent and significant relationship to energy conservation. He concluded that "the greater the expected probability that 'the energy crisis will affect your employment in the future', the more likely respondents were to have initiated a wide range of energy reducing measures in their own personal lives."[12]

FAMILY DECISION-MAKING

The various perceptions, expectations, and assessments of the energy crisis had a direct bearing on the decisions and subsequent actions of the households in this study. Before presenting in the next chapter the behavioral changes that were made, there is another aspect of the cognitive process that deserves attention. Just as families differed in their first-hand experience of the crisis and in their evaluations of its immediate and long-range effects, they also differed in the ways in which they reached decisions.

Much of the research in family decision-making has revolved around the questions "who decides about which aspects of family living" and "what factors determine their decisions?" Most of the studies concentrate on the use of financial resources for consumption or savings. One of the issues is to what extent "family" decisions represent the unrelated actions of individuals and to what extent they represent joint activities, especially between husband and wife.

Clearly the overall outcome of a family's decisions with respect to the energy crisis depends on hundreds of decisions made by all members of the family with respect to heating, travel, and the use of appliances. "Families do not make explicit decisions to consume energy at some level or up to some dollar amount," Morrison and Gladhart report from their review of existing literature on decision-making.[13] Rather, they say, "families engage in activites of their choice, presumably to meet particular family goals, and consume energy in the process...heating and gasoline bills are the *consequences* of the family's life style."

However, the energy crisis of 1973-74 apparently did require decisions in some families and it is important to ask who made them. The findings are of interest for two reasons. First, they add another brush-stroke to the research canvas on family decision-making. Second, the findings may suggest guidelines for those interested in promoting energy conservation, since they indicate the most promising targets.

Respondents in this study who reduced their use of energy were asked who had made the decisions. The distribution of responses appears in Table 4-1.

The position or ranking of decisionmakers followed much the same pattern across the various end uses of energy. Variation by metropolitan area was minor. Most noticeable were sex-related differences.

Women made the decisions two to four times as often as men with regard to household appliances, heating and air-conditioning. The decision to reduce use of the car was more evenly balanced between women (19 percent) and men (16 percent), though this was the area in which the proportion of joint decisions was the highest (52 percent). There were no notable differences among households in Hartford, Mobile, and Salem.

The extent to which husbands made decisions alone varied little by income. But as income increases there is a consistent shift of decision-making from wives to husband-wife collaboration. Except

Table 4-1. Decisionmakers in Energy-Conserving Households (in percent)

Source of Decision	Driving	Heating	Appliances	Air-Cond.
Husband & wife jointly	52	45	42	55
Wife or female head	19	30	39	27
Husband or male head	16	18	9	9
Whole household	10	7	9	10

for the car, women in the lowest income group made approximately half the decisions.

In short, the main pattern is for husbands and wives jointly to decide about energy conservation. This becomes more pronounced as family income increases. The overall pattern reinforces the conclusion of the Blood and Wolfe study that cooperative decision-making between husbands and wives is the predominant mode for those areas of family life that are not clearly identified with traditional sex-related roles, such as decisions about the man's job.[14] The decisions about energy use correspond closely with the pattern Blood and Wolfe found for choice of a place to live, choice of a doctor, and vacation planning.

The data from the three metropolitan areas coincide with two conclusions of Hill and Klein: (1) that joint decisions are more characteristic of middle class families, costly expenditures, and situations where family members have shared interests in the use of a product or service and (2) decisions by women are more characteristic of low income families.[15]

SUMMARY

This chapter has touched upon a number of aspects of the cognitive process in which families engaged during the energy crisis. This all took place in an atmosphere of strong distrust of pronouncements by the Nixon Administration and of the statements issued by corporations in the energy field. Self-serving economic and political motives were in fact blamed by a majority of the survey households for artificially generating the crisis.

Within this generally skeptical climate of opinion, however, families made different assessments of their situations and decided on different responses, colored by regional differences. Some saw the crisis as, in effect, a noncrisis or at most so weak in its possible effects on them that they made no change in their behavior. At the other end of the spectrum, some families perceived the events of 1973-74 as so powerful or potentially threatening that they mobilized considerable effort to oppose and resist the pressures emanating from the crisis.

Three other kinds of perceptions were discussed. Those who experienced a reduction in the availability of an important resource (for the most part, gasoline) changed their behavior to counterbalance the deprivation, however slight or temporary it may have been for some of them. Another perception was that of being financially squeezed by the inflation in energy prices. Finally, some families viewed the energy crisis as impinging on their values and norms, perhaps influenced by the behavior and expectations of their neighbors, but apparently not by their own attitudes about the energy crisis.

In any case, the last three assessments of the energy crisis all led in the direction of adjustments by the families. It is to these adjustments that we now turn.

Chapter Five

Family Adjustments

The changes that families make in their accustomed patterns as they respond to a crisis are mediated by their perceptions and assessments of the nature of the crisis, as seen in the previous chapter. The adjustments that follow can be thought of in two ways. Families' adjustments to a crisis can be described as a process extending over time and unfolding in phases. The analytical model used in this study conceives of a process that begins with the exploration of possible responses to a stressor event. New patterns are tentatively adopted, subject to attrition before a new level of stabilization is achieved. The next chapter treats adjustment in these terms.

Adjusting to a crisis can also be viewed in terms of its outcome. The model conceives of the effects of a crisis on families as diminutions (occasionally increases) in their capacities and resources for performing tasks for their members and for other social systems. To recall what was suggested in Chapter Two, the critical capacities include the families' state of integration, their adaptability in relation to their environment, and their cognitive competence. These depend on each family's material and nonmaterial resources. The particular character of a crisis will determine which of these elements are affected more or less than others.

Earlier chapters indicated, and the findings here will confirm, that the impact of the energy crisis of 1973-74 on family life was, for *most* families, so limited that it is questionable whether it can be considered "a crisis." However, the analytical model is useful in calling attention to the changes that did take place and to their effects on the execution of both utilitarian and affective functions that the family performs. Most of the changes described in this chapter concern adjustments that were made in the mobility of families, in the tasks involved in maintaining a home, and in their participation in the labor force.

The effect on family integration was slight. Among the families surveyed in Hartford, Mobile, and Salem, only 7 percent said that the energy shortage had had an effect on the way the family members got along with each other. Half of that small number said the crisis had led to arguments, grouchiness, and anger. Very few said it had brought the family closer together. There was no evidence of changes in families' adaptability as a result of the energy crisis.

Whether experience with the campaigns of information, propaganda, and exhortation that surrounded the events of 1973-74 produced changes in families' cognitive competence is difficult to assess. Coming on the heels of the discovery that many "official" pronouncements connected with the Vietnam War and the Nixon-Watergate scandals were false, large segments of the public seem to have brought a heightened skepticism to the energy crisis. Whether the crisis per se affected their competence in obtaining and processing information cannot be determined from the available data.

Health and a sense of well-being are important nonmaterial resources. Only 5 percent of the households reported that the energy crisis had affected their health, mostly in the form of more colds. However, this reached 17 percent in Hartford. Many more—slightly over one-third of the families—said the energy problem had had something to do with the way things had been going in general for their households. They mentioned primarily increased costs, reduced use of energy, and cutbacks in purchases, trips, and activities. A few said the situation made them more tense or more cautious.

The main impact on the performance of family tasks came as a result of changes in their material resources and in relationships with their environment. Previous chapters have made it clear that energy price increases pinched almost everyone's pocketbook. Shortages of gasoline affected many. A small number of households was drastically affected by loss of jobs and reduction of income. A larger number was inconvenienced by changes in the accessibility or availability of goods and services.

In tracing through the responses to these changes, the distinction between internal and external tasks is a useful one. When a family alters the ways in which it serves its members it can be said that in part the family has "absorbed the impact" of a crisis. If from the family's perspective the change is undesirable, then the family has paid at least part of the cost of the crisis. To the extent that externally-oriented tasks are modified, the burden of the crisis has been shifted away from the family.

CHANGES IN INTERNAL TASKS

Our discussion begins with the effects of the energy crisis on the handling of internal tasks, principally those affective functions having to do with leisure time and recreational activities. The respondents compared the amount of time spent at home during the peak of the gasoline shortage with the previous year. When they were asked about time devoted to "doing things with other members of the family," such as playing cards or talking, 21 percent said they spent more time that way than the year before, but 7 percent said they spent less time.[a] Some 18 percent reported more and 11 percent reported less time watching television.

It is not clear how to interpret the increase in time spent at home with the family or watching TV. Did this really add to the family's gratification of its members and to its sense of integration? In the study by Hooley, the interviewers asked: "Many have said that the Energy Crisis will keep us at home more, with our families. Do you think that is a good idea?" Two-thirds of the respondents said they thought so, but one-third said more time with the family meant increased tension and frustration.[1]

Recreation and vacationing, major American family pursuits, were markedly reduced during the energy crisis, presumably lowering the families' satisfactions from those sources. Two-thirds of the respondents (67 percent) in the three metropolitan areas said they had reduced their driving for recreational purposes.[2] One-third of the households (35 percent) indicated that their vacation plans had been influenced by the energy situation.[3] Within this group, 60 percent said that they stayed home; 19 percent cut down on the distance traveled; and 10 percent shortened their vacations.

Thus, the *affective tasks* of the family that were touched during the energy crisis had to do with relaxation and the enjoyment of leisure time. These may not be as crucial in satisfying the affective needs of family members as, for example, support for a family member under severe strain. But the changes that were made in recreational activities can be looked upon as inconveniences and as

---
[a]Unless otherwise noted, the differences among Hartford, Mobile, and Salem residents were not consequential. For example, the proportion reporting more time with their families was 23 percent in Hartford, 17 percent in Mobile, and 24 percent in Salem.

diminutions in the performance of functions that now engage a large share of the time and resources of American families.

The *utilitarian tasks* that the family discharges for its own members include personal caretaking, socialization of the young, and household maintenance. While these are primarily oriented inward toward the family, it is obvious that they also entail effects on other social and economic units. At the edges, it becomes arbitrary whether to consider certain activities "internal" or "external" tasks. In the following sections, we have divided tasks according to what seems to be their dominant characteristic.

The transportation of children, especially in suburban areas, is an aspect of parental responsibility. This study found that among households with school-age children, slightly more than one-third (37 percent) said that they had cut down on the amount of driving that was done to take children to school and to after-school activities as a result of the energy crisis. In the eddies and currents that the energy crisis produced, there were, here and there, contradictory results. The NORC survey found an increase (from 39 percent to 55 percent) in the proportion of families who drove their children to school in the winter of 1973-74 compared with the previous winter. This was related to the institution of year-round Daylight Savings Time as an energy-conserving measure.

The NORC study notes that in January and February of 1974 there were reports in the media about accidents involving children on their way to school.[4] Although highway statistics showed a decrease in accidents during the winter of 1973-74 compared with the previous year, many public figures voiced the opinion that accidents were being caused by the extra hour of darkness in the morning. Actually only 19 percent of the respondents in the NORC survey reported problems in connection with children's getting to school safely. Despite the apparent discrepancy between rumor and reality, the concern about children's safety accounted for more than half of the opposition to year-round Daylight Savings Time.

HEATING AND COOLING THE HOME

Turning now to the distinctly utilitarian task of maintaining the physical aspects of a household, we inquire into the effects of the energy crisis on keeping the house warm enough or cool enough. The gross findings are presented here to indicate the impact on families as a whole. The next chapters analyze the data with a view to their implications for conservation policy and equity among different social and economic groups.

Half of the households in our survey (49 percent) reported that they had lowered the temperature of their dwellings during the day or evening when people were at home during the winter of the energy crisis in comparison with the year before.[5] Here the regional differences are important. The proportions of households who could control the heat in their homes and who did lower the thermostat were 67 percent in Hartford, 23 percent in Mobile, and 39 percent in Salem.

If one asks how much of an effect did this response have on the families involved it is difficult to answer decisively. Overall, they reported an average drop of 1.5° Fahrenheit from 70.2° to 68.7°.[b] The regional differences follow the same pattern throughout these comparisons. Hartford, most vulnerable to petroleum shortages, made the most marked changes. Mobile, with much milder climates and less concern about fuel, changed its heating practices the least. Salem consistently fell in between Hartford and Mobile. Details on these differences are shown in Table 5-1.

Perhaps more revealing of the extent to which families experienced lower household temperatures as a loss of comfort or a "cost" is to compare their actual temperatures with what they considered "ideal" temperatures. As a group, the households' mean ideal temperature for the wintertime when people were home and awake was 69.9°. During the winter *before* the energy crisis, the families said they kept their homes 0.3° warmer than this. When they lowered their temperatures *during the crisis* the reported reading was 1.2° below their ideal. How many experienced this as discomfort or an improvement is not known.

The respondents were also asked at what levels they kept the temperature in their homes when people were asleep and when no one was home. Generally these were 3-4° cooler than the temperatures when people were home and awake. The reductions were of

Table 5-1. Differences in Mean Household Temperatures when People Were Home and Awake, Winter of 1972-73 and 1973-74

	Hartford	*Mobile*	*Salem*	*All Areas*
Difference from precrisis Winter of 1972-73 to crisis Winter 1973-74	−2.1°	−0.4°	−1.4°	−1.5°
Precrisis: Difference between actual and ideal	+0.6°	+0.1°	+0.2°	+0.3°
Crisis Winter: Difference between actual and ideal	−1.5°	−0.3°	−1.2°	−1.2°

[b]NORC reported an average drop of 2.5° from 70.5° to 68°.

the same order of magnitude. It is of interest that Hartford households tended to keep their homes 6° warmer in winter when people were asleep than Salem families, with Mobile falling between the two.

A smaller proportion of households responded to the crisis by spending money on their heating systems or on insulation in order to save fuel and, in the long run, money.[c,6]

With regard to air-conditioning, the families' adjustments were not dissimilar to what they did about heating. Two-thirds of the households said they reduced their use of air-conditioning from the summer of 1973 to 1974 by an average of 1.7°. This was a change from 71.2° to 72.9°.

Bearing in mind that air-conditioning is far more important in Mobile, with its high summer temperatures, than in the two other areas, it is notable that 62 percent of the Mobile households with air-conditioning reported cutting back. The comparable figures were 77 percent in Hartford and 54 percent in Salem. Mobile and Salem permitted their indoor summer temperatures to rise about the same amount (1.1°-1.2°), while Hartford households adjusted their air-conditioning so that there was an increase of 2.4°. Only 6 percent of the households with air-conditioning spent money to fix up their units.

In short, half to two-thirds of the families made minor but measurable changes in the temperature of their homes, summer and winter, in response to the energy crisis. The changes were for the most part under 1.5° (warmer or colder) except in Hartford where the changes were between 2° and 2.5°. Again, these adjustments do not bespeak serious interference with the ability to perform these utilitarian tasks in the families studied. Much smaller proportions responded by making repairs or changes in their heating systems and insulation.

A high proportion of families in all three metropolitan areas made adjustments in their use of electricity. Asked whether they had cut back due to the price, three-quarters of the Hartford and Mobile households said they had.[7] The proportion dropped to 58 percent in Salem, where electricity is practically the cheapest in the country. But even in Salem, three-quarters of the families (73 percent) said

---

[c]The percentages who made changes were:

		Median Cost
Weatherstripping on windows and doors	16.7%	Under $100
Installed storm windows and doors	12.5%	$300-$400
Insulated floors, walls, ceilings	10.2%	$100-$200
Fixed heating system	7.4%	Under $100
Changed kind of heating system	1.8%	$800-$900

they had reduced their lighting; in Hartford this was 88 percent and in Mobile 77 percent.

The proportion of households who reduced their use of appliances because of the price of energy, whether it was electricity or natural gas, was substantial. In Chapter Three the raising of prices by establishments in the utility field was described in general terms. It should be noted here that families had been adjusting to these increases for several years before the Arabs' oil embargo of 1973, a trend that was intensified after that event. Table 5-2 summarizes the increases in the residential rates for electricity and natural gas in the three metropolitan areas.

Reductions in the use of household appliances were made by one-quarter to one-half of the households who owned such appliances, as shown in Table 5-3.

In this connection it is relevant to note that half the households in the three areas told the interviewers that they had cut down on the use of hot water. This was quite constant across the three SMSAs.

Thus far we have been discussing impacts on the families' performance of *internal tasks*. The data from this and other studies seem to warrant two general observations. One is that substantial percentages of the families surveyed made some adjustments in their handling of these tasks. The proportions range from one-third to three-quarters of the households with respect to vacationing and recreation; driving children to school; maintaining the temperature of their homes, and in the use of electricity. The prevalence of the impact, so to speak, was substantial.

The other observation—admittedly more difficult to document—is that *in most cases* these adjustments did not have serious consequences for the viability of the family as a social unit. The impacts were more in the nature of inconveniences and some slight loss of comfort, though some of the changes may have been felt as positive.

Table 5-2. Percentage Increases in Residential Costs for Electricity & Natural Gas in Hartford, Mobile, and Salem, 1970-74

	% Increase in Price Per KWH for Electricity	*% Increase in Price Per MCF for Natural Gas*
Hartford	28	28
Mobile	41	67
Salem	45	31

Note: For Hartford the electricity rates are for 1970-73 and the natural gas rates for 1971-74.

Table 5-3. Proportion of Respondents Who Said They Reduced Use of Appliances Due to Price of Energy

Appliance	Percent of Owners Who Cut Back
Clothes dryer	46
Dishwasher	45
Fans (attic)	39
Space heaters	38
Clothes washer	33
Stove	29
TV (black/white)	23

Here subjective evaluations enter and it is difficult to know, for example, which families were in fact distressed by lowering their thermostats during the winter or by spending more time with each other at home. On balance, however, it appears justifiable to conclude that while the impact on internal task performance was extensive, it was not intensive. This is, of course, a broad generalization about the 1,440 households overall; how intense were the impacts on certain families remains to be examined in the next chapters.

CHANGES IN EXTERNAL TASKS

What happened in the performance of tasks that affect social systems outside the family? We look first at participation in out-of-the-house activities. Between one-quarter and one-half of the respondents stated that because of the gasoline situation they had reduced these activities, as shown in Table 5-4. A negligible proportion reported increases. But here again there is evidence of differential effects among families. Some 8 percent of the respondents said they were entertaining friends and relatives *more often* than in 1972. Perhaps this meant that people living nearby were walking over to visit or that people were visiting more frequently but driving shorter distances. These speculations are given some support by the finding that Warren and Clifford made in their Detroit study in which they reported that 11 percent of their sample said they were spending more time with neighbors.

Large areas of family activity are concerned with the acquisition of goods and services and with income-producing work. It is obvious that both consumption and occupational activities of families have

Table 5-4. Respondents Who Reported Less Time In Participatory Activities

	% Reporting Cut-back
Entertaining friends & relatives	24%
Visiting friends & relatives*	47%
Taking part in educational, recreational, sports events	29%
Participating in social, union, professional meetings	26%

*When respondents were asked, at another point in the interview, whether they had cut back on the amount of driving they did to visit friends and relatives as a result of the energy situation, 64 percent said yes.

significant repercussions on economic and social systems beyond their borders.

To begin with consumption activities, the respondents were asked whether there were any major purchases they had thought seriously about making but had decided not to make because of the energy situation. One out of five (22 percent) said yes to this. Among all 1,440 households, 14 percent mentioned appliances and home improvements and 10 percent mentioned cars in this connection. Most of this group cited the increased cost of operation as the main reason for not buying. One out of five families said they did in fact make some change in the kind of clothing they bought.

The most pervasive adjustments came in the use of cars in the form of lower speeds and curtailed driving. Largely in response to federal legislation, which set a 55 mph speed limit on the highways, drivers said they dropped their highway speeds an average of 7.9 mph to 53.5 mph during the crisis.[d] None of the studies probed beyond this to determine the effects that slower driving had on households. A remarkable lowering of the national accident rate and the number of deaths on the highways, however, point to one of the most benign effects of the energy crisis.

The buying, selling, and maintenance of cars were also affected by the energy situation. Nine percent of the households said they sold cars with a view to saving gas and 13 percent said they bought cars for that reason.[e] Half the owners of cars with air-conditioning cut back on its use. Several maintenance measures were taken: half of

---

[d]The precrisis speed reported in the survey (61.4 mph) was only slightly lower than the 63.3 mph on suburban highways reported for 1973 by the Federal Highway Administration of the Department of Transportation. The small difference is a source of reassurance about the validity of the self-reported data in this study.

[e]The NORC researchers were told that 12 percent of their sample had bought or used a car that gets better mileage in order to save gas.

88 Families in the Energy Crisis

the car owners said they had their engines tuned up to increase mileage and one-fourth changed tires for that reason, though only 15 percent changed their tire pressure.

In general, 79 percent of the households in the sample reported curtailing the use of their cars to save gasoline.[8] Almost two-thirds of the households (62 percent) said they cut down on the amount of driving they did to shop for groceries, clothing, housewares, and the like as a result of the energy situation.[f] One-third said they were spending less time going to the movies and eating out. Households were far less flexible in their adjustments in the religious and medical areas; only 4-5 percent cut back on trips to doctors or dentists or on their attendance at religious services.

Families living within the central cities in the three metropolitan areas made somewhat different adjustments from those living outside in suburban and rural areas. Among those in the central cities, 75 percent said they cut down the use of their cars in contrast to 82 percent outside the cities. Shopping by car was reduced proportionately more by households outside the cities (71 percent) than by the city dwellers (60 percent), but driving for recreation, children's activities, and visits were not curtailed in markedly different ways.

It is useful to look at the very widespread adjustment in the use of automobiles, reported by eight out of every ten households, in terms of the analytical model employed in this study. When people use their cars less, what compensating changes do they make and how do these adjustments further affect the family members? In the language of the model, what substitutions or rearrangements were made when car usage was decreased?

SUBSTITUTES FOR DRIVING

The respondents who had cut back on driving in general were asked which of several modes of transportation they had resorted to in order to save gas. Car pooling was mentioned most often and walking almost as much, as shown in Table 5-6. Bicycles and public transportation were cited by fewer people. But the adjustment was quite different when it involved shopping and recreation. Here the shift was heavily in the direction of making fewer trips and choosing

---

[f] "Gas Watchers' Guide," published by the American Automobile Association, contains estimates of the relative amounts of gasoline used for different purposes. In millions of gallons of gasoline consumed per week, the AAA estimates the breakdown as follows:

To and from work	290 million gallons
Social and recreational activities	382 million gallons
Family business	225 million gallons

destinations closer to home, with much less reliance on shared driving and walking. The most frequent substitute for chauffeuring children to school and after-school activities was to have the children bicycle or walk more; almost as many resorted to sharing the driving with other families. Among the workers interviewed only 15 percent reported changing their mode of travel to their jobs. Most of this shift took place, as Table 5-5 indicates, among those who had been driving alone and changed to car pool arrangements.[g] The fact that so small a percentage of workers altered their way of getting to work is an indication of the constraints that operated on families in their adjustments to the gasoline shortage. This is reinforced by the finding of the Survey Research Center at the University of Michigan, which reported that "more than three-fourths of those who drove to work said that they could not get to their jobs using public transportation, so that they could not reduce their gasoline consumption unless they joined a car pool, moved closer to their place of work, or found another job."[9]

The increase in car pooling for travel to work can be interpreted as an adjustment for which the family as a whole pays in one way or another. Half the car pool participants in this study shared the driving; 13 percent split the expenses; and 7 percent paid the driver outright. The result is either a financial cost to the family or less use of the family car.

Table 5-5. Changes in Mode of Getting to Work (n = 964)*

Time 1–Before Gasoline Shortage	Drove Alone	Pool-alter.	Pool-passenger	Pool-driver	Bus Street car	Walk	Total
Drove alone	670	67	11	15	14	4	781
Pool-alternating	1	57	1	1	–	–	60
Pool-passenger	1	1	44	–	2	–	48
Pool-driver	–	–	–	27	–	–	27
Bus, street car	–	–	–	–	25	2	27
Walk	–	–	1	–	–	20	21
TOTAL	672	125	57	43	41	26	964

Time 2–During Gasoline Shortage

*The table omits 15 persons who got to work by train, motorcycle, or bicycle either before or during the shortage.

[g]NORC reported a 7 percent shift to car-pooling; Gallup an 8 percent shift; and Warren and Clifford in their Detroit area study found 19 percent of their respondents stating that they were not using their cars as much to go to work. It is worth noting that NORC reported that 11 percent of their respondents were walking more to work.

90 Families in the Energy Crisis

The substitutes that families who cut down on their driving utilized for various purposes are shown in Table 5-6.

On the whole, then, households compensated for reduced driving of their cars by making fewer and more economical trips, sharing or doubling up with other drivers, and going to places closer to home. Some car-owning households increased their walking, bicycling, and use of public transportation, but much larger proportions did not avail themselves of these alternatives. In short, they absorbed much of the presumed inconvenience of having less use of their cars. To a limited extent, some families transmitted or shared the cost of adjustment with other families with cars.

The reported reduction in the use of vehicles other than automobiles was substantial though less than the cutback in car usage. Among households owning campers or motor homes and motor boats 55-60 percent said they reduced their use to save gasoline. One-third of those with vans or trucks said they had done the same thing. On the other hand, only slightly more than one-quarter of those who had motorcycles said they had cut down on their use in order to save gas.

Probably the most severe adjustment was felt by the 3.6 percent of the households in the three metropolitan areas who reported that someone in the household had quit or had been laid off their jobs because of the energy shortage. On the average, these workers had been unemployed for 3.3 months at the time of the survey in November 1974. The range was from one to twelve months. Except to the extent that unemployment compensation cushioned these separations from work, these fifty-five families bore the brunt of the

Table 5-6. Alternatives to Driving Utilized by Respondents Who Reduced Driving (in percent)

	In General to Save Gas (n=1,049)	For Shopping (n=891)	For Recreation (n=894)	To Get To Work (n=161)
Car pool and shared driving	31	20	17	69
Walking	26	14	9	4
Bicycle	17	8	7	4
Public transportation	13	4	4	1
Hitchhiking	2	–	–	–
Fewer trips	–	69	80	–
Combining errands	–	70	–	–
Going closer to home	–	32	24	–
Motorcycle	–	–	–	8

energy crisis in their lowered income and presumably lowered morale.[h]

Absenteeism and lateness, on the other hand, are adjustments that are at least partially transmitted to employers, though they may also involve loss of earnings. Among the employed workers in this study, 14 percent said they were late to work during the crisis on account of the gasoline shortage. A smaller number, 3 percent, said they were absent because of the energy crisis.

SUMMARY

What can be said then, by way of summary, about the nature of the adjustments that families made to the energy crisis and the effects these responses had on their task performance? Adjustments were made by very sizable numbers of families in their use of the car to provide satisfactions to the family members, such as recreation. Considerable proportions of households cut back on the conveniences of home heating, air-conditioning, and the use of electricity.[10]

But these adjustments, as well as others that were made in the consumption activities of the families, did not appear to have affected such vital areas as health, well-being or the basic financial condition of families, taken as a whole. Chapter Seven will examine these changes as they impinged on families with differing socioeconomic status. But on the average, the consumer functions that are related to utilitarian and affective tasks in the family were not notably affected in the energy crisis.

The role of a small proportion of families in the labor force was sharply affected. The weight of the crisis fell heavily on those families whose wage-earners were forced to leave their jobs. Except

---

[h]The sector of the economy which the worker left as a result of the energy crisis is known for most of the fifty-five persons involved and is as follows:

	No. of Persons
Services	14
Manufacturing	10
Transportation	7
Wholesale	2
Retail	2
Finance, insurance	2
Other	18
Total	55

The income and racial differences among these workers are described in Chapter Seven.

for these, the adjustments that most families made can hardly be said to have seriously affected their viability or even their life-styles.

This chapter has focused on the substance of the adjustments and changes that were made and on the effects on families. The next chapter looks into two aspects of adjustment as a process—the attrition that occurred in some of the early adaptations that were made and the repercussions on systems outside the family. In this latter connection, attention is given to conservation of energy as an outcome of family adjustments and as an impact on the economy as a whole.

✳ *Chapter Six*

Attrition, Repercussions, and Energy Conservation

Adjustment to crises can be described as a dynamic process unfolding in phases over time—as well as a set of outcomes, which was the subject of the previous chapter. The process of family adjustment during the two years following the energy crisis of 1973-74 is the focus of the first part of this chapter.[a] Here the prime question is whether the changes that families made in the early stages of the crisis were stable or fleeting and whether there was attrition in their initial adjustments.

The second part of this chapter deals with another feature of the process: the ripple effects that were set in motion by the families' adjustments. What were the repercussions on other systems? The paramount issue here—of particular interest from a public policy perspective—concerns the impact of family actions on the consumption and conservation of energy.

The model employed in this study suggests that the process of family adjustment to crisis can be pictured as a number of overlapping but distinguishable stages. In one of these the families confront stressor events by exploring possible responses. In another phase they adopt changes in attitudes and behavior, albeit tentatively and often temporarily. As the stressor events recede, the changes may undergo attrition. The process eventually reaches a point of relative stability. As we have pointed out, these are often in reality not discrete, sequential stages, but processes that intermingle and interact.

Exploration and experimentation in a situation of uncertainty early in a crisis involves the cognitive activities of acquiring and

---
[a]Chapter Eight reports additional data on the 1976-77 crisis.

weighing information about the present and future. Under these circumstances we have already seen that expectations can influence behavior. It will be recalled that one study of the energy crisis found short-term expectations to be more significant than long-term ones. Another study found that a person's concern about effects on his or her employment was the most powerful determinant of energy-related behavior.[b]

The Brandeis study saw evidence of families' trying to look ahead and choose appropriate action. For instance, though the percentage is very small, 4 percent of the households said that in the months following October 1973 they gave some thought to moving because of the energy crisis. Another illustration of exploration is apparent among the homeowners (17-27 percent) who considered fixing their heating systems or improving the heating efficiency of their homes by putting in weather-stripping, storm windows, or insulation. Approximately three-quarters of those who explored these possibilities followed through and actually had the improvements made; the others decided against it. Only 5 percent contemplated the more costly work of changing their heating systems and only one-third of this very small group actually did so.

Another indication of this phase in a crisis comes from answers to questions about the future. Respondents were asked—without specifying the conditions that might prevail in the twelve months following their interviews—whether they anticipated using more or less energy for a number of purposes. Some 17 percent said they expected to use less energy for heating and very few said they would use more. The respondents said that they expected their driving speed on the highways the following winter would be, on the average, 55 mph, but that if there were another gasoline shortage, this would be 53 mph.

More marked changes were anticipated in the use of electrical appliances. Here, 30 percent said they would use their air-conditioning less. A reduction in the use of dishwashers was forecast by 22 percent of the respondents. The most inelastic consumption item was TV; only 10 percent said they expected to cut down their TV watching. Only 2-3 percent said they would use these electric appliances more in the future. Clearly more respondents leaned toward making further adjustments in their use of appliances in the future than expected to reverse adjustments already made.

The weekly surveys taken by the National Opinion Research Center from the summer of 1973 through the spring of 1974 reinforce the observation that this was a period of experimentation,

---

[b]See Chapter Four, page 75 for details on the two studies.

exploration, and short-term fluctuations in perceptions and opinions. The proportion of people reporting that they had difficulty getting gasoline was 18 percent in November 1973; it moved up to 60 percent and then down to 12 percent by the end of May 1974. The number of Americans holding the federal government responsible for the crisis see-sawed up and down between 30 percent and 45 percent in this period, as did those holding the oil and gas companies responsible.

In the same vein, NORC found that almost 40 percent of their respondents felt gasoline rationing was necessary by the end of November 1973. Less than 20 percent felt that way in mid-January. This rose to 35 percent a month later and then dropped below 20 percent. Fluctuations in behavior were less marked during these crisis months, e.g., the proportion of drivers going to work alone in their cars varied only between 75 percent and 85 percent during this time.[1]

That aspect of a crisis which we have referred to as "unfreezing" and exploration of possible responses is evident in these findings. There was uncertainty about the future course of the energy crisis and ambivalence about the adjustments to be made. Certain options were considered and pursued by some families and dropped or never considered by others. Heavy financial investments in energy-conserving measures, such as replacing the heating system, were made by only a very few.

STABILITY OR ATTRITION A YEAR LATER

Notwithstanding this cautious and exploratory attitude, very substantial adjustments were in fact made in the use of cars, heating, and electricity at the peak of the energy crisis, as described in the previous chapter. A general question raised by this study's analytic model concerning these adjustments can be simply stated: were the responses made at the height of the energy crisis in 1973-74 stable or was there attrition following the easing of the gasoline shortage and the assurance from the president that "the crisis" was over? Was there a process of erosion that wiped out part or all of the changes that had been made in a crisis atmosphere?

In order to get at this question, the respondents were asked in November 1974 to look back and describe what changes they had made at the peak of the crisis from their customary patterns. During the interviews they were also asked whether they had made any further changes in the year that had elapsed since the peak of the crisis. It is therefore possible to compare their reported behavior as it changed from Time 1 (precrisis) to Time 2 (peak of crisis) to Time 3 (a year after the crisis). For example, one out of five families said they had spent more time at home at the peak of the crisis than they had before the crisis. But only one out of ten reported spending more time with their families a year after the peak in comparison with their allocation of time at the height of the crisis, as shown in Table 6-1. The proportion reporting less time with their families remained constant over both time intervals. Note, however, that the overwhelming majority of families made no adjustments at either time.

The situation with regard to television was similar. Between the pre-crisis period and the peak of the crisis almost one out of five families was spending more time watching TV. A year after the peak, only one-third of that number was giving more time to television. The proportion devoting less time to TV remained constant.

Turning to the family's entertaining and its participation in events outside the home, there were more noticeable changes here. One-fourth of the respondents said that during the crisis they were doing less entertaining and going less often to recreational, sports, and cultural events and to union and professional meetings. One-half had cut back on visiting friends and relatives. One year later only one-eighth of all the families were doing less of these things. There were minor increases in the proportions who said they were doing *more* entertaining and going *more often* to outside events.

Similarly during the crisis one-third of the respondents had cut down on eating meals away from home and on attendance at movies. A year later one-fifth of the respondents were cutting down on these activities. The percentage who were doing *more* eating-out and movie-going had doubled from the crisis level of 3-4 percent.

In other words, *a modest proportion of families was continuing to*

Table 6-1. Comparison of Time Spent with the Family and Watching TV Before, During and After the Peak of the Energy Crisis (in percent)

	Nov. 1973 Compared with Previous Year		Nov. 1974 Compared with November 1973	
	More	*Less*	*More*	*Less*
Time with family members	21	7	9	7
Watching TV	17	11	6	12

adjust their behavior so as to conserve energy a year after the crisis. Practically the same proportion had stopped adjusting and had reverted to precrisis patterns. Like the proverbial glass of water that can be called half-full or half-empty, there was, from one perspective, measurable attrition in the adjusting that families in this study reported. From another point of view, the process of adjustment was still active among some families a year after the oil embargo in 1973.

In order to obtain information on adjustments beyond November 1974 when the interviews were conducted, the 1,440 households were mailed a questionnaire in September 1975. The response rate was 60 percent and those who answered were a remarkably good cross-section of the original households. (See Appendix B for details on the Mail Questionnaire.) Data from the Mail Questionnaire are compared below with the original interview data *from the same families.*

We use two ways to measure changes in adjustments from one time period to another. One is to cite overall rates. For example, 73 percent of the households said in the interviews they had lessened their use of electricity during the year following the crisis; a year later 58 percent of the same families reported by mail using less electricity. A more revealing way is to trace the behavior of groups within this population and to see, for example, whether the early "savers" continued to save, increased their consumption of electricity, or kept it at the same level as the previous year. Both methods are used here.

The drop in the overall rate of electricity conservation from 73 percent in 1974 to 58 percent in 1975 has already been noted. Eight percent of the mail sample said they were *using more* electricity in 1975. Well over half of the households, in other words, reported *continuing efforts* to reduce their use of electricity.[2] But, again, there are signs of attrition. The proportion of conservers in the aggregate has decreased and the proportion of those using more electricity has increased. What does the finely-tuned analysis show?

Among those who had said in the interview that they were cutting back on electricity following the 1973-74 crisis period, more than half said by mail in 1975 that they were reducing still further their consumption (see Table 6-2). Four out of ten said they were at the same level of consumption. Only eight percent of these original conservers said they were using more electrical energy in 1975. The percentages for Hartford, Mobile, and Salem were very close to the overall rates shown in Table 6-2.

98 Families in the Energy Crisis

Table 6-2. Attrition in Electricity Conservation 1974-75

Original Survey (Nov. 1974)	September 1975 Consumption Patterns Compared with 1974		
	More	Same	Less
Electricity conservers	8	39	53
Electricity nonconservers	8	22	71
Air-conditioning conservers	14	33	53
Air-conditioning nonconservers	23	45	32
(Electricity: n=720)			
(Air conditioning: n=380)			

Among those who told the interviewers in their homes that they had *not* cut back on electricity after the crisis of 1973, conservation increased sharply in 1975. Seven out of ten of these earlier nonconservers were using less electricity in 1975. The differences among the three metropolitan areas were minor.

The pattern in all four groups shown in Table 6-2 is the same: the conservers in 1975 far outnumber those who have started to use more electricity. It is worth remarking that among those *who had not started to save on electricity during the crisis, the number of 1975 conservers is very substantial.* Fairly significant percentages retained their earlier level. Not many households were reporting more consumption in 1975 over 1974. In short, attrition in conservation of electricity has been minimal. Indeed, more people were making downward adjustments twenty-four months after the crisis than were not, except for the air-conditioning "nonconservers."

HEATING AND DRIVING BEHAVIOR

Among families who lowered their temperatures during the crisis winter, the mean of the reported decreases was 1.5°.[c] The mail questionnaire showed a small rise of 0.8° the following winter. The sharpest increase was in Mobile (1.9°) compared with Hartford (0.5°) and Salem (0.6°).

[c]Another way of examining attrition in heating patterns is to compare the percentages of households reporting low, medium, and high temperatures in the interviews and later in the mail questionnaire. The proportion keeping their homes between 68° and 72° remained constant at 76 percent. Originally there had been 20 percent reporting temperatures below 68°; in the mail replies this dropped to 14 percent. Conversely, those reporting temperatures above 72° increased from 4 percent to 9 percent. In short, there was some slippage in conservation behavior.

The change in heating behavior appears inconsequential when measured in degrees Fahrenheit, but the attrition becomes much more vivid when one tracks the shifts by groups among those who responded to the mail questionnaire. Practically half of the original conserving group abandoned that pattern and raised their thermostat settings in 1975. Almost as many among those who had originally kept their temperatures steady during the crisis said that they were setting higher temperatures at home in 1975. About 40 percent of both groups kept their temperatures unchanged between the crisis winter and the following winter (see Table 6-3).

Dramatic changes had initially taken place in the use of cars. More than three-quarters of the households reduced their driving. On the average a drop of 8 mph in highway speeds was reported. How much attrition was there in these adjustments?

The tendency to return to earlier patterns was, of course, severely restricted in the case of highways' speeds by the imposition of the legal limit of 55 mph.[d] But almost anyone who was driving the highways from 1973 to 1975 was aware of an increase in the speed at which motorists were traveling. The drivers in this study said that they had inched up on the average from 53.5 mph at the peak of the crisis to 55.1 mph a year later. For some drivers and for some parts of the country this was undoubtedly much more. The Federal Energy Administration reported at the end of 1975 that "drivers in many regions are growing less conscious of the 55 mph speed limit and enforcing that limit is getting difficult."[3]

As we turn to the amount of driving that respondents reported, it is possible to compare behavior at three points in time: (1) the peak of the crisis in 1973 and early 1974, (2) November 1974, and (3) September 1975. Figure 6-1 shows that a year after the crisis one-fourth of the drivers had made *further cutbacks* in their car use. This was "balanced" by roughly the same number who increased their driving.

Table 6-3. Changes in Heating Behavior 1973-75
(in percent; n=629)

Behavior in Crisis Winter (1973-74)	Behavior in Following Winter (1974-75)		
	Lowered Temperature	Increased Temperature	Kept Same Temperature
Lowered temperature (Conservers)	15	45	40
Kept same temperature	25	38	37

[d]Gallup reported in January 1975 that 68 percent of the drivers they interviewed said they had reduced their speed as a result of the legal limit.

100 Families in the Energy Crisis

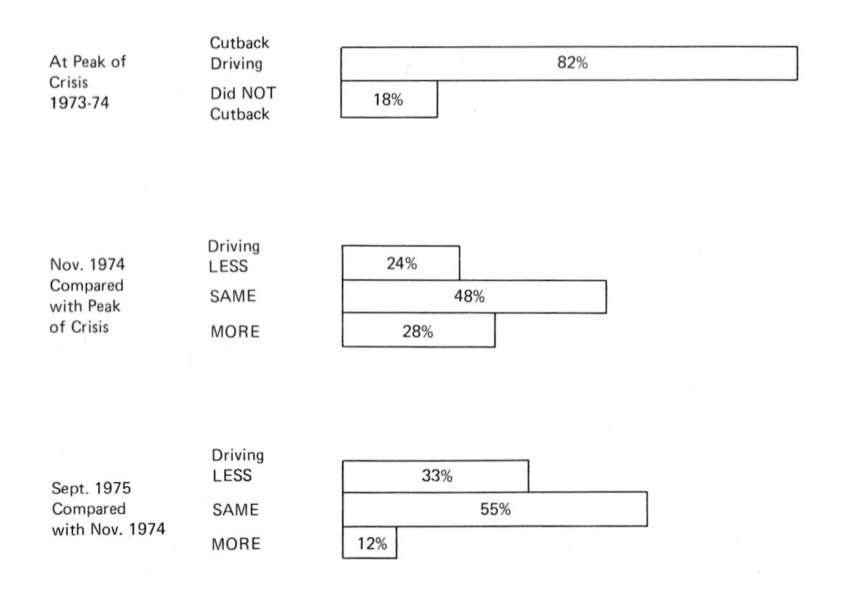

| At Peak of Crisis 1973-74 | Cutback Driving | 82% |
| | Did NOT Cutback | 18% |

Nov. 1974 Compared with Peak of Crisis	Driving LESS	24%
	SAME	48%
	MORE	28%

Sept. 1975 Compared with Nov. 1974	Driving LESS	33%
	SAME	55%
	MORE	12%

Figure 6-1. Overall Changes in Driving 1973-74 (n=682)

In September 1975 one-third were reducing their driving even more and only 12 percent had stepped up their use of cars. Approximately half of the drivers reported steady use of their cars from 1973 through 1975. The proportion of "conserving drivers" increased over time more than the percentage of heavier users. Hence, there was *some attrition but noticeably more downward adjustment in driving.*

This observation is accentuated by the data in Figure 6-2. Regardless of whether people had increased, decreased, or stabilized the amount of their driving in November 1974, by September 1975 many more in each category were cutting back than were increasing their driving.

Attrition was the most pronounced in Salem, where 37 percent reported driving more than they did during the crisis. This compares to 29 percent in Hartford and only 14 percent in Mobile. It might be expected that since the largest changes were originally made in Salem and Hartford, the greatest postcrisis attrition would take place in those areas, as it did.

At the time of the crisis not many working people altered their mode of travel to work. Only 15 percent said they had switched to

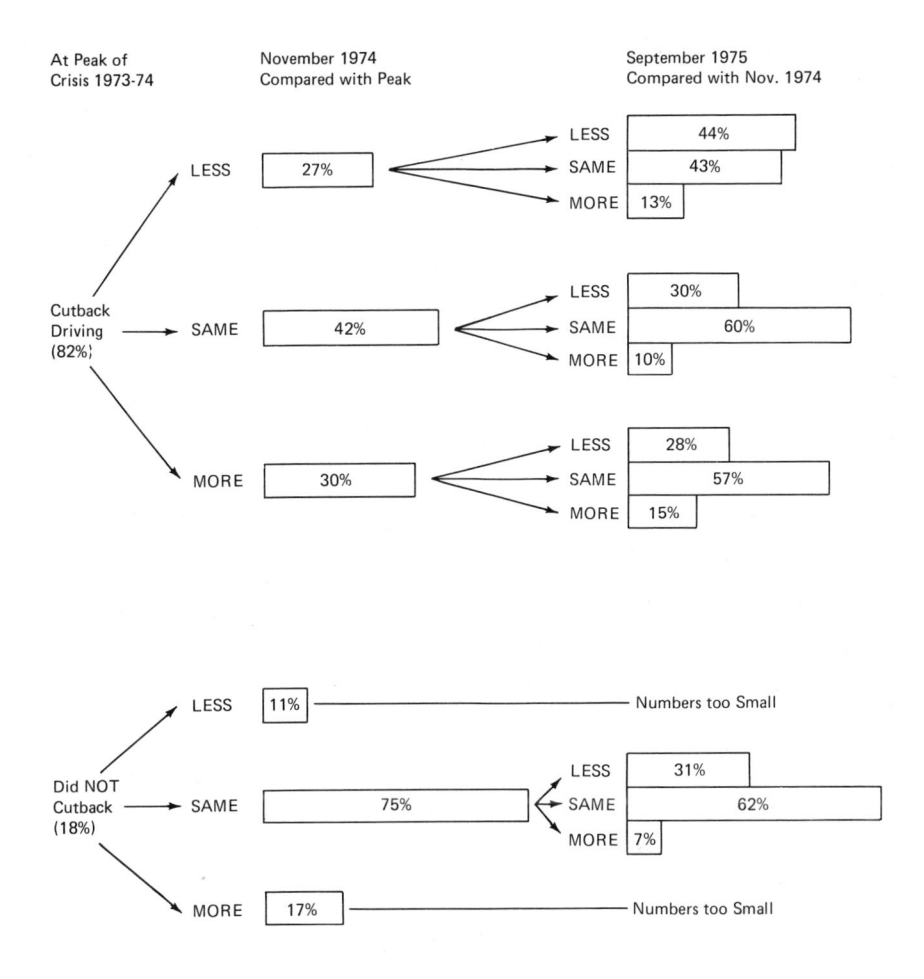

Attrition, Repercussions, and Energy Conservation 101

At Peak of Crisis 1973-74	November 1974 Compared with Peak	September 1975 Compared with Nov. 1974
Cutback Driving (82%) → LESS	27%	LESS 44% / SAME 43% / MORE 13%
Cutback Driving (82%) → SAME	42%	LESS 30% / SAME 60% / MORE 10%
Cutback Driving (82%) → MORE	30%	LESS 28% / SAME 57% / MORE 15%
Did NOT Cutback (18%) → LESS	11%	Numbers too Small
Did NOT Cutback (18%) → SAME	75%	LESS 31% / SAME 62% / MORE 7%
Did NOT Cutback (18%) → MORE	17%	Numbers too Small

Figure 6-2. Changes in Amount of Driving 1973-1975 (n=682)

another way of getting to their jobs. A year later the travel-to-work patterns were practically the same as those that prevailed before the crisis. For example, 76 percent of the employed workers drove to work alone in the precrisis period; this had returned to 74 percent late in 1974.

To sum up the process of adjusting the use of cars to the energy crisis, it is clear that while there was some attrition in the early adjustments, there was considerably less attrition than in the families' behavior concerning heating. On the other hand, there was a bit more attrition in car usage than in the conservation of electrical energy in the home.

ATTRITION BY INCOME GROUPS

It is of interest to know about the stability/attrition of the adjustments made by the different income groupings among the respondents.[e] At all income levels the overwhelming portion of families said that they had stabilized their adjustments a year after the crisis peak. But there were some discernible differences. The return toward precrisis behavior was more pronounced among higher income families in terms of visiting, going on recreational trips, attending meetings, going to the movies, and eating out. In fact, the attrition rate of the families above $10,000 income was two to three times as high, in these respects, as it was in the below $5,000 income group. And a year after the peak of the crisis, proportionately more lower income families reported making still further reductions in the activities noted above.

Just as reductions in highway speed varied directly with income, so the "bounce back effect" was roughly proportionate to income. On the average, families above $15,000 boosted their speeds 3 mph following the crisis; those between $5,000 and $15,000 increased by 1 mph, while the lowest income group increased by 2 mph.

It is also interesting to compare the attrition in car use during the twelve months following the oil embargo among families with one car and those with two or more cars. The differences are not large but their direction is clear. A year after the peak of the crisis 20 percent of the one-car families said they were driving more and 30 percent said they were driving less. It was just the reverse among families with two or more cars: 29-32 percent of them were driving more and 21 percent were driving less. In other words, reversion to precrisis car usage was greater among those with more than one car, presumably the higher income owners. Intensified conservation was greater among one-car owners.

The questionnaires mailed in September 1975 asked about changes in the preceding twelve months. Changes reported in car use were inconsequential when compared by income of the households. The same held for use of electricity, though more higher income families

---

[e]To some extent this anticipates the discussion of socioeconomic differences in Chapter Seven, but it seems more useful to complete the consideration of attrition and repercussive effects in this chapter by including income-related differences.

said they were using less air-conditioning in the summer of 1975 than was the case with lower income families.

On balance, then, stability rather than continuing change characterized the behavior of all income groups in the two years following the fall of 1973. Among the minority of households who shifted away from their initial adjustments to the crisis, the variations among income groups were on the whole not marked, but there was a tendency for more higher income families to report attrition in their behavior in the direction of precrisis patterns. This was somewhat less so for the lower income families. The most noticeable difference was in activities related to recreation in the first postcrisis year.

Attrition can occur in attitudes as well as behavior. This was the case with beliefs about the energy shortage, that is, whether it was "real" or not.[f] As Table 6-4 indicates, there was some erosion in the size of the group that doubted the reality of the energy shortage as well as among those who thought there was an actual shortage. The proportion who "didn't know" increased sharply and this accounts for the decrease in both "believers" and outright skeptics. The differences along income lines were unimportant. It may well be that their own experiences after the fall of 1973 had made some respondents less certain that the crisis was "phoney." On the other hand, practically half still felt in 1975 there was not a real energy shortage.

Table 6-4. Belief and Disbelief in the Energy Crisis, 1974 and 1975 (in percent; n=723)

	Believers	Disbelievers	Don't Know*	Total
Nov. 1974 Interview	35	60	5	100
Sept. 1975 Mail Response	21	48	31	100

*In the original interview, respondents were not given the option of answering "don't know." Those who did not choose a yes or no answer were counted as "don't know" responses. In the mail questionnaire, they were given an opportunity to check "don't know" and this may account for part of the difference between the two time periods.

The flavor of the comments about the energy shortage is caught in these notes written by respondents on the returned mail questionnaires next to the query: "Do you think there is a real shortage of energy at this time? (Nov. 1975)   Yes ( )   No ( )   Don't know ( )"

---

[f]See Chapter Four, pp. 67-68 for a discussion of the possible ambiguity surrounding this question.

Strongly suspect contrived shortages and genuine rip-offs. PGE increased 30% this week and is asking more. In this state of hydro-electric power???

Yes, but I also believe that there has been a deliberate reduction of supply by the oil companies.

There certainly is a shortage of oil and gas produced in this country, but there is no shortage of energy, because we keep increasing our dependency on foreign supplies. If this is cut off we're in a real mess.

Real shortage as opposed to contrived? No. Energy, does this mean natural resources? If so, yes, I believe that there is a need to develop other sources of energy.

I don't think there is a shortage but the big oil company men don't have to pay my bill so they don't give a dam.

Trick to make increased rates gradually acceptable.

No shortage of coal, only because utilities are not allowed to make reasonable profit and therefore cannot raise capital for expansion, do we face a shortage of *electricity*, not energy *per se*.

Due to addition of first child in the family more use of washer and dryer. I think that there is energy wastage, however. And I think that energy shortages will develop if usage patterns are not changed.

Environmentalists are making the shortage, we have plenty of coal. Let's use it.

There is also an acute shortage of intelligent, non-political, national energy policy.

I'd like to think there is and was a real shortage of energy but it all came about too suddenly. The sudden gas lines appearing at stations—without a gradual warning, months, yes, even years in advance of the shortage. In our day of modern science, it seems unbelievable to think we could have such stupid experts—people who are collecting enormous salaries—not to have foresight enough to see such serious energy shortages occurring at least a full *decade* hence. Also, when these shortages did, in fact occur and our lines were formed, why then, did they suddenly disappear just as suddenly as they occurred? Was it not the real fact of *price boosting* and not so much shortages that caused a return to normalcy. When, we, the people decided we couldn't afford that extra trip to the grocery store or extra weekend drive to the lake, then, and only then, did our oil prices come down. Our sugar shortage will verify this also—we are still using less sugar and will probably never use it as we once did.

ATTRITION SUMMARIZED

The general picture of the unfolding stages of the crisis and particularly the attrition in behavior and belief can be summarized in these statements:

The immediate reaction by families to the energy crisis took the form of uncertainty about its meaning and future course and was expressed in exploration of alternative responses, e.g., whether or not to install fuel-saving improvements in one's home.

There followed, as detailed in Chapter Five, adjustments in behavior on the part of a very substantial proportion of families. Eight out of ten households cut down on driving; half reduced their heating at home; and three-quarters cut back on electricity. About one-fifth to one-third altered such behaviors as time spent at home, eating out, and going to the movies.

In the course of the next two years, the majority of those who had adapted their behavior in the crisis situation continued in the same pattern or at the same level of adjustment. This group did not give evidence of attrition in their original adjustments. They "froze" their new behavior.

A small minority that had not originally modified their behavior made some adjustments in the year or two following the peak of the crisis. In effect, they were latecomers to the adjustment process.

There was some attrition on the part of a substantial proportion of households who partially reversed their crisis-induced behavior and turned back *toward* precrisis patterns, though apparently few returned completely to those behaviors. This attrition was most marked in terms of heating, where four out of ten households stepped up their use of heating fuels; it was less true of electricity and use of cars. Conversely, the proportion of families trying to reduce their use of energy in 1975 was highest in terms of electricity and lowest with regard to heating.

For the families as a whole there was considerable movement in behavior at the height of the crisis. This was followed by a limited, partial return to precrisis conditions.[4] The net result was a significant residue of altered behavior two years after the crisis. This is not to say, however, that the outcome seriously affected the capacities or performance of families in areas vital to their functioning. Nor is to imply that adjustments or burdens were borne equally by all families, an issue that will be taken up in the next chapter.

Finally, it cannot truly be said that the families' adjustments stabilized at the close of the period under review. It is only an artifact of research that we can point to a new equilibrium at the end of the study period. The reality of continuing adjustments—of backing and filling among families with respect to the energy crisis—is apparent in the continual changes that have taken place, not only in behavior but in attitudes and beliefs about the energy crisis. Indeed the uncertainty about whether or not there was an energy shortage persisted for at least 30 percent of the respondents as late as the fall of 1975, when they said they simply did not know one way or another.

The final aspect of the analytical model to be treated in this chapter has to do with the ripple or repercussive effects that family adjustments had on other parts of the social and economic system. The model suggests that adjustment by any unit in a social system produces consequences for other units. The ripple process can be illustrated if we inquire what led to the unemployment problems of the fifty-five families cited earlier.

RIPPLE EFFECTS

Of the twelve people who quit their jobs, nine of them pointed to the price or availability of gasoline as the reason. One said he quit because the company "won't use the heat or lights." Another said the company's juggling of work schedules to promote car pools made it impossible to catch his bus.

Among the forty-three who were laid off, seven said it had to do with petroleum problems. These included two shrimp boat operators, two service station employees, and a jet pilot. Five more were forced out of work because "materials were not available" for production. Others were victims of the indirect effects of the energy crisis. Typical of these was an employee of a truck repair shop who told the interviewer "the trucks aren't running any more" and a trailer salesman who blamed the rising cost of gasoline for his plummeting sales. The connection with the energy problem was not always clear or explicit: some people noted that business was bad and seemed to place the blame on the energy crisis. Economists working on input-output analyses chart these interactions or repercussive effects in dollar terms for the economy as a whole. Except for the investigation of residential energy conservation which is reported below, we did not undertake an exhaustive study of the ripple effects that flowed from households' adjustments to the energy crisis. Here are a few illustrations of the aftereffects of family adjustments, beginning with some typical excerpts from newspapers during the crisis period.

Vacationers Expected to Stay Close to Home
In Yellowstone National Park, rangers expect fewer people to stay longer. In San Diego, hotels are trying to entice tourists from Los Angeles, 100 miles away, instead of Chicago, 1,800 miles away ... On the eve of the nation's annual summer vacation ... the multi-billion dollar tourist industry is gearing for a change.

Lots of Football, Few Cars at Holiday Halftime
Traffic on New England's major highways was exceptionally light yesterday as the region passed the halfway mark in a holiday weekend long on televised football and short on gasoline.

Energy Crisis Inducing Return to City Stores and Attractions
The energy crisis may be slowing down the rest of the nation, but in many ways, it is pumping new life into the central city ... More people are pouring into the city, by train and by bus. And a lot of this traffic is in the off hours, which means people are coming into the city to shop and to play. Retail sales are up ... Real estate leaders are predicting a new boom in office rentals ... theaters are doing better.

Based on the data presented in this chapter, one can project with little difficulty some of the repercussions that followed—or might have followed if the families' behavior had lasted longer or been more widespread. For this purpose the repercussions can be conveniently identified under three headings: heating; consumption of electricity; and use of cars. We offer only a few examples of the myriad aftereffects that took place.

Conservation in heating led to more colds. If this had been more serious, presumably absentee rates at work would have risen and possibly demands on the health system would have increased. There was in fact some buying of clothes to compensate for lower temperatures, with benign results for the clothing industry. The same can be said about the increased buying of insulation and weatherstripping materials. In one of the notes written on the margin of the mail questionnaire, was this comment. "I heat the house with tree prunings and don't use any oil."

The reduced use of electricity had the effect of cutting down the demand for certain electrical appliances and/or boosting the demand for alternatives. A handwritten note from a respondent said: "Because of our extremely high electrical bills (over $110 monthly—sometimes over $150) ... (and we do not have electrical heating) we had our hot water heater removed and replaced by an oil heater. Our electrical bill is now at least 50% less." Another person wrote,

"Don't use the air conditioning we have. We use fans. Our bill dropped from $80 to $14."

The most visible and dramatic repercussions of adjustments by households took place as a result of the cutback in the use of cars. Purchases of large cars were reported down and the buying of small cars was up. One respondent wrote: "Stopped using car. Now using motorcycle. It's cheaper." Service stations that did tune-ups and other gas-saving maintenance presumably profited. The providers of public transportation and vendors of bicycles benefited, but only to a small extent. Much more affected—and adversely—were recreational establishments, restaurants, theaters, membership organizations, and others that saw their customers or participants coming less often or not at all for the duration of the gas shortage.

It takes little imagination to discern what follows. As the automobile industry, the restaurants, and the clothing manufacturers respond to changes in consumer behavior, their actions (e.g., stepped-up production or reduction in output) generate a new set of consequences, which redound to the benefit of certain families and the disadvantage of others.

From the perspective of the long-term energy problem and from the viewpoint of some civic leaders and conservationists, the most critical repercussion of the energy crisis of 1973-74 concerned the question: did the demand for energy in the household sector drop and if so how much?

Using the households involved in this study, we engaged in a systematic investigation to answer this question. Before proceeding, we must enter a serious caution. Focusing on what households did by way of conservation does not imply that household behavior was, could be, or should be the major point of concentration in a policy designed to save energy. First, it must be recognized that the household sector consumes only one-third of the energy used in the United States. Second, the energy requirements of a family's house and car and many appliances are, in the short run, fixed by their size and the type of construction and materials used. Hence, unless the family changes its dwelling or buys another car or shifts to another type of transportation, only limited savings in energy can be achieved using the family's present "stock" of energy-using facilities. Third, a conflict in policies continues to exist between a conservation ethic and the incessant, powerful attempts by advertisers to persuade, cajole, and pressure consumers into buying more and more energy-profligate devices.

Having registered an important caveat, we can turn to some questions of prime interest to policymakers in the energy field. One of these is: what kinds of energy consumption are most easily modified by the household sector? Column A in Table 6-5 shows the proportion of households in this study who reduced their consumption of energy for the major end-uses of families in the months after the oil embargo.

For whatever reasons, three-quarters or more of the families responded to the energy crisis by diminishing their consumption of energy for automobile travel and for electrical uses. Half did so for purposes of heating their homes and for heating water. But these findings per se lack any real meaning in terms of energy consumption and conservation. In order to judge the impact on energy savings, it is necessary to know what proportion of energy each of these end-uses consumes. From the perspective of conservation it would be ineffective to concentrate on end-uses that might be easily achieved but that have very little significance for energy-saving.

Column B in Table 6-5 gives the percentage of energy used by households for each of four major uses. The prevalence of energy conservation by families does not correspond uniformly to the amounts of energy used. It does in the instance of car usage. But space heating, which consumes almost as much energy as travel, was the end-use reduced by the smallest proportion of householders in a position to do so. By the same token, more families reduced their electricity consumption than their water heating, but the latter consumes double the amount of energy that is used for lighting and appliances.

Table 6-5. Percentage of Families in Sample Reducing Various Energy-Using Activities

	Col. A % of Families Cutting Down	Col. B[1] % of Energy Used in Typical Household
Car use	79	44[2]
Lighting, appliances	73	15
Water heating	52	8
Space heating	49	32

1. Source: Dorothy K. Newman and Dawn Day, *The American Energy Consumer: A Report to the Energy Policy Project of the Ford Foundation* (Cambridge, Mass.: Ballinger Publishing Company, 1975), p. 34.
2. Newman's figure for transportation includes travel by air, rail, and taxi in addition to cars. Other studies show transportation and space heating as approximately equal in terms of energy consumed.

ESTIMATES OF HOUSEHOLD CONSERVATION

In order to make maximum use of our data in dealing with this issue, we constructed estimates for each of the 1,440 households of the amount of energy consumed before the crisis and for the year after the oil embargo. The methodology for developing these estimates is summarized here.

For each household, five estimates or indices were calculated in millions of Btu's:

1. The Transportation Index—energy consumed in travel to work and in nonwork travel.
2. The Heating Index—energy used in space heating.
3. The In-House Index—energy used for lighting, cooking, hot water, and appliances, except for air-conditioning.
4. The Air-Conditioning Index.
5. The Family Energy Consumption Index—the total energy consumed by the family, i.e., the sum of the other four indices.

In order to arrive at these estimates, information on the number of persons in each household, the number of cars, the distance to the designated worker's place of employment, the kinds of appliances owned, the climate, and many features of the household was combined with energy-use data from the Newman-Day study and from standard engineering sources. These calculations produced precrisis approximations of the amount of fuel used in heating, the number of gallons of gasoline consumed, and the amount of electricity used. These were then converted into a common energy measure, the British Thermal Unit or Btu.[g]

Each household's responses to questions about their behavior in response to the crisis were used to estimate the change in energy consumption that had occurred. The difference between the precrisis and postcrisis estimates generated two figures. One permits an estimate for each family of the *absolute* amount of energy used (in Btu's) *before and after the crisis peak and therefore of the amount saved*, if any. The second figure is the *percentage* of precrisis energy saved; this facilitates comparison of *the extent to which different families cut down on energy consumption*.

---

[g]A British Thermal Unit (Btu) is the quantity of heat necessary to raise the temperature of one pound of water one degree Fahrenheit. The Btu's equivalents of common fuels are:

1 cubic foot of natural gas	1,032 Btu's
1 kilowatt hour of electricity	3,412 Btu's
1 Barrel of crude oil	5,800,000 Btu's
1 ton of coal	24-28,000,000 Btu's

A fictitious example will make this clearer. The Smith family consumed 150 million Btu's for heating annually *before* the winter of 1973-74. The Smith's answers in the interview indicated a drop to 125 million Btu's in response to the crisis. Consequently the Smiths effected absolute savings of 25 million Btu's and relative savings of 16 percent. If the Jones' household dropped from 70 million Btu's to 55, then their absolute savings (15 million Btu's) were less than the Smiths' (25), but the Jones household's relative savings of 21 percent exceeded the Smiths' 16 percent.

Table 6-6 presents the precrisis amount of energy used in typical households in each of the three metropolitan areas.

What appears in this study as a ripple effect of household adjustments in the energy crisis—namely energy conservation—is a matter of prime importance to those concerned with energy policies. The data in Table 6-7 have a direct bearing on household energy conservation. The table indicates how much energy was saved in each of the four components of home use in each of the three communities.

It is clear that across the board the greatest savings were achieved in transportation. Only in Hartford did conservation in heating energy approach the savings in travel. As might be expected, the savings in energy in uses other than heating and transportation were much less significant. To put this dramatically, all the Btu's saved in cooking, lighting, appliances, water heating, and air-conditioning in all three metropolitan areas were less than the energy that Hartford households saved in heating alone.

Regional differences are clearly the most important factor in connection with air-conditioning. Three-quarters of the Mobile households were equipped with air-conditioning compared with 54 percent in Hartford and 16 percent in Salem. Add to this the fact

Table 6-6. Precrisis Energy Consumption per Household (in millions of Btu's)

	Total	Hartford	Mobile	Salem
Transportation	161.4	171.5	143.4	167.8
Heating	112.7	160.2	43.9	112.3
In-House	74.8	79.5	65.3	80.0
Air-conditioning	15.2	3.8	39.1	0.7
Household Total*	365.3	416.5	294.0	359.9

*The Household Total does not precisely equal the sum of the four components, since households were not counted in a particular component if they did not report that usage, e.g., driving a car. Hence, the numbers on which the component averages are based are different from the number of households on which the total is based.

112 Families in the Energy Crisis

Table 6-7. Energy Savings per Household Resulting from Reported Changes in Behavior (in millions of Btu's)

	Total	*Hartford*	*Mobile*	*Salem*
Transportation	25.3	27.1	23.1	24.6
Heating	15.6	22.3	5.3	16.8
In-House uses	3.6	4.2	2.8	3.4
Air-conditioning	1.0	0.3	2.5	0.004
Household Total	45.7	54.3	33.7	45.5

that a central air-conditioning unit in Mobile uses five times as much energy as in Hartford and ten times as much as in Salem, and the differences in consumption are apparent. In fact, air-conditioning in a typical Mobile home costs the same as space heating, i.e., $96 and $94 respectively.

Relatively more households in Hartford (77 percent) reported reductions in air-conditioning than in Mobile (62 percent) or in Salem (54 percent). Moreover, Hartford households reported more of a reduction in use measured in degrees Fahrenheit than the other communities (Hartford, 2.4°; Mobile, 1.2°; and Salem, 1.1°). Nevertheless, as Table 6-7 demonstrates, the absolute savings in energy were much greater in Mobile than in the two other communities.

PROPORTION OF PRECRISIS ENERGY SAVED

In addition to knowing how much energy was saved in an absolute sense, it is also essential to understand how much was saved in relative terms, i.e., what *proportion of precrisis energy was saved* as an outcome of household adjustments. Table 6-8 shows this.

Overall, *the households in this study reduced their energy consumption by 12 percent in the year following the oil embargo.* The relative savings were practically the same in Hartford, Mobile, and Salem. Unlike the absolute savings, households in each area conserved almost as much in heating as they did in transportation. The in-house uses—cooking, lighting, use of appliances—were much less elastic; here the savings were only on the order of 4-8 percent compared with the 12-16 percent savings in heating and travel.

Before proceeding further it is important to pause and ask to what extent the reader can have confidence in the data on energy savings reported in the three preceding tables. A special study, described in Appendix C, was undertaken to determine how valid were the estimates based on respondents' replies to the questionnaire.

Table 6-8. Proportion of Energy Saved per Household 1972-73 to 1973-74 (in percent)

	Total	Hartford	Mobile	Salem
Transportation	15.5	14.6	16.3	16.3
Heating	13.3	13.8	12.0	14.8
In-House uses	4.7	5.1	4.3	4.2
Air-conditioning	6.9	7.7	6.2	5.4
Household Total	12.0	12.5	10.9	12.6

This was done by obtaining copies of households' bills for electricity, natural gas, and heating oil from a subsample of the 1,440 households. The subsample was stratified so as to insure an adequate number of families in each metropolitan area and in each income group. It was not feasible to conduct a validation study of the amount of gasoline saved by households, hence the Transportation Index was not verified.

The information obtained from the utility companies and fuel distributors was processed as follows:

1. For the twelve months before and the twelve months after November 1973, energy consumption (i.e., cubic feet of natural gas, kwh of electricity, or gallons of fuel oil) was converted into Btu's.

2. Where one type of fuel, e.g., fuel oil, was used for space heating and for no other purpose, a direct comparison was made between the amount that had been estimated from the respondents' self-reported data and the amount shown on the record of actual deliveries.

3. Where the same type of energy was used for heating and for other purposes, the number of Btu's was disaggregated in accordance with (a) the kinds of appliances actually owned by each household, using national averages for the amount of energy used by each type of appliance; (b) known differences in terms of metropolitan areas, e.g., the amount of air-conditioning used in Mobile as opposed to Hartford or Salem, and (c) differences in consumption according to household income, as estimated in other studies. The total energy consumption was then disaggregated into (a) the in-house uses such as cooking, lighting, and hot water heating, (b) air-conditioning, and (c) the remainder, space heating.

4. Finally, the number of Btu's for heating and for air-conditioning were further adjusted to eliminate changes in consumption due to year-to-year differences in temperature, thus leaving the changes that could be attributed to the respondent's actions. This was done by using actual Heating and Cooling Degree Days for 1973 and 1974 to produce an average year for each location.

114 Families in the Energy Crisis

These calculations produced actual and estimated amounts of energy used by each household, permitting us to answer the critical question whether the people who said they had saved energy did in fact save and whether those who said they did not, did not. Secondarily, the Validation Study asked how closely the actual savings corresponded to the estimates in Btu's and in percentages.

The results for heating are very reassuring, as Table 6-9 shows. The households' bills showed that on the average the families did indeed save energy. Moreover, the amounts saved—in both absolute and percentage terms—are comparable between the estimates and the actual amounts.

What is more, as the table indicates, the actual amount saved by the subsample of households in the Validation Study is very close to the amount estimated for the average of the 1,440 families in the total sample.

The results for In-House savings, shown in Table 6-10, were also rather close in terms of estimated and actual use, though not quite as close as the heating comparison. The results for air-conditioning, however, were dependent on somewhat more speculative assumptions and less information from households and did not produce usable comparisons.

The lion's share of the savings in heating energy was due to the resetting of thermostats. Despite the fact that very substantial conservation methods can be achieved through installing better insulation and storm windows, these methods accounted for a small part of the savings that were effected, as Table 6-11 demonstrates. Apparently the most expensive methods of heat-conservation were little utilized, though they can save much energy, and the most easily accomplished methods were used.

A study of residential heating conservation in suburban Boston areas offers a basis for comparison with the Hartford data in Table

Table 6-9. Actual and Estimated Savings in Heating 1972-73 and 1973-74 (in millions of Btu's; n=123)

	Precrisis Consumption	Postcrisis Consumption	Millions of Btu's Saved	Percent Saved
Estimated (based on self-reported data)	113.9	95.6	18.3	15.9
Actual (based on bills)	113.1	98.3	14.8	10.3
Correlations (Significant at ≤.001 level)	.65	.63		.30
Estimated for 1,440 households	112.7		15.6	13.3

Table 6-10. Actual and Estimated Savings in In-House Uses (in millions of Btu's; n=150)

	Precrisis Consumption	Postcrisis Consumption	Millions of Btu's Saved	Percent Saved
Estimated (based on self-reported data)	78.2	74.4	3.8	4.8
Actual (based on bills)	112.0	112.1	−0.1	0.0
Correlations	.30*	.26*		−0.4+
Estimated for 1,440 households	74.8	71.2	3.6	4.7

*Significant at ≤.001 level.
+Not significant.

6-8.[5] Donovan and Fischer reported that for the same time periods that we used there was a savings of 10.3 percent on the part of 8,000 households whose records they examined. This is lower than our finding of 13.8 percent in Hartford.

To sum up, the implications for energy conservation are evident. Reduced use of the car, slower highway speeds, and lowering of the temperatures in homes appear to be both feasible of accomplishment and significant in energy-saving. Comparatively less, though not an inconsiderable amount was saved by reductions in consumption of electricity, in cooking, heating water, and other uses within the home. Except for the anticipated differences between Mobile on the one hand and Hartford and Salem on the other in terms of heating practices and air-conditioning, there was little variation among the three areas.

To the extent that our estimates approach the realities of the residential sector's response to the energy crisis, an overall rate of

Table 6-11. Proportion of Heating Energy Saved by Various Methods by Households between Winters of 1972-73 and 1973-74 (in percent)

	% of Btu's Saved
Resetting thermostats	
During daytime	62.6
During nighttime	13.7
Closing off rooms	12.2
Adding weather stripping	7.2
Installing insulation	2.2
Installing storm doors and windows	2.2
Total	100.1

energy consumption of 12 percent—*before attrition set in*—is significant. Speculate for a moment on the likely results if the crisis had been more severe, more widespread, and longer-lasting. How much additional energy might have been saved by households? Could home-heating temperatures be significantly lower; would widescale insulating have cut consumption; would drastically diminished use of cars have been possible? A fuller discussion of the implications for policy in the light of the study as a whole appears in Chapter Nine.

The findings with respect to energy conservation can be interpreted directly in terms of the analytical model used in this study. The families' responses to the energy crisis rippled out through the economy and the society in countless channels and had repercussions on producers and providers of many goods and services and their employees.

The model for this inquiry reminds us, however, that the figures presented in this chapter are, after all, "averages." They obscure socioeconomic differences among families in terms of their resources, their responses, and the burdens and benefits that may have come their way as a result of the crisis and their adjustment to it. Not the least important of these are differences in income, race, and age, which must be taken into account in assessing the differential impacts of the energy crisis. The next chapter examines the experience of the 1973-74 energy crisis in this light.

❋ *Chapter Seven*

Different Families, Different Burdens

In the end, the effects of a crisis fall unevenly among families, but they do not fall randomly. Our model offers an explanation for this proposition.

Perhaps the most important function of the family as a social unit is to meet the needs of its members by performing the utilitarian and affective tasks that they require. To perform those tasks families draw on their material and nonmaterial resources. But the necessary resources are not evenly distributed. In advance of a crisis some families are better equipped than others and are therefore better able to withstand the impacts that lie ahead. Moreover, the features of a specific crisis may "single out" certain types of families that will be most affected, e.g., farm families, young families, poor families. In short, different burdens result when vital functions are not as well performed in some families as in others, either because certain families enter the situation with more meager resources or because their capacities are more seriously impaired by the particular change or both.

Although each family is unique in the particular stock of resources it commands, differences among them are not whimsically distributed. They are closely associated with such socioeconomic characteristics as age, race, income, occupation and employment status, and education. Certain of these are more important than others depending on the nature of the crisis. But in any changing situation the social and economic capacities that families share are closely correlated with the differential impacts they will experience.

The unique characteristics of the energy crisis of 1973-74 were such that they did not heavily involve most of the nonmaterial resources and capacities that the analytical model posits, that is, integration among family members; their competence to process information and make decisions; the support they get from relatives and friends; and their capacity to adapt to change. To a greater extent the energy crisis called into play the material resources that families possess and their abilities to handle relations with their environment.

This chapter addresses the question: How did the energy crisis affect the activities and task performance of different types of families and how did these changes affect their well-being? This raises the issue of equity, for it asks not simply *how* were the costs of the energy crisis experienced by families of differing socio-economic status, but *how fairly* were the burdens distributed, an issue that obviously involves values and judgments. It is not simple to confront questions of relative welfare and to compare satisfactions and hardships among families. Ultimately these are matters of personal, subjective judgment and are not easily accessible to scientific measurement by outsiders.

We take the view that *in most instances* families would not have chosen to make the adjustments that the energy crisis brought upon them and that it is reasonable to assume therefore that changed behavior was undesirable from the point of view of the families involved. We assume further that the greater the change, the greater the inconvenience or hardship. Thus, for example, we interpret a lowering of home heating temperature or a reduction in the use of the car as *per se* negative impacts on a family. True, the change might in time be welcomed as an improvement, perhaps in the health of the family. But in the following analysis, we shall assume that changed behavior—from going less often to the movies to losing one's job—represents undesired and undesirable effects on the families concerned.

The social and economic characteristics of families are interwoven and it will be seen that in this study income, age, race, and residence in Hartford, Mobile, or Salem are all related to each other. For the analysis presented in this chapter, we take income as the anchor characteristic of the families.

INCOME AS KEY FACTOR

Probably the most significant feature of a family's material resources is the flow of money that reaches it, because that is the primary means for acquiring many other resources, including the labor of

Different Families, Different Burdens 119

outsiders to perform some of the utilitarian and affective tasks for the family. In the energy field there is another and compelling reason to emphasize income. "The more money you have," write Newman and Day, "the more energy you use at home and in your automobile. This is regardless of any other condition—climate; how far you commute to work; the size of your house; your age; number of people in your household; and whether or not your house is protected from the weather by insulation, for instance."[1]

Our study population has been divided into four income groups as shown below in Table 7-1. While the study does not purport to be based on a national sample of households, the sample corresponds in general to the national income distribution, though somewhat skewed toward the upper end of the distribution.

It is important to note that Hartford has proportionately more higher income families and Mobile more low income families.[a] For example, one-third of Mobile's sample received less than $5,000 in income, in contrast to 7 percent in Hartford. Conversely over 40 percent of Hartford's families had incomes in excess of $15,000 and only 16 percent were in that category in Mobile. Salem's sample was rather evenly distributed among the income categories. It should be borne in mind, therefore, in interpreting some of the findings that region and income interact. For example, proportionately more low income families lived in Mobile's warm climate with high air-conditioning costs but lower heating costs compared with Hartford or Salem. But the two latter communities also have more middle and upper income families, presumably better able to pay for heating fuels.

Table 7-1. Income Distribution of Study Sample and All U.S. Households

Income Group	Households in Brandeis Sample 1973 No.	%	U.S. Population* 1972 %
Low (under $5,000)	256	17.8	24.9
Low Middle ($5,000 to $9,999)	327	22.7	26.6
Middle ($10,000 to $14,999)	419	29.1	23.0
Upper ($15,000 or more)	438	30.4	25.5
TOTAL	1,440	100.0	100.0

*Taken from "Number and Percent of Households by 1972 Household Income," *Consumer Income, Current Population Reports*, Bureau of the Census, Series P-60, No. 89, July 1973.

[a]Tables D-1 through D-5 in Appendix D present in detail the relationships among income, place of residence, work status, race, and age of household head.

The clustering of characteristics is apparent in the tables in Appendix D and in these comments on the sample as a whole. The low income group had several distinguishing features. The heads of half the families were retired. Half of them were sixty-five years old or older. One-third were single-person households. Three out of ten families were black, far more than in the other groups.

The low middle group was younger with more household heads employed and more two to four person households. The middle group families were slightly larger and almost nine out of ten household heads were working full time. The upper income category had proportionately more families with five or more members and more whites. Only 6 percent were elderly. Practically all their household heads were working full time.

It follows from the overlap among these characteristics that what will be said in this chapter about lower income families will apply to a higher than average proportion of black families and to households in which the head is over sixty-five, no longer employed, and often living alone. This should be borne in mind in reading the first part of this chapter, which discusses differences in adjustments and burdens based on income.[b] This section begins with a treatment of differences in the way in which mobility, that is, local travel, was affected, moves on to heating and other aspects of maintaining an adequate household, and ends by considering overall savings in energy as an indicator of the burdens borne by income classes.

The second part of the chapter examines evidence of other repercussions on families in their roles as consumers and as participants in the labor force. The differential impacts of both the gasoline shortage and the increases in prices are assessed in this section. Before setting forth our conclusions, the burdens of the energy crisis are described in relation to two particularly vulnerable groups, the elderly and the racial and ethnic minorities.

Beginning then with changes in family mobility, we consider first the matter of speed on the highways, and how income groups differed in their adjustments.[c] Respondents in the low income group reported that before the crisis of 1973-74 they were driving on the highways at an average of 58 mph. Each group said that, on the average, they drove faster than the next lower income group, with

---

[b]The phrase "lower income" will be used in this chapter to refer to the income groups under $10,000 and "higher income" will mean families with incomes above $10,000. When we refer specifically to one of the four income levels, we shall use the terms low, low middle, middle, and upper.

[c]Instead of presenting voluminous statistics in the text, we refer the reader to numbered items in Table D-6 in Appendix D.

the upper category of families driving at 63 mph (Item 1, Table D-6). In order to conform to the 55 mph speed limit, therefore, the higher the family income the greater the decrease in speed. The upper income families reported a drop in speed of 9 mph, compared with 6 mph for the low income drivers. This is reinforced in the study by the National Opinion Research Center, which found that the proportion of families driving more slowly rose from 40 percent for families under $5,000 income to 59 percent among families over $15,000 income.[2]

Our first set of observations illustrates the difficulty of determining who bore more of a burden. From a social point of view, lower speeds brought a drop in the rate of injuries and death on the highways. For some drivers, having to slow down was experienced as an inconvenience. One might say that the higher income families experienced more of a burden since they had the largest adjustment to make in order to comply with the new speed limit. But it could also be said that the lower income groups were still at a disadvantage since, even at the peak of the crisis, they were driving more slowly than the higher income motorists.

A clearer case of inconvenience or burden can be made in terms of having to curtail the use of one's car for a whole gamut of purposes. Actually there was little variation among income groups in the percentage of respondents who said they had reduced the use of their cars *in general* in order to save gasoline (Item 1, Table D-6). The variations among income groups within each of the metropolitan areas were somewhat larger, but were not consistently related to income. We must now ask whether the *effects* of cutbacks in car usage *for particular purposes* were associated with income differences and how they impinged on the performance of family responsibilities and the enjoyment of leisure activities.

EFFECTS ON VARIOUS FAMILY FUNCTIONS

In terms of two utilitarian tasks, the various income groups cut back about the same amount in their use of the car for shopping and for ferrying children (Item 2, Table D-6). The reductions were also much the same among socioeconomic groups when it came to the affective functions of providing recreation and spending time with family members. Except for vacations, there were no strong associations between family income and cutting back on these family activities— doing things with other members of the family, such as talking or playing cards; entertaining or visiting; watching television; attending sports, recreational, and cultural events; going to the movies; eating out; and taking part in social or professional meetings. There was a slight tendency for more lower income households to cut back on visiting, movies, and eating out. A stronger positive relationship between income and reduced use of the car was found by Matre in Texas.[d]

In our own survey data, very distinct variations were registered in connection with vacations, an activity that is closely correlated with income.[3] Almost twice as many higher income families said their plans for vacations were affected by the energy shortage compared with lower income families. Among those who acknowledged changes in vacation planning, the higher income groups shortened the time or distance to a much greater extent than the lower income groups. However, the outright cancellation of vacation travel plans fell much more heavily on the lower income groups—a loss of satisfaction that can be considered more serious than shortening a vacation.

Decreased mobility meant that some families *increased* the time they spent on affective functions. Here it was the higher income groups that reported a larger proportion of households devoting time to interaction among family members, to TV-watching, and to entertaining (Item 4, Table D-6).

The substitution of other modes of travel for the automobile was related to income differences, but here it is difficult without having much more data to assess who bore the greater burden. The higher the family income, the more families with cars turned to car pools and to bicycling (Item 5, Table D-6).[4] Walking, on the other hand, was increased by lower income families much more than by higher income families. These patterns were consistent across the three communities and were similar to the NORC findings.[5] Stearns reported that the energy shortage was related to decreased trip-making for middle income households and a significant modal shift for lower income households.[6]

A car is an important resource in American culture, but not every family has one. Those respondents in this study who did not have a car in the family fared poorly in the distribution of burdens stemming from the gasoline shortage.[7] Almost half (43 percent) of the carless households said they could not get around as much as

---

[d]In his survey of 621 respondents in Texas in 1974-75, Matre asked separately about driving related to work, to family responsibilities, and to pleasure. Using the same income categories as in the present study, he found that cutbacks in travel to work did not vary consistently with income, but that family driving and pleasure driving were reduced twice as often by upper income families than by low and low middle households. Professor Matre furnished us with data prior to publication; these are given in Item 3 in Table D-6.

they liked. Two-thirds of them attributed this primarily to getting fewer rides from friends, neighbors, and relatives and one-fifth to the increased cost of public transportation. Their shopping, recreation, visiting, religious activities, and medical care were all curtailed to some extent. While this informal support mechanism for the driverless was disrupted, the fall-off in assistance meant a modest savings in energy expenditures for their relatives and friends. The driverless households, it should be noted, are predominantly poor—nearly three-quarters of them have less than $5,000 income—and slightly more than half are one-person households.

There were other families who were especially vulnerable to the gasoline shortage, not by virtue of their income, though limited income undoubtedly made the adjustments more difficult, but because of health conditions. Connecticut's Energy Emergency Agency reported, for example, that it received many such appeals for gasoline. Among those who wrote were a sick and elderly man who had to drive twelve miles to the drug store; a mother of a leukemic child who needed to be taken regularly by car to a New York hospital; and a Vietnam amputee who had to travel weekly to Hartford for rehabilitation services.

What can be said by way of summary about impacts on families' mobility? There were some differences, but they seem not to have been striking in their extent or in their effects on family task performance.[8] Higher income families decreased their highway speeds more than lower income drivers. Lower income households had to call off vacations they had planned to a larger extent than more affluent families. Households without cars—predominantly poor ones—suffered deprivations because their relatives and friends gave them fewer rides. However, the impact on the performance of most affective and utilitarian functions for the family was not clearly related to family income.

DIFFERENCES IN HEATING HOMES

Keeping the house warm enough in the winter is one of the utilitarian tasks a family performs for its members.[e] Plainly one could consider a reduction from a family's precrisis temperature as evidence of discomfort and, if serious enough, hardship. It should be noted first that *precrisis* winter temperatures during the day and

---
[e]Note that nine out of ten households in every income group in Hartford, Mobile, and Salem controlled their own heat, except for the low income group in Mobile, where only 72 percent controlled their heat. Those who could not set their own thermostats were, of course, subject to the landlord's decisions and the study makes no separate analysis of these households.

124 Families in the Energy Crisis

evening when people were home and awake were 70-71° for all income groups (Item 6, Table D-6). Moreover, each group reported maintaining its heat before 1973 either at its "ideal temperature" or only one degree colder.

Among those able to control their heating, a larger proportion of higher income households lowered their temperatures than did the less well-off. The percentage cutting down on heat rose steadily from 35 percent in the low group to 61 percent in the upper group. The variation was 10 percent from low to upper in each community.

Much the same result was noted by NORC: "It is quite likely that, among homeowners, fuel conservation varied positively with income... among renters, the results are more ambiguous, with the possibility of a negative relationship between fuel conservation and income."[9]

But these reports do not really speak to the question of inconvenience or discomfort. In point of fact, the decreases in temperature were small and were quite similar among income groups. They ranged from an average of −1.1° for low income families to −1.9° for upper income households. There are two indications that whatever inconvenience there was in dropping the temperature a degree or two was experienced in rather even measure by the various income levels, *on the average*.[f] First, within each metropolitan area the drop in temperature did not vary more than 0.5° from one income group to another. Second, the differences between what each income group called its ideal and what it set as its temperature during the crisis winter were 1.5° or less and the differences were not related to income.

Speaking only in terms of averages, the personal costs of living in slightly cooler homes during the crisis winter were shared rather evenly among the different income groups. The same can be said about cutting down on the use of hot water. Very close to half of the families in each income bracket reported using less hot water.[g]

Electricity for lighting and cooking, sometimes for heating, and frequently for running labor-saving appliances can be as important as transportation and heating for fulfilling the needs of a household and its members. A high proportion of families of all types reported

---

[f]The changes reported above consisted of adjustments of thermostats. Heating fuel was conserved in other ways as well. More low income families shut the windows to save fuel and more higher income households closed off rooms, an option that was easier for them to exercise.

[g]Matre reported much less of a cutback in hot water heating in Texas, but the intergroup differences were also not striking; they ranged from 10 percent for low income families to 6 percent for upper income households.

cutting down on electricity in general (Item 7, Table D-6). The reductions varied inversely with income in Mobile and Salem, but in Hartford they were greatest among families in the $5,000 to $15,000 income range. The NORC surveys revealed little variation by income; Warren and Clifford reported somewhat more in Detroit.[10]

The same conclusions were reported by NORC and by Warren and Clifford as were reached in this study concerning reduced use of household appliances operated by electricity—there was no consistent pattern of change that can be related to the family's income.

The outcome with respect to air-conditioning was similar to heat reductions. The proportions of families who cut down on the use of airconditioners in Mobile, where this can be looked upon as a necessity in the summer, and in Hartford were much the same across income lines.[h] Too few cases are available to report on Salem. Again, the extent of discomfort apparently was not very different among income groups. In Mobile people permitted their homes to get warmer by 1-2° and in Hartford by 2-3°, but income made little difference.

Based on the data already presented, what can now be said about the burdens entailed in cutting down on the use of energy? The evidence is mixed. Reductions and resulting disadvantages in the use of heating fuels and electricity were on the average not noticeably different among income groups. The burdens stemming from curtailed mobility fell somewhat more heavily on the lower income households, including those without cars; the nature of the differences is reflected in two examples.

Among families whose plans for vacations were affected, more lower income households had to cancel their plans, in contrast to higher income families who more typically had to shorten their vacations. The second example concerns the shift to alternative modes of transportation. Here the higher income families characteristically shifted to car pools more than low income households, while the reverse was true of walking, to which poorer households resorted in larger numbers.

But we hasten to add two qualifications to these preliminary observations about the distribution of burdens. Thus far we have not dealt in a quantitative way with the extent to which different families reduced their consumption of energy and presumably therefore the satisfactions and welfare that rest on energy utilization.

---

[h]Matre also did not find much difference among income groups in their use of airconditioners, though he found a smaller proportion of families in Texas making this reduction in energy use. There the proportions rose from 33 percent among low income families to 45 percent among upper income families.

Most of the data from this and other investigations are couched in terms of the proportion of families in an income group who made a specific adjustment. But this does not get at the amount or the extent of the adjustments that different kinds of families made, a criticism that Olsen and Goodnight direct at the energy studies in general.[11] However, the Consumption Index, which was introduced and described at the end of Chapter Six, does permit one to compare differences among households in terms of both the absolute amount of energy involved and the percentage change from previous patterns.

The second reservation that must be expressed about the data presented thus far is that we have dealt only with averages for each of the income groups. And while there is considerable overlap between income and other socioeconomic characteristics, the data do not focus on groups that are particularly vulnerable to this kind of disruption. At the end of this chapter, therefore, we discuss more pointedly the families living in poverty, the elderly poor especially, and blacks and other minorities.

DIFFERENCES IN ENERGY CONSERVATION

Turning now to the data generated by the Energy Consumption Indices, we assume that a reduced level of energy consumption *ipso facto* constitutes a burden or cost to a family, ranging from a slight inconvenience to a major hardship, depending on the circumstances. On this assumption, how did the four income groups fare? Table 7-2 indicates the percentage by which energy use in 1972-73 was reduced in 1973-74.

Table 7-2 indicates that:

1. Families under $5,000 experienced the greatest reduction in energy use for transportation and heating. The inter-income differences were most pronounced in the use of cars, minor in terms of heating.

Table 7-2. Percentage Reduction in Energy Use per Household by Income Groups between 1972-73 and 1973-74 (in percent)

	All Incomes	Under $5,000	$5,000 to $9,999	$10,000 to $14,999	$15,000 or more
Transportation	15.5	21.0	13.9	14.5	14.4
Heating	13.3	14.9	11.1	13.2	14.3
In-House Uses	4.7	4.4	4.5	4.7	5.0
Air-Conditioning	6.9	6.2	7.0	6.6	7.2
Household Total	12.0	11.7	10.2	12.2	13.3

2. Above $5,000 the differences among income groups are not large, but the pattern is rather consistent: the higher a family's income, the more proportionately they reduced their use of energy.
3. For lighting, cooking, air-conditioning, and the use of labor-saving and comfort-producing appliances in the home, the income-related differences are not striking.

The meaning of these changes will be further considered in the summing up at the end of this chapter, but we pause here to take account of income differences as they relate to conservation policies, which were discussed at the end of the previous chapter. It is obvious that absolute savings in energy (in millions of Btu's) will be utterly different from the relative drop in energy use described in Table 7-2. This follows from the vastly disparate amounts of energy that are consumed in homes at different income levels. Our estimates of precrisis Household Total Energy Consumption are: 201.2 million Btu's annually for the average low income household; 302.5 for low middle income families; 370.0 for middle income families; and 498.3 million Btu's for those above $15,000. The absolute changes in energy use are presented in Table 7-3.

For those interested in pressing for effective household energy conservation, policies clearly should be directed at the higher income groups, where the greatest amounts of energy can be saved, as Table 7-3 indicates. On the average, families with incomes above $15,000 saved almost three times as much energy as those below $5,000. Quite apart from equity considerations, measures that would reduce energy use among higher income groups will bring the greatest yields.

This next part of this chapter looks at other effects that families experienced in their roles as consumers and as participants in the labor force.

The respondents were asked whether, because of the energy shortage, they had decided not to make major purchases. There were

Table 7-3. Absolute Reduction in Energy Use per Household by Income Groups between 1972-73 and 1973-74 (in millions of Btu's)

	All Incomes	Under $5,000	$5,000 to $9,999	$10,000 to $14,999	$15,000 or more
Transportation	25.3	10.9	17.3	25.8	40.3
Heating	15.6	10.4	10.9	15.2	22.5
In-House Uses	3.6	2.9	3.3	3.7	4.0
Air-Conditioning	1.0	0.6	1.1	1.2	1.0
Household Total	45.5	24.8	32.6	45.9	67.8

some differences among income groups. Decisions not to buy appliances figured much more prominently among lower income families, while cars were more frequently foregone as purchases by higher income families (Item 8, Table D-6). The differences in explanations are important to note. The lower the income of a family, the more likely they were to say either that they could not afford the purchase price or that the appliance would be too costly to operate. By contrast, the high cost of gasoline and its scarcity was, comparatively, a more important reason among higher income families. A slightly larger proportion of higher income families reported changing the kind of clothing they bought during the energy crisis than was the case with lower income households.

Turning now to employment, how were the income groups affected? It has already been reported that fifty-five workers in the households in this study were either laid off or quit because of the energy situation. We have compared the number of lost jobs to the total number of employed heads of households in each income category as a measure of the extent of unemployment. Expressed as percentages, the families under $5,000 income experienced a loss of 15 percent and the families above $15,000 a loss of 2 percent. The two intermediate income groups each had a job loss of 5 percent. Plainly by this measure, the low income families suffered the most from unemployment resulting from the energy crisis.

The employment loss was more severe for lower income families in still other respects. The number of months that the unemployed worker had been out of a job at the time of the interview was directly related to income level. It was 4.3 months for the low group, 3.6 months for the low middle group; and 2.6 months for each of the two highest income categories. At the time of the interview, the number of workers who had been rehired or who had found new jobs again favored the upper income families. Below family income of $10,000 only nine out of twenty-five workers were back on a job; above $10,000, sixteen out of thirty were.

We come now to other aspects of family life though, as it turned out, they did not figure importantly in the energy crisis. Only 5-6 percent of the families said their health had been affected and this was the same in all the income brackets. As for thoughts about having to move because of energy considerations, approximately the same proportion in each income group said this had been considered.

Respondents were asked whether "the energy shortage had any effect on the way things have been going for the household." Close to one-third at each income level replied that the shortage had had an effect on them (Item 9, Table D-6). Each householder was also asked whether, at the height of the energy shortage, he or she felt "that you had experienced more, the same or less inconvenience and hardship than other groups of people?" The vast majority replied that they had experienced the same degree of hardship as others (Item 9, Table D-6). There were some odd inconsistencies among the minority.

Compared with other income groups, a larger proportion of families in the $5,000 to $10,000 bracket said they had experienced *more* hardship than others—and a higher proportion said they had experienced *less* hardship than others! The differences were small, as they were in the following oddities: Proportionately more upper income families than low income families said they had been more put upon by the crisis. And more upper income families said that they had suffered less inconvenience than other groups, when compared with the lowest income level households.

Other energy studies found more notable and systematic differences in this regard. Lou Harris reported that in replying to a question whether people felt personally affected, the proportion who said either "a lot or a little" increased steadily from 35 percent in the low income group to 60 percent in the upper income group. Warren and Clifford calculated how many problems were reported and found that "overall, low income respondents (under $5,000) were more likely to report 0 or 1 problem due to the energy crisis, while the income group of $15,000-$24,999 was the most likely to report 4 or more affects of the energy crisis."[12] However, Stearns wrote that "respondents with less education and lower income levels perceived people like themselves suffering more from the energy crisis."[13]

How does one explain the seemingly contradictory tendency for *both the affluent and the poor* to feel that the energy crisis was more of a burden than it was for others in society? The answer apparently lies in the fact that both rich and poor experienced effects that they considered onerous but which were qualitatively different. The difference appears to be that the lower income families were more prone to be affected by the price of energy and the resulting squeeze on their budgets while, by contrast, the families with the most money were more concerned about being able to maintain the high level of energy consumption to which they were accustomed. This distinction is a matter of degree and emphasis; it is not absolute. Low income families were also affected by shortages—in some instances, grievously so. And lower middle and middle income families were vulnerable to the soaring energy prices. But at the two ends of the income spectrum, prices and shortages were, relatively speaking, the most serious problems.

THE AFFLUENT AND "ENERGY THIRST"

We want now to explore these two processes and outcomes—the "price vise" in which the lowest income families were caught and the "energy thirst" which apparently afflicted the most affluent households. The image of a vise grasping poorer families was chosen to convey a picture of families trapped between two rapidly closing metal jaws—the skyrocketing prices of energy and the climbing cost of food, clothing, housing, and all other goods and services. The phrase "energy thirst" was selected to apply to higher income families because, as energy supplies dwindled or threatened to, households with larger incomes and therefore with larger homes, cars, and energy requirements felt an unsatisfied "thirst" for energy to meet their needs.

Newman's point that energy consumption increases directly with income is reinforced by the data in Table 7-4, which shows ownership of various facilities and appliances by income. The exception is space heaters, which low income families must rely on to a far greater extent than the other groups.

From the point of view of the more moneyed households there is a perverse logic in the proposition, advanced earlier, that material resources differentially equip families to confront crises. As Table 7-4 makes very clear, the higher the income, the more appliances, and the greater the "need" for energy.

A number of factors operate to make the energy requirements of upper income households far greater than those of poor and moderate income families. One of these is the size of dwellings. Newman points out that the median number of rooms for the poor in her sample was 4.1 and for the well-off it was 7.0 rooms.[14] Families with limited incomes make fewer and shorter trips; they own fewer things that require energy for their operation.[15]

It is easier to absorb even a steep price increase for energy on an income of $25,000 than it is for a family living on $6,000. The

Table 7-4. Ownership of Energy-Using Facilities and Appliances In Sample Households (in percent)

	Low	Low-Middle	Middle	Upper
Number of cars	0.9	1.3	1.6	2.1
Percent in single family dwelling	84	80	89	94
Percent owning clothes washer	56	77	87	95
Electric dryer	23	43	60	77
Dishwasher	7	19	38	64
Space heater	55	28	22	22

former has much greater financial capacity and discretionary income; the latter is at the subsistence line, living with basic deprivations. Presumably it would also be easier for a household with three cars, a dishwasher, and a clothes washer and dryer to reduce its energy consumption than it would be for a family with one car and none of those appliances. But the need for energy on the part of the more affluent families, as Newman points out, is not so flexible or elastic. Their larger homes and cars demand a higher level of energy that, *at least in the short run* while they must depend on their existing stock of facilities, cannot be materially reduced except for some appliances and at a drastic cost in comfort, convenience, and—in the case of heating—maybe health. This is not to say that in the long run this dependence on large amounts of energy for higher income households cannot be reduced by replacing this stock with less energy-profligate facilities.

This line of analysis clarifies the burdens that higher income families felt in the energy crisis of 1973-74. The rigidity in their requirements for energy—which was played out this time only in the case of gasoline and pressure on their mobility—helps to explain why they felt so burdened and even more put upon than other groups. If one reexamines the data on mobility, it is clear that proportionately more higher income families in fact reduced certain activities and functions than did the lower income groups (Item 2, Table D-6).

THE POOR AND THE "PRICE VISE"

Lower income families were confronted not only by decreasing supplies of gasoline (and sometimes fuel oil), but were even more exposed to the double bind of rising prices for energy and for all other necessities. Energy costs account for a significant part of all family budgets—8-10 percent of median family income in Hartford, Mobile, and Salem, according to our estimates (see Table D-7). But these averages obscure important differences. Newman has calculated that energy costs in proportion to income are almost four times heavier for the poor than they are for the well-off.[i] This is despite the fact that energy consumption increases rapidly as income rises.

---

[i]Income-related differences in cost of energy and in energy consumption.

	Percent of average Income spent on energy	Millions of Btu's Consumed annually
Poor (average income $2,500)	15.2	207
Lower middle ($8,000)	7.2	295
Upper middle ($14,000)	5.9	403
Well off ($24,500)	4.1	478

Source: Newman and Day, *The American Energy Consumer*, p. 116.

This state of affairs takes on added importance when it is seen in conjunction with the phenomenal rise in energy prices that was well under way before the events of 1973-74.[16] Between May 1969 and May 1974, Newman reports, the price of electricity and gas rose by 40 percent; gasoline by 58 percent, and fuel oil by a "whopping 100 percent."[17] This during a period in which the overall Consumer Price Index increased by 34 percent and the price of food by 49 percent. The result was a drain on lower income families' resources. Rising food expenses had to compete with the precipitous upsurge in the cost of energy.

It could be anticipated in the light of these facts that continued increases in the prices of energy following the Arab oil embargo would have more serious effects on the families with the least financial resources. And so it was, judging by the primary reasons respondents gave for lowering their temperatures, cutting down on driving, or using less electricity. The burden of the rising prices for energy was much more keenly felt by the lower income families (Item 10, Table D-6). Moreover, more of them said that price was a more compelling motivation for conservation than shortages or a sense of civic duty.

All this was made palpable in an article on conditions in the Midwest that appeared early in 1975 in a dispatch from Milwaukee:

> Last weekend, when temperatures here dropped below zero, Christine Robinson was forced out of her small flat by the cold and spent the night with friends.
>
> Marshall Glass watched the thermometer inside his home drop to 40 degrees. His children, their breath frosting in the cold, spent two nights in a relatively warm hallway.
>
> An earlier freeze caused a bad leak in one of the pipes in Virginia Pirtle's house. The pipe is needed to feed water to the toilet, but she cannot afford to have it repaired ...
>
> The Robinson, Glass and Pirtle households are among hundreds here that have lost their heat at one time or another this winter when fuel bills went unpaid ... Mrs. Robinson receives welfare assistance, Mr. Glass is a recently laid-off wage earner and Mrs. Pirtle gets Social Security payments.[18]

Newman describes the general situation of the poor with respect to energy in these terms:

> In summary, the poor use much less energy than others and use it largely for necessities. They spend a larger proportion of their income on the energy they use, pay a higher price per unit, and cannot afford the

out-of-pocket costs of equipment for conserving it... The poor, therefore, are doubly disadvantaged, because they pay more than others for the little energy they must have, and haven't the resources to make the fuel they use go further and make them more comfortable... Unlike some conventional wisdom, poor people buy and use cars conservatively. Their gasoline usage is almost entirely work-related, and far below the usage of other households.[19]

This assessment was shared in a paper issued by the Department of Health, Education and Welfare.[20]

IMPACT ON THE ELDERLY

There are two groups in American society who are well represented among the poor: the elderly and the minority groups. It is important to assess the difficulties they encountered in the energy crisis. Evidence of the effects on the elderly can be found in a series of hearings before the Senate's Special Committee on Aging and in a report prepared for the Federal Energy Administration.

The report to FEA makes these points about the elderly:[21] In 1973 16 percent of the elderly lived below the poverty line, as defined by the federal government. The percentage of elderly living alone increases with age. Almost 80 percent of this group among the elderly had incomes of less than $3,000 in 1970. As people grow older they are faced with more frequent and longer illnesses and their ability to meet the cost of medical services is reduced by higher prices for all commodities and an increase in rent or home heating fuel costs can force many elderly people to do without needed medical supplies or services. For people over sixty-five energy expenditures increase dramatically from the lower middle income level to the upper middle income level, but *the elderly poor spend a much higher proportion of their total budget on energy than any other age-income group.*

Although the FEA report does not furnish quantitative data dealing with the impact of the energy crisis of 1973-74 on the elderly, it does depict the consequences of rising prices and shortages on their welfare. The hearings before the Senate committee include pages of testimony not only from national experts in the field of the aging and in energy, but local reports of the actual effects of the energy crisis. The testimony contained illustrations such as the following:

> The Idaho Community Action Program Directors Association reported that persons interviewed "are more concerned about the cost of energy

than with shortages ... An elderly couple in their 80's who received $113 a month Social Security subsisted a large part of the winter on potatoes and oatmeal for some time in order to pay their fuel oil bill."

A man in Lakewood, Florida, wrote: We have cut down on food to meet the electric bill but we cannot cut much more as food prices are also high.

Another older man wrote: Something is drastically wrong when the electric bill approaches the same total of a house payment bill. What is this State and our country coming to if situations like this cannot be controlled?

A woman commented: I am a widow depending on Social Security and I find the electric bill way out of bounds. I need to run the air-conditioning due to high blood pressure and slight heart irregularity, but the fuel adjustment limits this and it is so unfair. Due to this expense I am denied some of the essentials.

An elderly woman living on Supplementary Security Income has medical bills beyond what is covered by Medicare. Because of the high monthly cost of these bills, she is still attempting to pay her fuel oil bills from last winter. Now it is almost October, when heat will be needed again.[22]

The comments of these people illustrate the devastating effects that price increases have had on the lives of older poor people. A theme that ran through the hearings was caught in the phrase: Too often the elderly are left with the impossible choice—to heat or to eat.

THE BURDENS FOR BLACKS

"About the only certainty in the energy crisis situation," Vernon Jordan of the National Urban League predicted early in 1974, "is that black people will bear a disproportionate burden of the sacrifices and penalties." This would be so, he argued, because blacks are disproportionately poor, are concentrated in the most vulnerable sectors of the labor force, and would be hard hit by high gas prices. "White commuters still get to center-city offices on time, but factory jobs are generally in fringe locations that make black workers dependent on their automobiles."[2,3]

"Beyond the immediate economic impact," Jordan continued, "is the more insidious use of the energy shortage as the all-purpose alibi to justify further erosion of black rights. Although school busing uses up something like one-one-hundredth-thousandth of all gas used in the country, some Congressmen want to end school busing as an energy-saving measure!"

Much of Jordan's analysis and predictions would have applied to

Different Families, Different Burdens 135

Puerto Ricans, Chicanos, and other minority groups.[j] In the light of his statements, what does the available information show about the way minority families fared in the energy crisis?

In this study almost half of the black families had incomes of less than $5,000 (see Table D-5). There were fewer car-owners and homeowners among blacks (Item 1, Table D-8), and fewer black families could control their heat. It should be recalled here that there was a concentration of black respondents in Mobile and that the local conditions in that metropolitan area influenced some of the total responses from black families, especially with regard to heating.

Among car-owning families the loss of mobility was not substantially different among blacks and whites. Virtually the same percentage reported cutting down on driving in general; for specific purposes the differences were minor (Item 2, Table D-8). Blacks turned somewhat more to public transportation and less to car pools than whites. Nor were the discomforts entailed in heating and cooling changes distributed very differently along racial lines (Item 3, Table D-8). However, blacks did cut back on electricity measurably more than whites. Black householders were more skeptical about the reality of the energy shortage and more prone to blame the federal government for the situation and less likely to blame the oil and gas companies than were whites. When they were asked whether they felt more put upon than other groups in the energy crisis, the same proportion of blacks as whites said yes. However, *fewer blacks said they had experienced less inconvenience* or hardship than others (Item 4, Table D-8).

The real differences in burdens borne by black and white families followed a pattern similar to the one we have seen involving the poor and the nonpoor. The price squeeze was more burdensome for black households than for white, as reflected in their reasons for decreasing their use of energy (Item 5, Table D-8). The most dramatic difference was the loss of jobs due to the energy crisis. Eleven of the fifty-five displaced workers in the sample households were black, which means that their rate of unemployment was twice that of the white households. At the time of the interviews, only four of the eleven black workers were back at work in contrast to twenty-one of the forty-three white workers. The blacks who had been displaced were out of work 4.5 months and the whites 3.0 months. One of the thirteen Spanish-speaking families among the respondents reported the loss of a job.

---

[j]There were only thirteen families of Spanish-speaking surnames and background in this study, hence it was not practical to make a separate statistical analysis of their responses.

Overall, our data indicate that while there were no striking differences in the burdens that black and white families experienced in day-to-day living as a result of changes in transportation and heating, blacks were, as Jordan predicted, proportionately more disadvantaged both by the sharp increases in the cost of energy and in the extent of unemployment traceable to the energy crisis. The greater impact on black families is not by any means due entirely to the fact that so many of them are in the lower income groups, though this accounts for some of the difference.

"Black households," Newman and Day comment in their study, "are at the lower end of each income class and have less wealth in each one than white households. Therefore, they have less buying power than those with whom they are being compared."[24] Beyond income, however, are two important aspects of the status of black families and other minority group families in American society that have a direct bearing on energy matters. One is that blacks' more precarious position in the labor force makes them more susceptible to job and income loss when economic changes (resulting from energy shortages, in this case) lead to retrenchment of production and firings. Since blacks tend to have less seniority and to occupy the least skilled jobs, they are more vulnerable to such economic readjustments.

Another facet of the peculiar status of blacks and other minorities concerns housing. Proportionately more of these families live in substandard housing so they need more energy to heat their homes than many white families at the same income level. The price squeeze then affects them with double force, particularly since, as Newman and Day observe, blacks pay more per unit for electricity and natural gas than whites do.[25]

A study in Galveston, Texas, set out to ascertain "whether or not the predominantly disadvantaged minority groups in the study area (i.e., Blacks and Mexican Americans) were more affected by the fuel shortage than the dominant Anglo group." Galveston felt the energy crisis less than other parts of the country.[26] It had a similar experience to Mobile's.

Kuvlesky reached two main conclusions. First, "ethnic status most often produced only slight differences in perceived impacts." Only two family patterns showed a substantial relationship between ethnicity and perceived impact—traveling to a doctor and getting children to school on time. Second, although the differences in perceptions of impact were slight, they followed a clear and consistent pattern. Mexican-American youths always perceived impacts more often than the other two groups. Whites perceived impacts the least. There did not seem to be any definitive explanations of these differences.

If the study in Galveston found that ethnic status produced "only slight differences" in perceived impacts on life-styles, two researchers working in North Carolina went much further and concluded from their study that "there is little evidence that the shortage discriminated against members of socially disadvantaged groups in our samples."[27] Moreover, they did *not find* that members of groups with multiple disadvantages, e.g., elderly, poor, black persons, were disproportionately discriminated against by the shortage, nor that the impact on the disadvantaged "increases disproportionately as the shortage endures and worsens."

This conclusion by Schwartz and Schwartz-Barcott seems to conflict with much of the evidence presented in this chapter. But their discussion at the end comes back to what we call the "price vise" and the "energy thirst" as they impinged on the poor and the affluent respectively. The energy shortage, they suggest, may not have been a unitary phenomenon.

> It had a number of different dimensions that tended to strike a balance overall... Thus, rising prices might have discriminated against the poor more than the rich, while the government's allocation program may have reversed this discrimination... In trying to determine the impact of unavailability, one might be advised to distinguish among different types of unavailability (e.g., unavailability because of price, consumer perceptions of sufficiency, or empty storage tanks) and to look for different impacts from each of these.[28]

Before setting forth our own summary and conclusions based on the information in this chapter, a brief comment is in order on policy and action with respect to the equity issues discussed here. It is beyond the scope of this inquiry to describe fully, much less evaluate, actions taken or policies considered during the crisis period, but we do note the following as symptomatic of the responses to the inequities that took place.

As early as February 1974 a number of consumer and advocate organizations sponsored a national "Citizens Energy Conference" to focus public attention on the minorities and the poor in the energy crisis. By August of that year the first national program aimed at the special energy needs of low income households got underway under the Community Services Administration, formerly the Office of Economic Opportunity. The program was intended to "enable low-income individuals and families, including the elderly and the near-poor, to participate in energy conservation programs designed to lessen the impact of the high cost of energy and to reduce energy consumption." A major emphasis of the program was on assisting low income families to winterize their homes more effectively.[29] (One must wonder, in passing, which objective took precedence—protecting the poor from disastrous price increases and actual shortages or promoting energy conservation?) In connection with delinquent payments of utility bills and the "shut off" that often followed, CSA in some states began to pay the bills for the poor and the elderly. A number of federal agencies had moves under way to address the inequities in the energy situation and in January 1975 seven of them entered into a working agreement to concert their efforts.

SUMMARY

This chapter began with the assertion of several propositions: (1) families draw on their material and nonmaterial resources to perform essential tasks for their members; (2) material resources are not randomly distributed among families but are closely correlated with socioeconomic status, hence (3) the burdens of a general or social crisis will be distributed among families in accordance with the systematic ways in which resources are distributed. The main question to be addressed in this chapter was how were the burdens of the energy crisis shared among different types of families—and how fairly? Income, poverty and age, and race were the main characteristics explored in the analysis.

What has emerged has given heightened importance to material resources as the main key to understanding the distribution of burdens among families in the energy crisis. To put this more completely, *qualitatively and quantitatively different resources had the effect of setting differential constraints and opportunities within which families had to adjust to the energy crisis and had to absorb its costs and burdens.*

It will be useful to go back to the "beginning" of our analytical model to see more clearly what led to the results described in this chapter. Many families, regardless of socioeconomic status, were subjected late in 1973 and early in 1974 to three stressor events: (1) a shortage of gasoline, (2) a sudden spurt in prices for energy, on top of several years of rising costs for energy and for other goods and services; and (3) appeals to engage in voluntary conservation of energy. The opportunities and constraints in adjusting to these pressures on families were strongly shaped and colored by their material resources, and, by what is closely related to them, their socioeconomic status. The development of this line of interpretation can best be done by contrasting the situations of the higher income families with the lower income families.

Perhaps in order to emphasize a point the impression has been created that there was a sharp dichotomy between the "price vise" acting on the poor and an "energy thirst" affecting the more affluent. In fact, all income groups were subject to both of these processes and effects. For example, the *shortage* of gasoline was given as the prime reason for reducing car use by *40-42 percent of the families in each income bracket* in Hartford and by 50-52 percent of all income groups in Salem. By the same token, a very substantial proportion of *middle and high income families gave price* as their main reason for cutting down on all uses of energy!

Nevertheless, the opportunity and constraint structure surrounding the more affluent families made their adjustments different in several important ways from the responses of the poorer families. First, the upper income families were better able to absorb the price increases. Their financial resources gave them more of a cushion, as illustrated by adjustments in vacationing. Higher income families shortened their vacations in time and/or distance, but they did not have to eliminate them as was the case to a greater extent with low income families.

But while more money meant greater flexibility in responding to price pressures, the unique resource situation of the more affluent families brought its own inflexibilities and strains in relation to the shortage of gasoline and the admonitions to save energy. Their existing stock of transportation and housing resources demanded a higher input of energy than the low income households, and *in the short run* gave them limited maneuverability in the face of scarce gasoline and urgings to cut back. It will be recalled from the Energy Consumption Index data that the richer families did not in fact cut back as much as the poor as a percentage of their precrisis consumption!

It is quite possible, of course, that higher income families in making their adjustments stopped short of encroaching on their life-styles and accustomed standards of living. Even when gasoline was hard to come by, they did not report greater cutbacks in driving than the least affluent families. The fact that they lowered their highway speeds more than the lower income drivers resulted from the new speed limit and from the fact that they started out driving faster before the crisis.

From the point of view of conservation as a desirable policy, it is the better-off families who can make the largest contribution to energy savings. In terms of millions of Btu's saved, they did so in the 1973-75 period. *In the long run*, policies addressed to further reductions in energy consumption among higher income families will produce far greater results than trying to cut down on low and moderate income households. But such policies cannot shrink from setting limits on the size of cars of affluent families, the amount of unused space that can be heated in their homes, the kind of energy-saving improvements that will have to be made in their dwellings, the use of appliances for purely luxury purposes, and the like.

Low income and poor families are more hemmed in by constraints than they are liberated by opportunities in adjusting to stressor events. Their limited scope for adjustment is related to a web of factors that reflect their resources—small incomes, poor housing, insecure jobs.

The situation is especially clear with respect to jobs. Unemployment as a result of the energy crisis and all it entailed for families was a burden that fell harder on poor families and black families. Beyond this the need of many low income wage-earners to reach their jobs by car exposed them to harsh pressures from the gasoline shortage and the zooming prices for gas.

Mobility to jobs is linked to choice of housing. As Newman and Day point out, "the problem of needing a car for the journey to work could be solved partly if the working poor had a choice of housing; but their housing alternatives are severely limited."[30] Housing opportunities are even more restricted for low income black families and other minorities. Since the poor occupy substandard housing more often than middle class families, they must burn up more energy for the same amount of space at higher per unit prices.

The overarching explanation is that the lower a family's income, the closer it is living to the line of what is essential for survival—in the use of energy for space-heating, water-heating, cooking, lighting, and the like. And, as we saw with the older people who were eating less or foregoing health services, their need for a minimum amount of energy may require inroads into other necessities when energy prices skyrocket. When supplies are not available, the poor and the old can freeze in the absence of any public intervention.

As for responding to appeals to conserve energy, again the lower income households have less room for doing this even when they might want to.[31] In the Newman-Day study, it was found that

> half the poor and one-third of the lower middle households are dependent upon a landlord for repairs and any major energy conserving improve-

ments. Some poor households do without what is common in others. About 15 percent of the poor do not have central heating; almost 10 percent share a bathroom with another family or have no indoor toilet at all; 8 percent have no running water. Almost half of all poor households have no thermostat or valve to control room temperature...."[32]

In short, the lower income families are caught between an already minimal standard of living and the pressures from rising energy prices, shortages, and exhortations to save energy. The more the pressures increase, the greater the strains on the families. In policy terms, there does not appear to be much waste or "fat" to be eliminated from the energy consumption of the lowest income groups. On the contrary, policy initiatives will have to insure their health and welfare by compensatory devices to protect them from constantly increasing prices and from shortages as they develop.

To address the question how fairly were burdens distributed among families, let us take an example that brings the value issues to the surface—the cost of getting to work by car. Having studied the impact of inflation in gasoline prices, Morgan concluded that "rising gasoline prices will affect more families at the upper end of the income distribution because they are more likely to be headed by those who drive considerable distances to work."[33]

In our study, the proportion of workers who reached their jobs by car was between 84 percent and 93 percent for the three income groups above the $5,000 family income line, but 72 percent of those below that line also had to depend on cars to get to work. Again it was true that higher income families had, on the average, longer distances to travel than wage-earners in low income families.[k] But more than a third of the workers in the families below $5,000 still needed to travel by car more than five miles to their jobs.

The same increase in the price of gasoline will mean that proportionately more higher income families will have to pay more in dollars and cents than low income households. By our criterion, however, the families with lower incomes will feel the price increase, dollar for dollar, more keenly because it cuts into their budgets and their level of satisfactions more deeply than it does for families with larger incomes.[34] Perhaps that is what was reflected in Stearns' comment that "Better educated, older respondents analyzed the energy shortage in specific objective terms, such as likely changes in

---

[k]For instance, 61 percent of low income families have less than five miles to travel compared with 31-44 percent of the other income groups. Only 18 percent of the low group travels more than ten miles compared with 27-37 percent for the other income groups.

gasoline prices. By contrast, the lower income, less educated, and the blue collar respondent had a more subjective response: he reported feeling markedly affected by the energy crisis in diffuse personal terms."[3][5]

This investigation has shown that the distribution of the lighter discomforts of the energy crisis was not strongly related to family resources and socioeconomic status. In two critical respects—the loss of jobs and the rapid erosion of purchasing power—it was. For those families who lost jobs and those who could no longer afford adequate heating or lighting or necessary travel, the burden was heavy and it was carried disproportionately by families of lower socioeconomic status.

In Rhode Island, where many poor families suffered fuel cutoffs because of unpaid bills, the governor advanced $300,000 in state funds to keep oil tanks refilled, hoping the legislature would approve the expenditure later. The TVA reported rises in energy consumption one-third over the previous year and stated that many families were paying their bills late or paying only two-thirds of the amount.

As the consumption of energy for heating rose higher and higher, there were reports of increased income in the energy industry. The General Public Utilities Corporation, serving Pennsylvania and New Jersey, reported earnings gains of 67 percent. *The New York Times* noted a "new stampede" on the part of the energy industry to find new sources of oil and gas.

A NATIONAL EMERGENCY

By the end of January and the beginning of February the severe weather had led to emergency situations in the North and East. Thousands of additional schools were closed. The administration announced that 1.8 million people had been forced out of work, half of them in Ohio, where the governor led a fifteen-minute prayer meeting on the fuel crisis. The secretary of labor eliminated the one week waiting period for unemployment compensation benefits for workers who had been laid off in eighteen states.

Natural gas had simply run out in certain areas of the country. California imposed restrictions on its use, including a ban on all luxury consumption, to permit supplies to be diverted to the areas in need. Under the law, the price of natural gas sent across state lines was being controlled; intrastate gas was going at much higher prices. Governors were calling for "equitable" sharing of the burdens, but with different definitions of what would be equitable.

Congress produced the emergency energy bill requested by the president in time for his fireside chat on February 2. The measure allowed the president to shift natural gas to areas of shortage and suspended for six months federal price ceilings for gas purchased by interstate pipelines to replenish the reserves depleted by the severe weather. The president called the development of a national energy policy "one of our most urgent projects" and asked that sacrifices be "borne fairly among all our people." The next day, in the first use of the new bill, the FPC moved to increase the flow of gas from the Southwest to the Eastern regions of the country.

As some areas began to feel an easing of the natural gas situation, oil imports shot up by 50 percent in the first week of February over the previous winter. The American Petroleum Institute reported that the nation's inventories of home heating oil had fallen by 11 million barrels in one week, considerably more than the 6.5 million barrel figure that the industry's researchers gave as a maximum if supplies were to remain above the critical reserve level through the winter. The only comforting news came from the Environmental Protection Agency, which announced that overall fuel economy in 1977 model cars was 6 percent better than the previous year. The average of 18.6 miles per gallon was a 34 percent improvement over 1974.

The severe winter and the energy shortages called up a variety of responses. In New York City, the *Times* reported on February 2 that "the freeze has converted tension and hostility between tenant and landlord into open warfare." In some declining neighborhoods tenants banded into groups that collected the rent, purchased fuel, and provided maintenance. These groups were sometimes able to work out delayed payment arrangements with fuel companies for part of their bills. "It is possible," declared a *Times* report about one neighborhood, "merely by walking in this area ... to see which buildings are operated by tenant groups. They are usually the ones without broken windows and with heat."

In Columbus, where most of the city's public schools were closed for a month because of the gas shortage, the superintendent of schools observed what he felt to be "the greatest outpouring of community spirit since World War II." To compensate for the school closings, the city undertook a "schools without schools" program involving many segments of the community. Students attended one day of formal classes at one of the open schools and maintained contact with teachers during the rest of the week by mail and phone, meeting occasionally in homes, churches, banks, hotels, and restaurants. The three major commercial television stations turned over as much as six hours of programming time a day during which teachers offered condensed fifteen-minute lessons. Class schedules and lessons appeared daily in the newspaper. High school seniors participated in classes at local universities, and all grades participated in a variety of field trips.

Warmer weather returned as February wore on. People were streaming back to work as the power situation improved. By the end of the month the Commerce Department estimated that unemployment caused by the fuel shortage had dipped to 218,000. However, a Library of Congress study suggested that the winter of 1977 would cost American households an average of $139 more in heating costs than they had paid the previous year.

The West was facing a different kind of shortage. Going into its third year of drought, this region anticipated a critical lack of power produced by hydroelectric facilities, a prospect that Oregon had confronted early in 1973.

Meanwhile, the Carter administration was proceeding to formulate a comprehensive energy plan under the direction of the president's advisor on energy matters, James R. Schlesinger, the former secretary of defense. In advance of that plan, the president sent to the Congress a proposal to combine all or part of nine agencies into a Department of Energy, which would have nearly 20,000 employees and a budget of more than $10 billion.

At the same time, the White House announced that it was sending out letter-questionnaires to 450,000 Americans (300,000 selected at random) seeking input on energy policy. An unsolicited reply appeared in *The New York Times* of March 11 from Senior Editor John B. Oakes. Questioning whether it would be possible to make much use of the data from the questionnaires before the energy program was unveiled on April 20, Oakes felt that the opinion-soliciting had the ring of a "public relations stunt." He asked whether Carter intended to lead the people or to be led by them. "Determining the least common denominator of acceptability would hardly produce the kind of energy program the desperate situation calls for." Despite Oakes's misgivings, 28,000 responses had arrived at the White House energy office by the middle of April, where a spokesman commented that "there is a strong desire for conservation as a national policy." Next to conservation, deregulation was the most common suggestion. International aspects received comparatively little comment.

CARTER PROPOSES BROAD POLICIES

President Carter went on television to present the broad goals and strategies of his energy policies to the American people. Aware that the conservation measures he was proposing might harm him politically, he said, "I'm willing to give up some of my own personal popularity among the people of this nation to require them to face the brutal facts." On April 20, he presented to a joint session of the Congress a detailed legislative program, commenting that the time had come "to draw the line" on wasteful use of energy. In contrast with Nixon's ill-fated Project Independence (i.e., independence of foreign oil by 1980), Carter set these as the goals for 1985:

1. A reduction in the annual growth rate in energy consumption of more than 2 percent.
2. Reduction in gasoline consumption of 10 percent.
3. Cutting by more than half the imports of foreign oil.
4. Insulating 90 percent of American homes and all new buildings.
5. Increasing coal production.
6. Using solar energy in more than 2.5 million homes.

The specific measures that the president proposed were not as draconian as some had feared or as forceful as some had hoped. Perhaps the most controversial feature was to be a standby tax to take effect if national gasoline consumption exceeded desired goals. The tax would begin at 5 cents a gallon and could increase by 5 cent increments to a total tax of 50 cents per gallon in ten years if consumption targets were repeatedly missed. The plan also proposed a "gas-guzzler" tax on cars with poor gasoline mileage and corresponding rebates for buyers of energy-efficient cars. Standards for fuel efficiency would increase to 27.5 miles per gallon in 1985, by which time the maximum tax would be $2,488 and the maximum rebate would be $493.

The Carter plan sought to reduce energy waste in existing homes by offering a tax credit of 25 percent of the first $800 and 15 percent of the next $1,400 spent on home improvements that would save energy. The plan included increased funding for the existing weatherization program for low income households and a 10 percent tax credit for businesses undertaking conservation measures. Among the other features in the plan were major sections intended to reduce the nation's reliance on natural gas and oil while developing use of coal and alternative sources of power.

The Carter program immediately ran into a whirlpool of conflicting interests. Although the president had called for the "moral equivalent of war," *The New York Times* noted that "the nation faces what some regional officials are calling 'the economic equivalent of civil war.'" "In the Southeast," the *Times* stated on April 26, "state officials pledged everything short of secession from the Union to save oil and natural gas supplies for the region's growing industrial base." On television's "Meet the Press," the head of a major oil company said the Carter program would discourage the development of domestic crude oil. A spokesman for the coal industry felt that despite its intentions, the program would actually hinder the expansion of coal use. The representative of a privately owned electric utility suggested that hundreds of millions of dollars would be added to consumer bills.

Warm weather came to the East and the North with the spring months. The crisis of 1977's winter was over. But the American people's representatives sitting in Washington were being asked to adopt a program of energy conservation that began to touch the life-styles of many American families, to impinge directly on regional interests, and to affect the production levels and sales of key American industries, most particularly the auto industry and the many-sided energy industry itself.

This is where the situation stands as of this writing. Before we compare these developments with the 1973-74 crisis, we turn to a description of Crisis II as it emerged in the three metropolitan areas we have been studying.

THE SITUATION IN HARTFORD

The rather relaxed stance toward energy matters that characterized the Hartford area before Crisis II is suggested by the Hartford *Courier*'s account of conservation measures being undertaken "at the start of another heating season" by the town of Enfield: "although the crisis atmosphere of the 1974 energy crunch has long passed, the town government is still taking steps to cut down on energy consumption." Awareness of energy questions persisted, but the sense of urgency had receded. The Christmas lights shone more brightly in Hartford's Constitution Plaza than at any time since the Arabs' oil embargo.

As the cold weather settled in, energy consumption and prices mounted rapidly. By mid-December, electricity usage had reached an all-time high. Within a few weeks, home heating oil prices moved up from 46 cents a gallon to almost 50 cents. The governor suggested that the federal government restore price controls on home heating oil. An oil shortage, dismissed out of hand at the beginning of the winter, seemed imminent. Worries were voiced that industries in other parts of the country, forced to switch from natural gas to oil, would divert some of Connecticut's oil supply. At the end of January, the Federal Energy Agency allowed emergency oil imports, which it was hoped would avert the threatened shortage.

In fact, despite the severe winter, Connecticut escaped the large-scale disruptions of work and school that afflicted other states in the Northeast. The reasons lie, in part, in its overall energy situation.

Only a relatively small proportion of Connecticut's energy is derived from natural gas, and much of that limited amount goes to residential users. The state was therefore less vulnerable than other areas, though it experienced some curtailment of gas from its pipeline suppliers during the winter. Its comparatively secure position was further strengthened by the fact that its industrial consumers of natural gas are generally able to switch to alternative energy sources on short notice.

Moreover, Connecticut has considerable peaking and winter storage facilities, which in 1976 held large reserves of expensive synthetic forms of energy. Indeed, one of the unrealized fears was that Connecticut would be punished for its prudence in storing up reserves by suffering more drastic curtailment of its pipeline supplies. This would have forced the state to draw more heavily on its high-priced reserves. That this did not come to pass did not entirely soften Connecticut's antagonism toward states where reserves had not been built up and where industrial users on "interruptible service" had not developed their capability to switch to energy sources other than natural gas.

Another mitigating factor concerned electricity prices. The only major form of energy that did not participate in the general price rise was electricity. A series of actions by the Public Utilities Control Authority and the courts resulted ultimately in a rollback of electricity rates. One of the major issues involved in the battle over the rates was whether the utilities must pass along to their customers savings achieved by employing less expensive types of energy in the production of electricity. The reduction in electric rates thus reflected in part the lowering of production costs obtained by using nuclear energy. The rate rollback, termed "a judgement for consumers" by the governor, was one of the few heartening aspects of the energy picture for the average family.

State government in Connecticut was already engaged in a number of activities that flowed from the crisis of 1973-74. It was involved in ongoing weatherization and emergency payment programs for low income families; it had mounted an educational campaign to promote conservation in the state; it was giving increased attention to the energy that would be used by new and existing buildings. New legislation provided tax incentives to encourage the use of solar energy and to lower the legally permissible temperatures in public buildings from 68° to 65° in the winter and to raise the limit to 78° in the summer.

As the winter of 1977 worsened, the state government was concerned and watchful, though it did not undertake any major new administrative or legislative initiatives. Largely this reflected the reality that for most sectors of Connecticut's population there was no crisis situation.

Some energy officials commented that the area of action open to the state, in the absence of a clearly defined federal policy, was limited. For the most part, it was felt that the state was far better prepared to handle the energy problem of 1977 than it had been to cope with the more far-reaching difficulties of 1973-74. Nevertheless, the state's energy stance contrasted with the flurry of activity in Washington, and some energy officials voiced fears that the state was returning to a pre-1974 position.

The original Connecticut Energy Agency with about thirty-five employees had become the Department of Planning and Energy Policy with a staff of sixteen. When the state undertook a general administrative reorganization in 1977, it was decided to terminate the separate energy department, with a commissioner reporting directly to the governor, and to incorporate it in the Office of Policy and Management, with a further reduction of personnel. Whether this move reflected a lowering of energy as a priority or whether it would impair development of a vigorous policy was unclear.

On the local government level, the picture was similar to that of three years earlier, with emphasis being placed on in-house conservation and comparatively little action being taken to promote public conservation. There were, of course, exceptions. Some towns moved to give tax breaks to homeowners switching to solar energy. In West Hartford the three year old Energy Committee undertook a Home Energy Program comparing ten homes in terms of heating efficiency and publishing the results as a guide for home insulation.

The towns of Bloomfield and Wethersfield adopted provisions for the recycling of motor oil. A Bloomfield study showing that 27,000 gallons of motor oil had been sold locally in the previous year (not including service station sales) encouraged the state's Department of Planning and Energy Policy to propose laws requiring motor oil sellers and gas stations to arrange to receive used motor oil, which could then be recycled into home heating and industrial oil. In Wethersfield, the town developed a plan to use its recycled motor oil to heat town buildings.

For the most part, however, local government measures were restricted to improving insulation in town buildings and installing various energy saving devices. In some cases, these improvements produced major savings. The city of Hartford estimated that in the period since the Arab oil embargo, it had improved its fuel oil efficiency roughly 20 percent.

The need to improve insulation was driven home with particular force to local school boards, many of whom saw their heating budgets rapidly outstripped by the cold weather and rising prices. Some districts turned down thermostats to 65° and asked children to wear sweaters to school. Others invested, or considered investing, in capital improvements. In Tolland, a physics teacher removed three hundred 100-watt bulbs from the high school without adversely affecting lighting. Similar reductions in lighting were made throughout the district.

Despite the overstrained budgets, no steps were taken that had any considerable impact on school activities. In one situation reminiscent of 1974-75, Plainville closed its high school swimming pool to save on energy costs. However, it was found that the swimming team would only be able to use the local YMCA pool for practice between 7 and 9 a.m. Within two weeks, the school board reversed its decision and reopened the pool, despite the admonitions of its chairman, who declared that it was the school board's duty to set an example to the community.

When the weather turned warmer in February, it could be said that most people in the Hartford area had not undergone serious disruptions in their daily living or in their incomes. As the ice melted in choked harbors, tankers that had been unable to make deliveries restored supplies of oil and petroleum products. Nevertheless, as one official at the Department of Planning and Energy put it, "this winter we came closer to scraping the bottom of the petroleum barrel in New England than we ever have."

But the winter took its toll, especially among low-income families, for some of whom there was indeed a crisis in 1977. In some respects the hardest hit were the working poor, who were ineligible for the "one shot" fuel payments available to welfare families and who lacked government support as a bargaining factor in dealing with fuel companies. But for all segments of the low-income population, the situation was threatening and, at times, devastating.

Although the gas and electric companies agreed not to drop any customers during the severe weather, those dependent on oil and too poor to be given a credit account found great difficulty in obtaining deliveries. Unable to accumulate sufficient cash to pay for a minimum delivery, they were forced to rely on aid from outside sources which was not always readily available. Many landlords in poor neighborhoods, their rents exceeded by their fuel bills, lost their buildings to the winter cold.

In the second half of December, the Hartford Community Renewal Team in conjunction with various community leaders announced the formation of a "fuel bank" patterned after the city's food bank. Funded entirely by private donations, the fuel bank provided low income families up to 100 gallons of heating oil, usually on a one-time-only basis. Similar fuel banks were established in surrounding towns, and the state set up Operation Fuel as a statewide operation. Unlike the fuel banks in cities such as New Haven and Waterbury, which soon ran out of funds, the Hartford fuel bank survived the winter, receiving $62,000 in contributions that were used to aid more than 800 families. Local television personalities played a key role in supporting the fuel bank and bringing the misery of heatless families to the view of the public.

State relief agencies found themselves similarly overtaxed. The state's Emergency Energy Assistance Program, providing welfare families with one-time-only fuel aid, reported aiding 700 families in November and December compared with less than 300 families the previous year. In the middle of January, the governor announced the creation of a $250,000 fund for welfare families who had already received fuel aid, since the $1 million in federal funds for fuel and utility emergencies had shrunk to $400,000. Within seven days, one-fifth of the $250,000 appropriation was spent.

The end of winter left a residue of unpaid fuel bills. According to a bulletin published by the state's Low Income Planning Agency in June, 97,000 Connecticut customers faced imminent termination of utility services. It was hoped that the federal money allocated to provide up to $250 to families with unpaid heating bills would allow many low income customers to begin the next winter with a clean slate, but there was little long-range optimism. The weatherization program for low income homes, half of which have no insulation, was proceeding with renewed force over the summer of 1977, but could only be expected to save a fraction of the heating costs involved.

Officials at the Low Income Planning Agency were particularly concerned with provisions in the Carter energy proposals for the redistribution of funds from the proposed fuel taxes. The Carter proposals included a progressive rebate system, with the highest rebates going to those with the lowest incomes. However, as a bulletin published by the agency suggested, "For low-income people who have no money whatsoever to spare, it would be inadequate to provide a 'rebate' when there is no money to expend in the first place."

Overall, then, people in the Hartford area were not as seriously affected by Crisis II as were people in Ohio, Pennsylvania, and New Jersey. Most of them did not experience as sharp a shock as the gasoline shortage three years before. But the poor felt the closing of the "price vise" that was described in the previous chapter. For three years the cost of heating, driving their cars, and running their homes had risen along with other items in the cost of living. For low income families, the cold weather and the further price increases during the winter of 1977 simply drew the vise tighter.

THE CRISIS IN MOBILE

After an unusually cold autumn, temperatures in Alabama turned still more sharply downward in the middle of January. Large industrial users of natural gas in the Mobile area had their supply interrupted, but all were able to turn to alternative fuel sources. Other parts of the state faced curtailments to all but residential and small commercial users. The Alabama Gas Corporation announced that the cold weather had resulted in reduced allocations and that large industrial users would be allowed only enough gas for plant maintenance. The company urged conservation efforts, recommending daytime thermostat settings of 68°, 60° at night in residences, and 65° and 50° in commercial establishments.

With a significant percentage of homes heated by electricity, the Alabama Power Company had difficulty in meeting the increased demand and was forced to interrupt service briefly to industrial, commercial, and residential users. The company joined in the pleas for conservation and obtained permission to reopen for a short time a generating plant fired by coal that had been closed down because it violated air pollution standards.

As the temperature in Mobile plummeted to a record 12° and residents took a rare look at falling snow, the state went through a four day cold snap, burning natural gas at two and a half times its normal rate, critically taxing supplies and reserves. The Alabama Gas Corporation released figures showing that while in late September residential and small commercial customers had accounted for only 24 percent of consumption, during the four days of the cold snap, their usage made up 97 percent. In many parts of the state, this change forced shutdowns of industrial plants and schools.

At the end of January, the governor estimated that 25,000 people were out of work in Alabama because of the natural gas shortage. He urged conservation and ordered all state buildings, including elementary and secondary schools, to turn thermostats to 65° and to 55° in nonworking hours. As the situation deteriorated, he ordered all state offices and facilities not "necessary to the health and protection of the citizens" shut down for a day. The order was greeted with confusion in some areas of the state where the energy situation was under control. Officials expressed uncertainty as to whether they were included in the order. It should be noted that what little state apparatus had existed following Crisis I to cope with energy problems had been largely dismantled.

Although Mobile schools closed for one day because of gas shortages, the city remained largely immune to the problems which mounted in the rest of the state as another spell of cold weather hit. Schools in the northeast of the state closed and the president of the Alabama Gas Corporation declared that "if this weather continues for a week, we just couldn't stand it."

There was an ironic reversal of the trucking situation that had plagued the state during the 1973-74 crisis, when the truckers were on strike and Governor Wallace had turned to the National Guard. Three years later the same governor ordered weight limits increased for trucks bringing extra supplies of propane into Alabama and specifically allowed them to exceed the speed limits.

The Public Service Commission issued an order preventing any Alabama utility from cutting off service to delinquent accounts during the severe weather and announced that it had placed pipeline crews on standby in case of emergency.

With the beginning of February, the weather began to moderate. The governor announced that the one day closing of state facilities, which had generated considerable confusion, would not be repeated. But he continued the lowered thermostat settings in state buildings. As the weather grew warmer, the flurry of energy activity at the state level died down as quickly as it had begun.

One of the main reasons Mobile escaped the winter comparatively unscathed was the presence of recently discovered natural gas resources in its backyard. Since 1976, natural gas had been flowing from what appear to be extensive finds located only fifteen and sixty miles from the city of Mobile. Five of the major oil companies and at least four independents now have operations in the area. According to *Business Week* of March 22, 1976, the new drilling may transform Mobile into something of a boom town. Since 1973, almost $900 million has been invested in capital expansion, a figure approaching the amount invested in the preceding fifty years.

Although it is unclear how much of this new gas will be consumed in the Mobile area, the presence of an intrastate gas source has already provided the margin between shutoffs and uninterrupted service for many industrial users. Despite the new gas findings, local distributors were involved in legal battles over a proposal by an administrative law Judge that would divert increasing amounts of gas away from city distributors to pipelines servicing the northern part of the country. "It's like another civil war," declared one official. In the view of Mobile Gas Service Corporation, the plan would expose Mobile to the danger of shortages by allocating a fixed amount of gas with no provision for extremely cold winters such as 1976-77. Although some doubt was voiced that the plan would ever take effect, it raised the spectre of regional competition for energy sources and, as in Hartford, the attendant bitterness.

The Alabama Power Company found itself involved in battles of a different sort with the state Public Service Commission. Although its average annual bill for residential customers increased from $205.70 in 1973 to $315.26 in 1976, the company demanded further rate increases, citing the fact that it had lost its bond rating and was finding it difficult to obtain credit. In December and January, the company threatened to lay off 4,000 employees if it was not granted a rate increase. In the middle of January, it began to lay off employees at construction sites across the state. At this point the Public Service Commission granted a temporary emergency rate increase which was made permanent in late April as an increase of 14.9 percent. Several groups at the PSC hearings testified to the hardships the rate increases would bring to those on fixed incomes. And the governor, on more than one occasion, denounced the utility companies for charging excessively high rates. By the end of the winter, utility prices had become a highly politicized issue.

Faced with increasing difficulties in meeting demand, the Alabama Power Company shifted the emphasis of its marketing from off-peak load building to conservation. The company published a pamphlet with ten specifications for new homes, emphasizing the use of the electric heat pump and improved insulation, which, it stated, would save up to 50 percent in heating and cooling costs. The company undertook extensive advertising and met with builders and realtors to promote its new scheme. The company's figures indicated that through 1976, average residential use of electricity had increased annually—with the exception of 1974, when average consumption dropped, perhaps in response to the conservation pressures brought to bear by the energy crisis of that year.

Interestingly, from 1971 through 1975, average residential consumption of natural gas for Mobile Gas customers declined annually, with the exception of 1973. In 1976, partly because of an unusually cold autumn, average consumption reached its highest point since 1970, and company officials figured that the average residential gas bill for the year ending in April 1977 was $212.00, as compared with an average bill of $106.91 in 1973. Nevertheless, officials estimated that since the decline in average use began, residential customers had been turning down their thermostats by about 3°. In 1976, the total amount of gas sold to residential customers was below that of 1970, although the number of such customers had increased by almost 6,000.

With its immediate energy problems slight, the city of Mobile undertook few new major conservation measures. The city did hire an energy consultant to recommend means of saving money and considered switching from mercury to sodium street lights; it did impose stricter controls over the use of city cars. Little effort was made by the city or by civic groups to encourage conservation. No general attempt was made to deal with the problems of low income families, who, as elsewhere, were hardest hit by the rising prices and cold temperatures. The energy-related problems of the poor were far less dramatic in Mobile than in Hartford where winter is of greater length and severity, but they were real enough. The Mobile Area Community Action Committee reported that many low income families had had their electric service terminated and had been unable to pay for its resumption. The poor in outlying areas, who often heat with butane, propane, wood, or coal, often had difficulties in obtaining fuel.

Several hundred families came to the Community Action Committee for assistance with energy bills, and the organization spent $5,000 helping them with $25 per family on a one-time-only basis. Because of a shortage of funds, MACAC aided families only where this small amount, on occasion supplemented by the Department of Pensions and Securities or the Catholic Social Services, would make it possible for the family to pay its bills. If a family could not meet its outstanding bills even if it received this assistance, the MACAC's policy was not to provide the $25 grant. It is not clear what options were open to these families. During the summer of 1977, MACAC received $200,000 in federal funds to pay back energy bills for qualifying families, but the long-term outlook for the poor, many of whom live in housing impossible to insulate, remained gloomy.

In summary, the Mobile area was for the most part not seriously affected by Crisis II. Although other parts of the state experienced layoffs and school closings as a result of natural gas shortages, Mobile, buttressed by recent findings of natural gas in its immediate vicinity, was generally able to proceed with business and school as usual. The poor were squeezed hard by the unseasonable temperatures and mounting costs for heating. But all families were trying to cope with gas and electric bills that were much higher than they had been in 1973. No organized conservation campaign was under way, but, as one community leader put it, "the cost of energy has supplanted patriotic desire to conserve" as the main impetus for cutting down on energy consumption.

CRISIS II IN SALEM

In March 1976, Oregon was beginning to experience its worst drought of this century, a fact of compelling importance in an area in which water means energy. But the shortfall in rain and its consequences for the flow of cheap electricity from hydroelectric dams did not become the focus of public attention until months later. The dominant issue in the energy field, as the November election neared, was a statewide nuclear safeguards initiative which, after much heated discussion, went down to defeat. The debate over nuclear energy was revived as the need for alternatives to hydroelectric power became more pressing in the face of a deepening drought.

By the end of the fall, fears of an energy shortage were growing. Salem received only one-fifth its normal rainfall between October and January. The snowpack on the Cascade Range was only one-tenth of the normal amount, which had immediate, depressing effects on the skiing industry and serious implications for the area's water supply after the winter. The Bonneville Power Administration, source of most of the electricity used in the Salem area, warned industry that curtailments might become necessary if the drought continued.

However, the crisis was blunted in Salem for several reasons. The Willamette Valley, with its underground water reserves trapped in sand and gravel, turned out to be something of an oasis in a parched state. Moreover, the city of Salem enjoys high-priority rights for the use of water from the Santiam River. Because water from the Santiam that is not used in Salem flows on through the Willamette River and out to the sea, Salem citizens apparently did not feel compelled to conserve water or, for that matter, electricity.

Despite the mounting gravity of the situation, a random telephone survey by the Oregon *Statesman* indicated that Salem area residents were not actively concerned either by the cold in the East or by the drought in the West. Only one person contacted reported that he was conserving water and electricity. The prevailing feeling about energy, according to the paper, was "I just figure it'll be there when I need it."

This is not to say that the Salem area was unaffected, nor that there was no response to the national situation. Efforts were being made in Salem and across the state to conserve electricity. The governor had appealed to the people of Oregon in straightforward words: "The years of cheap and plentiful electric energy in Oregon are over. And they'll never be back."

The price of electricity from Portland General Electric stood 113 percent higher than in 1970. Salem Electric had raised its rates in 1971 for the first time in thirty years and had not raised them again; the company's lower rates were made possible by the fact that, unlike Portland General, it does not generate its own power, but is a member of a power pool including Oregon, Washington, and Idaho, controlled by the Bonneville Power Administration. However, it is expected that the BPA will raise its rates in the near future by as much as 60 percent!

The two suppliers of electricity to the Salem area reported a modest cutback in usage. Portland General Electric, which supplies the bulk of the energy to the area, reported a 7 percent drop in consumption from the previous year; Salem Electric found 8 percent. But the rate of conservation in Oregon and the Northwest generally was still considered well below the standards set by environmental groups such as the Sierra Club, Friends of the Earth, and the Oregon Environmental Council.

These groups deplored the massive consumption in the area. In January, they described the Northwest as the "energy black sheep" of the country, with 80 percent of its power hydroelectric, the lowest electrical rates in the country, and close to twice the normal consumption of electricity per capita. The groups warned that conservation should be at the heart of any changes in electric utility rate design.

Natural gas, a significant issue in Mobile, was not a subject of concern in Salem, where representatives of the Northwest Natural Gas Company reported having more gas than they could dispose of. The company acquired nearly 1,000 accounts since the beginning of 1977 in the Salem area and is searching for more. Early in the year, Northwest Natural Gas diverted supplies to Los Angeles so that that city, in turn, could allow other supplies to flow to the east.

Despite the relative abundance of natural gas and the threatening outlook for electricity, it is worth noting that new homes were not switching from the prevalent form of heating fuel. Salem Electric reported that of 318 new houses it had hooked up after January 1, 1977, 313 continued to depend on electric heating.

State government in Oregon has a longer history of active efforts to deal with issues in the energy field than most states. Before and after the national crisis of 1977, the state legislature passed sixteen measures concerned with energy. The Department of Energy helped to prepare the legislation and was also heavily engaged in conservation programs, including media advertising, traveling conservation exhibits, and promotion of energy-saving through educational programs in schools and colleges.

The laws enacted in Oregon during 1977 included several designed to encourage weatherization of homes by requiring private and public utility companies and oil dealers to offer weatherization information and services to their customers. One of the new acts, anticipating the Carter program, offers tax credits to homeowners for weatherization, as well as outright grants to elderly, low income households for this purpose.

In addition, the new laws provide cash grants to low income, older taxpayers to help meet heating costs; tax credits for persons installing solar, wind, or geothermal facilities; prohibition of certain energy-using devices; and the promulgation of standards for public buildings and homes in their use of lighting and the installing of individual electric meters in multiple dwellings. The legislature approved the use of funds for the development of non-nuclear sources of energy, a proposition that will have to be submitted to a voter referendum in the fall of 1977.

Other legislation provided that the Department of Veteran's Affairs, the largest single lending institution in the state, processing over 20 percent of annual home sales, require as a condition for loans that homes meet state weatherization standards. The department estimates that over half of the homes for which it arranges loans are in need of weatherization services.

In addition to these measures, representatives of the governor proposed, and the legislature approved, the creation of a state Domestic and Rural Power Authority which would buy its power directly from the BPA, hopefully with the status of a preferred customer. The move brought sharp opposition from private utility companies. The governor also backed a move to allow persons sixty-two or over with household incomes below $4,000, to qualify for utility relief up to $100 a year. Concerned to raise more funds for highway maintenance, the governor supported a proposal for a 2 cent increase in the gasoline tax. A 1 cent increase had been voted down, despite support from the trucking industry.

At the local level, the city of Salem took a number of actions, particularly in the area of mass transit. Aided by federal money, the Salem bus system began in October 1976 a three month experiment of free Saturday service. The program was an immediate success, attracting 4,600 riders on its first day, 3,000 more than usual. The response continued, and the Saturday policy was extended.

A few months later, the city began offering free commuter passes to the downtown area and immediately added 1,200 to its former total of 3,600 daily riders. The city estimated that 1,000 cars had been put out of use by its new program. The only limitation to the success of the program was the fact that bus service was confined to Salem city limits. However, Marion and Polk counties are attempting to form a mass transit district, which will extend bus service to outlying areas.

The city also reported a significant degree of in-house conservation, estimating savings in city buildings since the 1973-74 energy crisis at 1.2 million kilowatt hours per year. This has been achieved largely by placing a 68° limit on heating and by reducing lighting in hallways and walkways. However, because of the increased cost of electricity, the electric bill for the Civic Center (the largest city facility), which was $97,000 for the year beginning July 1972, was $200,000 for the comparable period in 1976. The city was also trying to reduce the use of vehicles by its employees.

Looking back over the winter of 1977, although the Salem area passed through the national crisis relatively unscathed, the drought in the Northwest may bring power shortages in the coming year that can eclipse those experienced in 1973. In that event, Oregon's efforts to prepare itself will be put to the test.

TESTIMONY FROM THE HOUSEHOLDS

Information on the 1977 crisis was obtained directly from a subsample of the households originally contacted in 1974, in addition to the foregoing description of what happened in Hartford, Mobile, and Salem. Respondents were asked how they had been affected by the 1976-77 events, what steps they had taken this time to conserve energy, and what opinions they had about national policy, including President Carter's proposals. On some of these points it was possible to compare their 1977 answers with what the same group of families had said three years earlier.[b]

The findings from these interviews are compared in the footnotes with valuable data from the Gallup, Harris, and ORC surveys. In some instances we used the same wording as the Gallup poll in order to make direct comparisons. Again, we find comfort in the fact that while our sample is small, at many points our findings are remarkably similar to those of the national surveys.[1] However, our sample is small, and some of the differences reported below may be attributed to sampling error.

Turning first to job loss, it should be noted that the three metropolitan areas we studied were not as hard hit by unemployment during the crisis as were cities in Ohio, Pennsylvania, and other states. Nationally, a 7 percent loss of jobs due to the fuel shortages was reported by Gallup in February 1977.

Three out of the 154 households we contacted—one in each metropolitan area—said that someone had been fired or had lost a job due to the energy situation in 1976-77. It is of interest that among these same 154 families, a loss of three jobs was also reported in 1973-74.

The high cost of energy was much more widespread as a problem. One-third of the families (37 percent) said the cost of gasoline and

---
[b]See Appendix A for a description of the sample.

heating was a serious problem for them.[c] Most people (42 percent) said it was "just an average problem" and only a few (18 percent) found prices to be no problem at all. As might be predicted from what was said in Chapter Seven about the poor and the "price vise," half of the low income families said that the cost problem was "serious." Two-thirds of the black families said this. Still, the cost of energy affected some families at all income levels as is evident from the fact that one-fourth of those above $15,000 acknowledged this to be a serious problem for them.

What did these families say about energy conservation in 1977? As a group, they said they kept their homes slightly cooler during that winter than they did during the first energy crisis, but the difference was negligible.[2] The households in Salem reported approximately a one degree drop and the families in Hartford went up almost half a degree. Low income families reported temperatures more than 1° lower in 1977 than in 1974.

Asked whether they cut back on the use of air-conditioning, 60 percent said they had done so in the summer of 1977. Among these same families, 80 percent reported cutting down on the use of air-conditioning in 1974. The Hartford families we interviewed evidenced more attrition in the three years than did those in Mobile, where three out of four households in 1977 said they were cutting down.

There is ample evidence of the erosion that took place in observance of the 1974 law setting a 55 mph speed limit on America's highways. For example, in 1974, the state police in Oregon cited 7,121 truck drivers for breaking the 55 mph limit. In 1975, the number of violations climbed back up to almost 12,000. In 1976, citations for both cars and trucks were up 16 percent over 1975. In view of the upward movement of highway speeds, the self-reported average of 55 mph in our 1977 interviews is clearly open to question as any highway traveler can testify.

Among car-owning families, six out of ten in 1977 reported cutting down on the use of their cars.[3] This was a 20 percent drop in the proportion of conserving households, since eight out of ten were reducing their driving three years ago. The greatest attrition occurred in Hartford, where only half the families said they were cutting back on their use of cars during Crisis II. Gasoline availability in Hartford has not been a problem since the first crisis and long lines at service stations are but an unpleasant memory.

Two features of the Carter energy package were designed to lower

---

[c]Generally, there was little variation among the three areas and the four income groups. Where the variation is worth noting, it is mentioned in the text.

gasoline consumption by increasing taxes on gas-guzzling cars and by raising taxes on each gallon of gas sold. The families were asked in the interviews whether they would buy a smaller car if the price of big cars was increased by the government.[4] Half of the households (53 percent) said they would buy smaller cars under these circumstances, and half (49 percent) said they would drive less if gasoline taxes went up by 10 cents a gallon.[5] Understandably, the upper income group showed less interest in cutting back car use because of increased financial costs.

While half of the households thought they would drive less or use smaller cars if the government raised the cost of car transportation, these features of the Carter proposal drew the greatest antagonism when the respondents were asked for their opinions. Three-fourths (75 percent) were opposed to increased taxes on gasoline and heating fuels.[6] Just over half (56 percent) objected to the proposal to place heavy taxes on gas-profligate cars.[7] The latter proposition drew more support from middle income households than from those below $15,000.

Significant numbers of households continued into 1977 their efforts to save electricity. Almost half (42 percent) said they used less electricity than in the preceding year; a like number (42 percent) indicated that they were using about the same amount. Only 10 percent said that they had stepped up their use of electricity.

There was, in fact, a higher rate of conservation of electricity reported in 1977 than these same families reported in the mail questionnaire conducted in 1975, when only 30 percent of the households said they were using less electricity than the year before. Going still farther back with the same families, the percentage of electricity-savers at the peak of the 1973-74 crisis was two-thirds (68 percent), higher than in either of these subsequent periods. In other words, electricity conservation started at a comparatively high level of two out of three households in Crisis I, dropped to three out of ten one year later, and rose to four out of ten during Crisis II.

With respect to energy conservation, it can be said by way of summary that substantial proportions of families made efforts in the 1977 crisis to save gasoline and electricity, though not at as high a level as in the first crisis. A very small drop in home temperatures was reported from the first crisis winter to the second, three years later. How vigorous an effort to save energy was made and how much was actually saved are hard to assess. But there did seem to be a fairly widespread commitment to make some attempt to reduce the use of energy in the home and in the use of the family car.

This inclination was reflected in the respondents' views on the broad question as to whether consumers have the right to use as much energy as they want to or can afford to. Two-thirds of the household respondents in this survey (66 percent) said that they did not agree that consumers have such an unlimited right to use energy.[8]

However, this support for the principle of conservation in the abstract was not translated into comparable support for President Carter's program.[d] Only one-third of the households in Hartford and Salem expressed agreement with the president's policies on energy, and one-fifth were in disagreement.[9]

It is worth remarking in this age of mass media that three months after the president went to great lengths on television and in the press to put his program before the public, one-fourth of the respondents said they were not informed about it, hadn't looked into it, or did not understand it. The remainder included 15 percent who chose not to comment, and 10 percent who were neutral or said they saw both good and bad in the proposals.

The lack of strong backing for the Carter program as a whole must be qualified by attitudes toward specific features of it. On this level the reactions were mixed. Two-thirds (68 percent) agreed that government should give tax refunds to people who install extra insulation or buy storm windows or solar heaters—a finding that seems consistent with the willingness of half (48 percent) of the respondents to make such energy-saving improvements if the government refunded 25 percent of the cost.[10]

But two strategies that Carter proposed for energy-saving evoked strong opposition from the respondents, as they did in the congressional debate. Three-quarters of the households surveyed did not agree that government should tax fuels and gasoline to discourage consumption and half did not want extra taxes on "gas-guzzlers."[11]

On two equity issues, however, there was more agreement with Carter's approach. Two-thirds of those questioned (66 percent) approved of the government's helping low income people to pay for rising heating bills. This may well be related to the very widespread difficulty that families had in meeting the costs of heating and gasoline, regardless of their income. Virtually all the black families favored such aid to low income households.

There was even stronger support for measures to be taken by the government with respect to inequities among regions of the country. Three-quarters (73 percent) thought the government should make

---

[d]So few persons in Mobile commented on the Carter proposal that their responses to this part of the interview have been excluded from the analysis, which is based on 102 responses from Hartford and Salem.

different parts of the country help one another with energy problems, for example, by taking natural gas or fuel oil from one state and using it in another state.

Opinion divided more evenly on an issue involving environmental considerations—that is, the risk of polluting the ocean and beaches as a result of off-shore drilling for oil and gas. Some 45 percent believed the government should allow the oil companies to drill offshore, regardless of the risk of pollution, and 40 percent said no to this.[12]

The uneven, somewhat contradictory picture of attitudes toward energy conservation and government policy suggested by the above data—a generalized commitment to save energy, but not at the cost of personal sacrifices in extra taxes—ought to be seen in juxtaposition with opinions about energy shortages. Half of the respondents (49 percent) still were not convinced that there was a real shortage during the winter of 1977.[13]

On the other hand, the extent of skepticism is less than it was in 1977 among this same group of families. Perhaps more significant is the fact that those who said that they believed there was a real shortage of energy increased from 32 percent in the first crisis to 42 percent in the most recent crisis. A review by Montgomery and Leonard-Barton concludes that, "these percentages represent a steady, sizable shift in public awareness since those days of stunned surprise in 1973, when only one-third of the people believed in the crisis."[14]

The most marked increase took place in Mobile, which was relatively untouched in the earlier period and more directly involved in the cold winter of 1977. A shift also took place among the black families, who were overwhelmingly skeptical about the 1973-74 shortage, but rather evenly divided on the question of the reality of the shortage in 1977.

THE 1977 CRISIS IN RETROSPECT

To interpret the events of 1977 in summary form, we return to concepts used in this book to describe crises, namely, the onset, the phase of initial responses, and the state of affairs after the stabilization of changes.

The interim between the end of the oil embargo in 1974 and the freezing temperatures in the fall of 1977 can be seen as both aftermath of Crisis I and prelude to Crisis II. Once the gasoline shortage was over, the energy problem rapidly receded as a national crisis, though a residue of activities and efforts to cope with energy problems remained. For example, a considerable number of families persisted in their attempts to save energy. This seemed more and more, however, to be related to the uninterrupted, upward march of prices for gasoline, fuel, and electricity.

At the federal level there was a real lull. True, some millions of dollars were given to the states and then to localities to pay heating bills for poor families on an emergency basis, and assistance was being given to low income householders to weatherize their homes. Except for the fact that the energy issue was injected into the presidential campaign, little was happening nationally "on the energy front."

State and local governments during the interim were taking some steps to conserve and to plan for the future. Measures were adopted to encourage industry and households to save energy by insulating buildings or by switching to solar heating. Again, largely in response to prices that were outrunning budgets, state and city officials were finding ways to lower energy consumption in their own operations.

But all this intercrisis activity was low key. In fact, there had been noticeable attrition in the adjustments that had been made in response to the first crisis. For example, it seems fair to conclude that fewer households and establishments were continuing their conservation efforts at the 1974 level. There was a relaxation of attention and action in government; in two of the states we studied, for instance, the state government's resources for energy planning had been sharply curtailed or dismantled.

This was the legacy of the first crisis and was the situation in which the nation found itself toward the end of 1977, when a hard winter and a natural gas shortage catapulted the country into a second and more far-reaching energy crisis. Clearly, in both quantitative and qualitative terms, far more people were adversely affected than in 1973-74, as the 1977 shortages hit them where they worked, where they lived, and where they went to school.

A brand new administration in Washington reacted quickly. There were wags who said in the press that in its first months in office every administration needs a "good" crisis to demonstrate its effectiveness, one that can be rather easily mastered. Immediate steps were taken by the Congress and the administration to ease the genuine hardships that parts of the country were experiencing. Other than emergency financial aid to low income families and a new round of thermostat-lowering and exhortation, there was not much that state and local governments could or did do.

A crisis atmosphere—real enough for millions of families—prevailed for a time. The denouement closely resembled what happened in 1974. The crisis period, only a few months in each case, came to a rather abrupt end and public anxiety lapsed back to its former level.

It must be pointed out that by a curious twist of fortune, each of the metropolitan areas in this study escaped the worst effects of Crisis II. Hartford was less dependent on natural gas than its neighbors in the Northeast. Natural gas had been discovered near Mobile not long before the second crisis. Because of the specific water situation in and around Salem, that area turned out to be an oasis in a parched region.

Perhaps the outstanding difference between the two periods lies in the initiative that the Carter administration mounted to press for national energy policies that would do more than react to an immediate crisis and would be addressed to the chronic problem of energy in this country. More modest, but also more feasible than Nixon's wild dream of energy independence by 1980, Carter put on the table a set of proposals that would make a beginning on reducing the country's reliance on petroleum and reduce its energy consumption in general. While they seemed modest proposals to some, they presaged changes in Americans' level of energy consumption and aspects of its life-style, especially where untrammeled use of cars was concerned. Some of the proposals won general acceptance; those that cut most deeply into patterns of living or into economic arrangements generated strong resistance.

The Carter proposals and the lively debate they generated were symptomatic of a more general change that had been under way since the 1973 oil embargo—energy was becoming politicized. In the maneuvering to hold on to resources or at least not to see them reduced, each region of the country was in political competition with other regions, each state with other states; industries were protecting their flanks, and consumers were beginning to exercise political muscle. Energy-related issues were reaching the ballot box, as in Oregon, where state loans to stimulate non-nuclear methods of producing energy will be submitted to a referendum in the fall of 1977. White and blue collar families, banding together in consumer organizations, are challenging rate increases by utilities.

The poor are not so well represented in the political arena in which energy issues are being fought out. One of the results of Crisis I was a federal program of emergency assistance to low income families who cannot meet fuel bills. But this is generally on a one-time-only basis, and it turns out, as it often does in income-related programs, that the working poor do not qualify for the same benefits as the lowest income families, even though they may be just as much in need.

Looking back one can say, without facetiousness, that we have now seen two crises come and go. In each instance, the responses to shock and to hardship have been immediate. But in both periods there was a reluctance to take more long-term measures, as in Salem, where despite the grim outlook for electricity, new homes are still being built with electric heating, rather than with natural gas, which in that area may be a more promising source of home heating in the long run.

Verbally and in abstract terms, the American people express their understanding that energy problems call for basic policies affecting production, distribution, and consumption of many goods and services. The Harris poll found at the peak of the 1977 crisis that 70 percent of those contacted wanted the president to "impose a tough energy conservation program on both consumers and industry."

But one wonders about the breadth and depth of this commitment when it comes to concrete measures. It seems clear, as President Carter said, that voluntary conservation falls short of what is needed. It remains to be seen whether he was also right when he said, as late as the end of July 1977, that the American public "is not paying attention" to the energy problem.

Chapter Nine

Energy Conservation and Public Policy

In the fall of 1973 it was the Arabs' oil embargo that precipitated this country's first acknowledged "energy crisis." In the winter of 1976-77 it was unusually cold weather and a natural gas shortage that brought about the second energy crisis. In both instances these were only the outcroppings of a far more deep-seated, long-standing problem of energy scarcity. That problem is under intense discussion as of this writing as the country debates the energy proposals presented by President Carter with this blunt statement:

> The diagnosis of the U.S. energy crisis is quite simple: demand for energy is increasing, while supplies of oil and natural gas are diminishing. Unless the U.S. makes a timely adjustment before world oil becomes very scarce and very expensive in the 1980's, the nation's economic security and the American way of life will be gravely endangered. The steps the U.S. must take now are small compared to the drastic measures that will be needed if the U.S. does nothing until it is too late.[1]

In several respects the nation's energy problem has worsened since the events of 1973. The United States is more dependent than ever on imported petroleum—more than 40 percent at this time. Consumption of energy continues to increase. Drought in the far western states threatens to reduce the amount of hydroelectric power that is generated.

In the light of this continuing crisis it is timely to ask what can be learned from the experience of 1973-74 and especially from the adjustments that American families have made. This chapter examines the implications of that experience for energy conservation policy in the United States.

It will be helpful first to consider some aspects of the situation which constitute important constraints on energy conservation policy. This is necessary because conservation measures which might be acceptable to families cannot be assumed to be feasible on that criterion alone. The actions and responses of families impinge directly and forcefully on other parts of the society and what happens in the residential energy sector has serious repercussions on other aspects of social policy and social concern.

We shall discuss three main constraints that must be taken into account in framing conservation policies: (1) economic productivity and the standard of living enjoyed by many American families; (2) the environment; and (3) equity. These are political constraints in the political sense that policy alternatives are supported or opposed by various groups in American society depending largely on how they perceive their interests to be affected. Two additional sources of constraint, though important, lie beyond the scope of this inquiry; they are the interests of the main regions of the country and the interests of particular industries, especially those concerned with automobile production and distribution.

The most important constraint is that imposed by the requirements of the national economy and by concerns about economic growth. This is so ubiquitous and so obvious that it is characteristically accepted with little examination. The constraint is a virtually ironclad enclosure beyond which conservation policy, and policy in many other areas as well, may not venture. It is, simply stated, that *energy conservation policies must be confined to those which are the least injurious to economic activity.*

ECONOMIC PRODUCTIVITY A MAJOR CONSTRAINT

Energy conservation measures must not jeopardize the level of productivity. On the contrary, they are to be taken primarily as a means of assuring that sufficient energy will be available for continued high levels of productivity. Measures which would reduce the level of production are typically considered "impractical," not "cost-effective." They are usually rejected out-of-hand, without further analysis which would take other costs (especially social costs) and benefits into consideration.

Perhaps for this reason, the tendency has been to urge or force conservation on households through lowering the consumption levels of *current usages*. Policy has not been directed at reducing the number or variety of usages or at retarding or prohibiting new and additional ways of consuming energy. Conservation in the residential sector thus gets defined in terms of how to get consumers to cut down on present usages—to drive more slowly, to heat their households at a lower temperature, to cut down on unnecessary lighting, and so on.

But at the same time, little attention is given to the bombardment of consumers with new products which increase their energy usage. The television sets, television game accessories, frost-free refrigerators, radar ovens, and hair driers keep arriving on the market, beckoning householders to step up their use of energy. The advertising inserts of Sunday newspapers testify weekly to the infinite imagination of human beings and its translation into new types of energy-consuming gadgets. It would seem much simpler and direct to regulate or curtail the production of energy-consuming appliances than to produce them to a surfeiting level and then turn around and admonish consumers to conserve electricity.

Several features of President Carter's proposed program were designed to reduce residential consumption of energy. This was the purpose of the tax on gasoline, the tax on gas-guzzling cars, and the improved insulation of homes. The first two of these have already been perceived as a curtailment of production and attacked as a threat to profits, jobs, and the general level of economic activity. The argument is advanced that these matters are better left to the operations of the "market."

The present study is confined largely to consumer conservation in existing energy usages and does not treat the supply side of energy-using items. It is, therefore, important to stress that the study thus neglects an important aspect of energy conservation and does not adequately examine the constraint on policy mentioned above— the tacit assumption that conservation measures must be confined to those which do not threaten industrial production.

Closely related to this concern for maintaining production is the dedication of millions of American families to a life-style and a level of comfort and convenience that would be altered by serious and effective conservation measures. The resistance to change on the part of many upper and middle income households—for instance, in their leisure travel and the number of cars and other vehicles they operate—forms an important constraint on policy alternatives, especially considering the political and economic influence that such families wield.

Another type of constraint on energy conservation policy—much less politically powerful, we believe—is that of environmental considerations. We include here health issues, such as air pollution from industrial processes and from cars. While these considerations impose constraints on energy policy, it is significant that they are substantially downgraded when industrial production is threatened. As a simple example, one response to dwindling supplies of petroleum and natural gas is a switch back to higher sulphur level coal, whose use had earlier been restricted for environmental reasons. The alternative of reducing energy use through curtailing production was hardly given serious consideration. Nevertheless, though relatively weak, the possibly deleterious impact of various energy conservation or energy substitution measures on the environment constitutes a modest limitation on energy conservation policy, and a somewhat greater limitation on energy production policy.

In addition to constraints related to the level of industrial production and environmental impact, there is a third, still less powerful constraint on energy conservation policy. This is the matter of equity, by which we mean the attempt to distribute costs and benefits of public policy in appropriately fair increments across various socioeconomic segments of the population. Precisely what constitutes "appropriately fair increments" is a matter of debate, but it is our view—to be elaborated later on—that current policies treat lower income groups inequitably. We believe that the relatively little attention given to equity as a constraint on conservation policy results from a deliberate, though usually unvoiced, stress upon the level of production and environment as being more hard-headed and "practical," as well as from the complexity of the equity question and its susceptibility to different interpretations.

Another important preliminary consideration in interpreting this study's findings for implications regarding energy conservation policy has to do with the dual nature of the energy shortage. There is, on the one hand, the long-range development of energy shortages, especially in oil and natural gas, and the increasing cost of producing these fuels from existing deposits in this country. This situation was documented long before the Arab oil embargo and it persists today as a growing, gnawing concern—perhaps not critical in the short run but truly catastrophic in the long run. Within the long-term developing shortage there occurred the dramatic, episodic crises of the oil embargo and the natural gas shortage.

The present study was directed at the more visible impacts of the two recent crises. But its findings are applicable to the long-term energy problem as well, for families continue to experience the less flamboyant but nevertheless discernible impacts of incremental changes in the energy situation. Examples are the rise in the price of natural gas, the gradual increase in fuel oil prices, and the across-the-board increase in petroleum prices by the OPEC countries. Quite obviously, energy policy must adapt continually to incremental events reflecting the basic background reality of modern industrialized countries: the gradual depletion of energy resources and the increasing costs (in money and energy itself) of extracting and producing equal amounts of energy in the future.

While the long-term shortage and the immediate crises can perhaps be analytically distinguished, they are hardly completely distinct, since the threat of the latter serves to add to the significance of the former and to give it greater gravity. One can but reflect with some chagrin that were it not for the already crucial natural gas shortage and the lurking threat of a future oil embargo, long-run energy-conserving policies would command even less attention and support than they do at present.

The three constraints and the dual nature of the shortage are related in ways which are both interesting and important. For example, the production of fewer automobiles or of automobiles which achieve more mileage per gallon would represent a comparatively long-run measure, a measure which, as noted above, is highly constrained by the tacit mandate for high levels of industrial production. The lowering of driving speed represents a short-run solution and one which is less directly threatening to production levels. Investment in home insulation represents a long-run measure, while turning the thermostat down represents a short-run step.

Another illustration of the interweaving of the considerations noted above has to do with changes in families' standard of living that might be necessitated by specific policies. If there were serious efforts to stem the avalanche of new energy-using devices that blanket the market, cries would likely be heard from two quarters—from those who hold economic growth to be a paramount value and from those who can afford to buy more and more gadgets and pay for the energy they require.

In the treatment of policy implications of our study, we assume an awareness of the above considerations, pointing out specific points of relevance only when it seems especially warranted.

Before turning to the policy implications of this study, we want to call attention to a comprehensive, theoretical treatment of energy conservation written by Olsen and Goodnight. One part of their work sketches nine social and psychological perspectives that are applicable to the problem of promoting behavioral change. The second part analyzes alternative strategies for implementing conservation programs and the third part explores potential long-term social implications of various policy decisions. The key concepts are summarized in the following quotation:

> 1. The problem of replacing private rational expediency with public responsible constraint can be approached at three levels: (a) cognitive, or altering individuals' perceptions, attitudes, or values pertaining to the relevant situation; (b) behavioral, or altering the incentives, social exchanges, or influences being exerted upon people; and (c) structural, or altering the organizational, community, or societal social context in which people act.
>
> 2. These three contrasting approaches to promoting collective responsibility require quite different action strategies: (a) the cognitive approach stresses information, education, and persuasion to change people's minds; (b) the behavioral approach stresses direct inducements and constraints to change people's actions; and (c) the structural approach stresses the exercise of social power to change the overall social environment.
>
> 3. Each approach poses a unique central problem for the implementation of social change: (a) with the cognitive approach, is there any assurance that when people change their minds they will necessarily also change their actions? (b) with the behavioral approach, is there any assurance that the inducements and constraints utilized will necessarily produce the desired results? (c) with the structural approach, is there any assurance that power will be employed for collective rather than personal ends?
>
> 4. Each approach also possesses a unique advantage, if employed successfully: (a) the cognitive approach maximizes individual voluntarism of action; (b) the behavioral approach maximizes the speed at which change can be implemented; and (c) the structural approach maximizes the extent and permanence of change.[2]

PUBLIC ACTIONS AS STRESSOR EVENTS

These are useful concepts and questions to keep in mind as we consider the policy implications of the data from the 1973-74 crisis. Much of this discussion is equally applicable to Crisis II, but our data on that crisis are not as extensive. Moreover, it is still too early to assess the aftermath of the 1977 crisis as clearly as we can identify outcomes of the first crisis. Therefore, the discussion of policy makes use of the 1974 data plus what we learned from the mail questionnaire in 1975 about post-crisis changes in the behavior and attitudes of the households in the study.

The pluralistic nature of American society is well illustrated in the complexities of relationship between levels of government and between industry and government recounted in Chapter Three. A large part of this activity had to do with the preliminary testing out of various courses of action. Throughout this book, we have discussed such testing activities on the part of households in terms of the cognitive processes stipulated in our analytical model. The model can be applied to social systems other than the family. Here is an example, in the case of government, of the typical backing and filling associated with a system's initial response to a relatively new situation.

Governmental responses to the shortage had direct impacts on households as well as indirect impacts through their effects on establishments. Several characteristics of this public response to the oil embargo have obvious implications for energy conservation policy, especially for the short-run policies but also for the long-run policies and activities of governmental units. We consider them briefly here.

An important aspect of public policy during the oil embargo was the fragmentation of authority at different governmental levels, exacerbated by the lack of clarity regarding the respective powers of different governmental units. How much prerogative did a governor have over the activities of the schools? What types of authority did local governments have to regulate energy use? Such questions applied not only to the control of actions of establishments and households by state and local governments, but even more sharply, to control over governmental activity itself at those levels. Much of the vacillation, many of the false starts, were attributable to the lack of clearly defined authority: in many cases, the necessary authority did not exist. The experience of the energy shortage provided the occasion for clarification of some of these prerogatives and for legislative action to define, redefine, or expand these prerogatives, especially at the state level.

In this sense, the confused testing of the feasibility and legality of different modes of adjustment in 1973-74 left the governmental structure somewhat better prepared to confront such a crisis. But the events of 1976-77 left little doubt that more needs to be done by way of clarifying existing prerogatives, enacting additional authority, and preparing contingency plans. Although it is unrealistic to expect a perfect dovetailing of contingency plans at different governmental levels and among units at the same levels, some of the major points of conflict and confusion can be reduced in advance.

A study of the course of the first crisis in Hartford, Mobile, and Salem indicates that there was little sense of priorities among energy conservation measures. As a result, much of the effort was mainly "symbolic," having perhaps the side effect of reminding the public of the importance of the energy crisis but having little effectiveness in terms of units of energy saved. The experience with admonitions to "turn off the lights" when not in use and the hurried passage of ordinances permitting a right turn on a red light in order to minimize engine idling time are examples of measures which must be considered highly marginal in bringing about energy savings of any real magnitude. In terms of our model, cognitive processes in public decision-making were notably deficient. There was little evidence of sorting out very effective conservation measures from marginally useful ones. Part of the reason was the concern for impairing industrial productivity and a shrinking from the long-term adjustments that effective conservation would require.

As a result of the oil embargo and the experience of the winter of 1976-77, better information as to energy consumption and potential savings in various usages is now widely available. Plans for energy conservation both in the long run and in anticipation of possible short-run crises should be worked out in terms of the conservation effectiveness of different measures in relation to the costs—in energy, money, good will, political clout—involved in putting them into operation.

A third characteristic of governmental action with respect to the energy shortage may be characterized as "confused signals." Perhaps the greatest source of confusion was that regarding the actual extent of the crisis. Different reports of the allegedly critical shortage of petroleum, refined gasoline, heating oil, natural gas, and the availability of different grades of coal kept succeeding one another in a confusing stream. Rumors circulated that the storage tanks of the oil companies were full, that ships were waiting to unload oil because so much was already in storage that there was no capacity to receive it. The federal government found that it was lacking crucial information regarding the state of affairs at any given time. Allotment policies underwent almost continuous change, due in large part no doubt to the need for correcting errors made previously on inadequate data and on hasty estimates. These confused signals at the macro level made it difficult for individual families and establishments to make adequate assessments and adjustments. In terms of our model, their cognitive processes were impaired by poor data.

How serious was the immediate crisis, and how grave was the long-run situation? There seemed to be better data about the long-run situation than about the nature of the situation at any particular time. Our interviews with oil, gasoline, and public power providers were characterized by complaints about the difficulty in adjusting to the situation because of the lack of clarity about the dimensions of the shortage, the regulatory policies in operation at any given time, and the anticipated changes in these policies.

A city official in one community put it bluntly. The big problem, he said, in responding to the energy crisis was not a lack of statutory authority but a lack of clear, up-to-date information from Washington. Since information was slow in coming and was inconclusive when it arrived, public officials and the citizenry they were supposed to keep informed were left with serious doubts as to the reality of the crisis. This state of affairs, he said, undermined efforts to plan ahead for genuine and sustained conservation.

The orchestration of a clear and consistent set of policies by federal, state, and local governments in more detail than we are able to enter into here, would help to reduce the confused signals which made concerted action difficult at all levels and in all sectors of the society, including the household level.

Early adjustments, in terms of our model, made in the public sector represented confusion, false starts, and overreaction. Given the situation just described, it was only to be expected that there would be overreaction in the confused grasping for effective conservation measures. Examples of such overreaction abound. The most notable, perhaps, was President Nixon's announcement of Project Independence, a $10 billion program which was to make the United States energy independent by 1980.

The setting of speed limits (prior to legislative authorization) at 50 mph by presidential admonition and the subsequent retreat to 55 mph, partially in response to the intimidating tactics of the truck drivers, is another example of overreaction. The truck driver strike arose from a squeeze situation which could readily have been anticipated and was indeed anticipated by a few observers, but was given little attention by the federal government until the strike became violent.

The truckers were caught between limitations on the amount of gasoline or diesel oil they could receive, the higher costs, the lower speed, and the restrictions on the prices they were able to charge for transport. The situation was known, but there was little time to give it due deliberation, and so the action was taken without adequate assessment of its repercussions. A similar example of hasty overreaction was the institution of year-round Daylight Savings Time without prior regard to the difficulty of picking up school children in

178 Families in the Energy Crisis

the morning darkness and without any systematic decisions or activity regarding the adjustment of school time schedules to avoid the difficulty.

On the basis of the crisis experience, one should be able to anticipate with some degree of confidence that better data, better coordination of different governmental levels and different social sectors, a clearer set of conservation priorities, and a better understanding of the side effects of various conservation measures would minimize the hasty overreaction which occurred.

EXECUTIVE LEADERSHIP DEFICIENT

A final aspect of the situation surrounding American households in the energy crisis of 1973-74 had to do with executive leadership, primarily at the federal level. Presidential leadership was crucial in two respects. First, the White House had strong prerogatives to propose legislative on energy. New legislation was obviously called for and the president's role in the proposing and negotiating process was critical. Second, beyond the limits of what could be legislated, there was the need to gain the support of various levels of government, various sectors of the economy, and people throughout the country. This support was needed for enactment of desired legislation, for mobilizing a willingness to undergo a reasonable amount of sacrifice for ends which seemed appropriate and just, and for voluntary action to "do one's share" in a great conservation effort.

In retrospect, the actions of Presidents Nixon and Ford left a large gap in the needed presidential leadership. The reasons for this are fairly clear. There was understandable uncertainty about the effects and the duration of the Arab oil embargo. There was a lack of adequate data as to the state of affairs at any given time. There was widespread doubt about the authenticity of the crisis, exacerbated by the declining confidence in the Nixon Administration's credibility. There was the novelty of the situation and the unanswered question as to how much support or opposition could be expected for various measures. There was the lack of clearly defined authority at different levels. Perhaps most important of all, there was the tug and haul of competing interest groups in their struggle to protect themselves against the sacrifices that might have to be made.

We see the main deficiencies during that period to be an initial overreaction followed by half-hearted leadership in developing public concern about energy. President Nixon, for example, proposed staggered working hours, special bus lanes, preferential parking for car pool vehicles, year-round Daylight Savings Time, and a 50 mph speed limit. As the months went on, there was little presidential follow-up on these matters.

One obvious reason was the lifting of the embargo in March 1974. In any case, interest in conservation soon diminished while the president and the Congress squared off with fundamentally different positions on how to increase energy supplies and distribute available energy. Roughly, the Republican presidents favored the market as a regulating mechanism, allowing prices to rise, thus discouraging excessive energy usage and at the same time making energy production more profitable as an incentive to expanding capital investment. The Democratic Congress was generally more favorable to regulation and to various measures which would in effect reduce the profits of energy producers and at the same time reduce the burden on consumers.

With the country divided on how to proceed, one could not expect the White House to work a miracle of consensus. Both President Nixon and President Ford had a legislative program, but neither could get it passed—until the compromise Energy Policy and Conservation Act of 1975. But the presidents could have gone to the people more often and more forcefully than they did to reinforce the need for long-range measures, though admittedly there were strong differences as to what these measures should be. One need only conjure up the Roosevelt style of "going to the people" to recognize the paucity and ineffectiveness of presidential leadership in the wake of the embargo. Nixon and Ford did not get the major issues of the debate before the American people nor did they push for a workable resolution of the different points of view.

In relation to our own data on the attrition of energy conservation measures such as driving speed, use of cars, and household heating temperature, it is impossible to assess what impact more forceful presidential leadership might have had in sustaining higher levels of conservation and in preparing the public for more effective measures on both the supply side and the consumer side of the energy equation. With the passing of the immediate crisis, and in the absence of such forceful leadership, it is noteworthy that household conservation activity remained as high as it did.

President Carter has taken more initiative and employed a more aggressive type of leadership than his predecessors in placing his energy program before the country. His move to centralize and consolidate energy policy and programs in a new Cabinet position is one evidence of this. At this writing it is still too early to determine what the outcome will be in terms of public support for Carter's legislation and in those millions of acts of energy conservation that must accompany the new program if it is to be effective.

POLICY IMPLICATIONS OF THE ENERGY SAVINGS EFFECTED DURING CRISIS I

It will be recalled that we employed four types of measures of energy savings: (1) the number and percentage of households engaging in a particular energy-conserving activity; (2) the intensity or duration of such activity; (3) the number of Btu's actually saved; and (4) the percentage of precrisis energy consumption that was conserved.

For each type of energy usage, how great comparatively were the savings effected? What proportion of the relevant households (who had the potential for effecting savings in that usage) actually reported conservation behavior? How intense was the conserving behavior? How much attrition occurred in this behavior through time? What are the implications of the fact that this increment of energy-conservation is used up and that additional increments may be more difficult to accomplish? Our findings supply the answer to all but the last of these questions and they provide a basis for policymakers to draw the inferential answer to the last question.

Quite obviously, *the overwhelming volume of energy savings was accomplished in the area of transportation*, primarily in the use of the car, *and in home heating*. What do the data show?

In transportation, an overall saving of 15.5 percent was effected; this amounted to 25.3 million Btu's per household per year. Some 82 percent of the families with cars cut down on their driving and reduced their highway speeds by an average of 7.9 mph to 53.5 mph.

Compared with home heating and other possibilities for conservation, our data show that transportation by car was the single greatest source of household energy conservation. What potential might there have been for greater savings in this usage? One part of the answer is that approximately one in five of the households with cars did not cut back on their driving. They represent a residue of potential additional savers who apparently were not sufficiently impressed either by higher prices, limited availability, or a sense of civic duty to reduce their driving. They thus represent an untapped reservoir for potential future savings.

Other implications for energy saving in use of cars arise from the experience with attrition in this mode of saving. Data from the 682 households responding to our mail questionnaire of September 1975, indicated little overall change in the situation since November 1974, a year after the crisis. Surprisingly, as of September 1975, more households had cut down on their driving than had increased it. Thus, our data indicate very little attrition in the overall use of the car; rather, a slight increase in these savings between the height of the energy shortage in 1974 and the fall of 1975.

The situation was somewhat different with the average highway speed at which people drove. The households reported an average increase in driving speed from the low point of 53.5 mph at the peak of the shortage to 55.1 mph a year later.

From our reported data, it would appear that substantial savings were achieved in the driving sector; that four out of five households drove less; that there was a substantial saving through lowered highway speeds, and that these lowered speeds suffered some attrition over time but still remained substantially lower than previously, as reported almost two years after the shortage.

The policy relevance is clear. Can the one-fifth of households who did not cut down on their driving be induced to do so? Can lower driving speeds be achieved; specifically, can the savings lost through gradual resumption of higher driving speeds be regained? On the negative side, there is an implication rather than a question: Since it is presumably easier to get drivers to cut down on the first few miles of average highway driving speed than on additional miles, it is apparent that some of the "cushion" of potential savings through this means has already been used up and is no longer available to effect *additional* savings. On the other hand, to the extent that there has been attrition in this mode of savings, there remains this smaller "cushion," representing savings effected at the peak of the shortage which presumably could be recaptured.

Home heating is the other overwhelmingly important avenue of household energy conservation. An annual average saving of 15.6 million Btu's per household was effected at the height of the energy shortage compared with the preceding year, a reduction of 13.3 percent in energy use for this high-consumption purpose.

What is particularly striking about this energy saving is that *it was effected by only half of the households* who controlled their heating and thus had potential for such saving. The other half of such households did not cut down their heat at all. Clearly, the households which could have lowered their home heating temperature but did not do so represent a still untapped potential for additional savings of considerable magnitude.

The experience with attrition among those who did cut down at the peak of the crisis is relevant for potential energy conservation in the future. Among the half of the households who lowered their home heating temperature at the peak of the shortage, for an average of 1.5°, the following winter's experience indicated an average rise of 0.8°, or an attrition of about half of the earlier fuel saving. Obviously, greater savings would have been accomplished if this attrition could have been contained.

Our September 1975 responses from 629 of the original 1,440

respondents give some indication of the percentage of households involved in the attrition. Of those who belonged to the half of the households who had lowered their heating temperature at the peak of the shortage, 45 percent reported restoring a higher temperature, 15 percent reported an even greater cutback to a lower temperature, and 40 percent reported no change since the peak of the shortage. Hence, 55 percent or over half of those who had initially cut back either maintained or exceeded the fuel savings they had effected at the height of the shortage. The attrition applied to only 45 percent of those who had initially cut down.

Clearly, the energy savings in the home heating area were substantial. But there is a large potential reservoir for further saving among those who did not cut down at all. Anything done to lower the rate of attrition over time would effect additional savings. But here, again, it is important to note that, to the extent that these conservation patterns are already in operation at any particular time, they represent a cushion of adjustment already used up. Succeeding increments of saving will be more difficult to achieve.

In the prime conservation areas of car transportation and household heating, a total of 40.9 million Btu's were saved per household. This figure is impressive—it represents 11.2 percent of the average household's 1972-73 energy consumption. How could larger savings be achieved? As indicated, they would come from inducing those households to conserve who have not yet done so; by inducing households to conserve more intensively; and by minimizing the attrition over time.

The Btu savings in lighting, cooking, air-conditioning, and other in-house uses were much less significant than in travel and heating. Here only an average of 4.5 million Btu's per household were saved, roughly one-tenth of what was achieved in transportation and heating. While additional savings might be achieved in these uses (especially in higher income homes), policymakers must ask how much effort should go into promoting conservation in this area compared to the payoff in energy saved in travel and heating reductions.[3]

An important question in attempting to encourage further savings is the question of who makes the decisions in the household regarding energy-saving behavior. It will be recalled that in the largest number of households, most energy-saving decisions are made jointly by husband and wife. Regardless of whether the decision applied to the car, the heating, air-conditioning, or appliances, approximately 40-50 percent of the decisions to conserve were husband-wife decisions.

Women's decisions were next in importance, accounting for roughly one-third of the family determinations to cut back on appliances, on heating, and on air-conditioning. Men and women made almost an equal number of decisions about cutting down on the driving.

Clearly, inducements to conserve should be addressed primarily to joint decision-making by wives and husbands, with women as the secondary target for reductions in heating and use of appliances.

PRICE, DUTY, SCARCITY AS MOTIVATORS

Beyond the question of who decides to conserve energy in a particular usage is the question of why the decision is made. Although our findings do not afford a definitive answer to this question, they do afford pertinent data, especially as to the reasons given by respondents for undertaking conserving behavior in various usages. Granted all the reservations surrounding self-reported data, especially where matters of motivation are concerned, it is nevertheless pertinent to know the reasons given by household informants for saving energy. Respondents who had conserved were asked the principal reason for the energy conservation and given an explicit choice of price, problems of availability, civic duty, or other.

The high cost of energy was the preponderant reason given both for reduced car usage and for lowering home heating temperatures, accounting for approximately two out of five families who conserved in each usage. The second most frequently given reason for reduced car usage was the shortage of gasoline, mentioned by 35 percent of the conservers. Availability of fuel was not an important reason for reduced temperatures in most cases, accounting for only 6 percent of the conservers. A "felt duty to save energy" was given as the most important reason by 24 percent of those who reduced their car usage, and by 38 percent of those who reduced their home heating temperature.

These responses shed some light on various policy options to achieve greater energy conservation among households, but they are not definitive. One of the most prominent policy options has been to increase prices in order to discourage usage. Those who favor this option have the support of much economic theory regarding price-related behavior. The fact that price was mentioned most often as the principal reason for both main types of conservation gives this viewpoint further support.

Additional evidence for price as a significant regulator of energy use comes, in a negative sense, from other studies.[4] The National

Opinion Research Center, as reported, found that renters who do not directly pay heating costs appear to save on energy less than those who do pay out-of-pocket heating costs. The Federal Energy Administration reported that early research indicates that "between 20 and 40 percent more electricity is used in buildings with master-metering than in those where tenants pay their own bills.[5]

There is ample counterevidence, however, on the effectiveness of price as a regulator of consumption. The steady upward march of gasoline prices since 1973 has not significantly reduced the amount of gasoline consumed. One of the most controversial features of the Carter energy package is the proposal to tax gasoline up to 5 cents a gallon annually to a maximum of 50 cents, for each year in which gasoline consumption exceeds stated targets. It remains to be seen whether the proposal will be adopted and, if adopted, what effect it will have on consumption levels.

While price represents a readily available policy option, availability is a little more complex. Although controls might be exercised directly on availability—through gasoline allocations to states, for example, as was done in early 1974—its application would be somewhat more difficult with heating fuels such as natural gas and electricity, though it would not be as difficult with petroleum products. Quite obviously, to the extent that fuel is not available, consumers cannot use it. One application of the availability dimension which does have direct policy relevance is that of rationing, but the relationship between our data on reported availability and the rationing option is too tenuous to warrant a firm conclusion.

There was of course a clear example of the use of legal prohibition as a means of attaining energy conservation—the federally enacted 55 mph speed limit. Granted that there has been both lack of enforcement and attrition in this area since the peak of the crisis, there have nevertheless been significant savings—in lives as well as in energy. Americans take slowly to imposing legal restrictions on themselves, but various forms of mandatory conservation may well have to be applied in the future to other aspects of household energy consumption.

The situation regarding civic duty is also somewhat complex, but permits further analysis. Even in the face of the difficulty in securing gasoline and in a situation of rising prices for both gasoline and heating fuels of various types, approximately one out of four households gave duty as their principal reason for conserving car usage and approximately three out of eight gave it as the principal reason for conserving on home heating. This would seem to indicate that appeals to duty might be a more effective strategy for conservation in certain energy usages than has generally been recognized.

Extreme caution should be exercised in drawing inferences from the "duty" data, however. First, there is the question of the validity of such self-reported data, especially when the answer chosen seems to place one's reported behavior in a favorable moral light. Second, even taking the answers at their face value, we do not know the extent to which the effectiveness of appeals to civic duty depends on simultaneous high prices and the threat or condition of shortages. Even in those numerous households that gave duty as their principal reason for conserving, we cannot be sure that they would have conserved at all had it not been for the contributory operation of the price and availability factors. In this connection it is significant that in the case of car usage, our data show all three factors operating strongly, along with a regulatory limitation on highway speeds. A much higher proportion of households saved on car usage than did on home heating, where only a sense of duty and price were widely operative.

We can use our data to answer this question, however; did the specific purpose for which energy was consumed account for differences in behavior among those who were duty-conscious compared with the price-conscious and those who saved energy primarily because of shortages? The data show that regardless of the purpose of a car trip (i.e., shopping, recreation, visiting, or chauffeuring children) the proportions who cut down and who did not cut down were much the same among those motivated by duty, price, or scarcity. Nor did those motivated by duty turn to walking as a substitute for the car any more or less than the other two groups.

A similar finding emerges from a comparison of the three kinds of motivation among those cutting down on space-heating and those cutting down on hot water. The households who lowered their temperatures out of a sense of civic responsibility behaved substantially the same as the other groups when it came to cutting down on hot water.

These findings suggest that a feeling of civic duty as the basis for conserving energy is not per se a more or less powerful motivating force than other reasons for conserving, if one can judge by the behavioral outcomes as reported.

One other aspect should be taken into consideration in regard to a sense of duty as the reason for conservation. This has to do with the widespread doubt that the energy shortage was authentic. As we have seen in previous chapters, our data indicated little difference in actual conserving behavior between those who thought the crisis "real" and those who thought it "phoney." Other studies report similar findings. Nevertheless, one would have to assume that a greater degree of belief in the authenticity and seriousness of the shortage could only have a supporting influence on the motivation to save out of a sense of civic duty.

This last conjecture receives some support from a study in which the researcher employed the term "eco-conscious" to describe a person who understands that the supply of energy resources is finite and that conserving energy is the social responsibility of every citizen. Hogan found that families where both husband and wife valued eco-consciousness were more likely to have adopted practices in the home to conserve energy than families where the level of commitment was lower or where the husbands and wives differed in their commitment.[6]

Would a clearer set of reported facts to the American people and stronger admonitions to conserve energy have increased the energy-saving behavior of these households? We cannot say for sure. But we hazard the guess that a federal administration with greater credibility than was the case in 1973, with a clearer explanation of the existing state of affairs regarding energy stocks and energy usage, with a stronger determination to do all that it could to confront the crisis, periodically reinforcing the admonition to save energy, could have achieved higher levels of conservation than were achieved during the shortage of 1973-74. It also might have lessened the subsequent attrition.

CONSERVATION "CUSHION" PARTLY USED UP

In concluding this section on the energy conservation implications of this study's findings, two interrelated observations appear to merit serious concern. The first is the circumstance that during the energy-shortage period of this study, the most readily available and presumably the most "painless" adjustments were made by those households which were the most easily induced to conserve energy, for whatever combination of reasons. One may speculate with some degree of credibility that it might have been possible, given a longer or more serious acute shortage period, to have induced these households to increase their energy savings and/or to have induced other households which did not save energy during the 1973-74 shortage to do so for the first time. But it would probably have been more difficult to do so.

Further, these increments of energy savings would probably occasion greater inconvenience, discomfort, or actual hardship. One might say, to use the vernacular, and to mix metaphors, that our reported savings from the 1973-74 shortage represent "skimming the cream off" the energy-saving potential of these households. To effect greater savings would require greater inducements in terms of the scarcity of energy, price, and a sense of civic duty, and would probably be more costly in disadvantageous effects experienced by the households.

There is however an important side to conservation that will be discussed in the following section, but which is critical to an understanding of where energy savings can come from. As Chapter Seven made clear, the higher the income a family has, the larger the amounts of energy it uses, and the greater its potential savings in energy. The data from this and other studies make it unmistakably clear that the amount of energy the lowest income groups can conserve is small indeed compared to higher income households. What we do not know—and what calls for further study—is how seriously did the reduced energy use affect the welfare of families, say, in the $20,000 and over category and how much more can they be called upon to alter their accustomed use of energy in the interest of the nation as a whole.

This brings us to our second point. To the extent that any of these savings persist, a "cushion" of possible energy conservation has already been used up and is not available for additional increments of savings. To this extent, the households are in a more precarious position, as is the national society, in that this series of minor, relatively painless adjustments is not available for further increases in savings.

In this connection, the comparatively short duration and limited intensity of the 1973-74 energy "crisis" should be realistically assessed as a relatively minor crisis in energy availability. Viewing in perspective the events recounted in Chapter Three, one notes a great deal of anxiety, a flurry of adjustive behavior, a good deal of confusion, and some personal inconvenience caused by difficulty in getting gasoline. But "the crisis" which received such attention in newspapers and on the television screen was experienced by most households as at most a small number of readily endurable inconveniences. The crisis of 1976-77, as we pointed out at the end of Chapter Three, was both more intensive and extensive in its impact on households.

Today the United States is in a more vulnerable position with respect to total energy supplies than it was in 1973. It is even more dependent than it was then on imported petroleum, with the possibility of another embargo still present. More fundamental, however, is the prediction, based on several studies, that the world's supply of fossil fuels is running out faster than was thought to be the case even a few years ago.

It is not yet clear whether the political process and the balance of interests in this country will produce a program of conservation and alternative energy production that can cope effectively and in time with the short- and long-term pressures of the energy situation. Whether the Carter proposals are adopted or weakened, it is more than likely that America's families in the course of the next decade will be making more basic adjustments to the energy situation than they did in 1973-74.

EQUITY

The above considerations lead directly to the question of equity, by which we mean an appropriate, equivalent sharing of the costs or benefits of a national condition, event or policy. The effects of the energy shortage were spread unevenly over households of different incomes, age groups, and ethnic groups as indicated in Chapter Seven. What do our findings suggest about energy policy in relation to equity?

The question of equity is complex and we shall discuss it under a number of headings, some related to conservation behavior and some related more to impact on the households involved and on their living patterns. The questions most relevant to energy conservation but with equity implications are: Which types of households use the most energy? Which effected the greatest energy savings in 1973-74? And which experienced the heaviest burdens as a result of the shortages and of the conservation, both voluntary and enforced, that took place? Our analysis will be principally in terms of income groups, though age and race will also receive attention.

It is clear from the present study as well as from other studies that there are tremendous differences in energy use according to income groups. In relation to average household consumption, the well-to-do use much more than their proportionate share of energy of all types, and the poor use much less than their share.[7] Thus, in times of shortage as well as in times of greater energy availability, the below average income families are in effect conservers, and by contrast, the above average families are the most profligate consumers.

This condition prevailed before the oil embargo, during the embargo, and after the embargo. It applied, as our figures show, in the number of cars owned, average driving speed, amount of car use, amount of energy expended for home heating and cooling, and in appliances. Any consideration of the equity implications of energy conservation policies must, to be valid, take full cognizance of this disparity.

In this connection, our data as well as data from other studies indicate that two groups are especially low in energy use—blacks and the aged. There is some indication that the low energy use for these two groups is not solely a result of their being disproportionately at the low-income end of the scale but that even holding income constant, these groups utilize less energy.[8]

It would seem, then, that in terms of energy conservation potential, the greatest avenue of savings would lie in the direction of reduced energy consumption among those who use it the most profusely—middle and upper income whites. Less saving, even proportionately, should be expected from those lower-income households which already are using less than their share of the nation's energy supplies.

The actual energy savings effected during and after the energy shortage reflect this skewed distribution of energy use. More well-to-do drivers, driving at a higher average highway speed to begin with, cut down their average speed by more than did lower-income, slower driving car owners. In terms of car usage, our data indicate a peak saving of 40 million Btu's for households above $15,000 per year income as opposed to 10.9 million Btu's for households below $5,000. This enormous difference exemplifies the possibly misleading aspects of the equity question.

One might react to this and other differences indicating higher energy saving on the part of the well-to-do with the conclusion that they have been the public-spirited citizens, willing to make more than their share of sacrifice for the common good, and that they have saved more than their share, while the poor have saved less than theirs.

But this gross difference must be evaluated in the light of the energy-use patterns of these two groups. Our data indicate that the number of cars per family increases as one goes up the income scale. Obviously, a decrease in highway speed involving a larger number of cars per family will result in a greater saving, even assuming that the total mileage is constant. But actually, the upper income families drive a much greater distance per year—well over twice the distance driven by the poorest group. (The figures are 20,000 miles vs. 8,000 miles per year.[8]) Further, as indicated in Chapter Seven, nearly three-fourths of the carless households are in the lowest income classification—below $5,000 per year. One can hardly expect gasoline savings from people who do not buy gasoline to begin with.

A similar relationship applies to household heating. Higher income families have more rooms per household and a comparable reduction in household temperature results in a far greater saving in these larger dwellings which are already using more fuel for this purpose. Thus, as we indicated in Chapter Seven, *the above-$15,000-income households saved on the average slightly more than twice the Btu's expended for home heating than did the under-$5,000 households.* But if one looks at the percentage of fuel saving over the previous year, the difference not only disappears but indicates a *slightly greater percentage of saving over previous fuel use in the lowest income group.* In the area of other in-house energy uses, such as appliances, much less energy is expended than for transportation and home heating. Here, likewise, the amount of Btu's saved rises as one goes up the income scale. The percentage saved in this usage is slightly greater for the upper income groups. But even with these savings, they still use more energy for this purpose than do the lower income groups.

We turn now to the differential effects of the energy shortage on household living patterns, as these are related to the question of equity. Here again, two questions are central. What kinds of inconvenience or hardship were experienced by different types of families? And how did the rise in prices for gasoline, fuel, and electricity affect different types of families? The two questions are closely intertwined, but we shall nevertheless try to discuss first the more or less direct impact of the energy shortage and of conservation measures on household life-styles and well-being, and second the impact of the sharp rise in energy prices on different types of households.

The situation with regard to inconvenience or hardship has none of the possible ambiguity that applies to the earlier questions of usage levels and savings effected, for our data show quite clearly a greater inconvenience or hardship borne by the poor. Possibly the greatest hardship was caused by layoffs and unemployment attributable to the energy shortage. As Chapter Seven indicates, these layoffs fell inordinately on the poor and low income families. Further, the amount of time a person was unemployed as of the date of the survey was significantly higher for the poor than for the more well-to-do. Again, while the more well-to-do tended to shorten their vacation trips, the poor tended to stay at home. Among the poor who had no automobiles, especially the aged poor, greater difficulty was found in getting around through rides from friends.

While the percentage of households turning down their heat was greater in the upper-income groups, there is an indication that among those who did so in the lowest income group, there was a perhaps small but highly important number for whom this represented genuine hardship—having to go without heat completely or with a temperature well below comfort levels or health requirements. This was due less to the unavailability of fuel than to the increased difficulty in maintaining heat as prices went up and the choice came to be, grossly, one of adequate heat or adequate food. This brings us to our second question as to the impacts of increased energy prices on families of different income and other characteristics.

To refer to increased energy prices as a "price vise" is perhaps to give the misleading impression of a relatively minor and temporary inconvenience. This may well have been the case for those families well above the $15,000 income level. But for many families, the drastic increase in fuel prices made critical inroads into their ability to maintain an adequate household. At the time of the energy shortage, the poverty level was at $5,038 for a household of four, and the budget for a barely adequate level of living was calculated to be $8,181.[10]

An increase in energy prices works with special disadvantage on the poor, since they spend nearly four times as great a percentage of their income on energy as the well-to-do. Although they were able to curtail some of their energy usage, they found themselves in a losing struggle with the price increases. Even with some reasonable amount of curtailment in energy usage, other parts of the household budget had to suffer. Again, the burden fell inordinately on households with heads who were sixty-five and over, who comprised almost half of the lowest income group in our survey, but less than one-tenth of the households with incomes of $15,000 and over. The other extremely vulnerable group is blacks, with whom almost the same proportions prevail. There is little surprise then, in the fact that our tables show that the lower the household income, the greater is the reporting of "price" as the principal consideration in energy conservation.

From this discussion of our findings, two implications for energy policy emerge with respect to conservation and equity. The first implication is that since the poor are so close to the minimum possible use of energy, there is little to be gained in squeezing out from them the last drops of energy savings, in contrast to the large potential for savings from the more well-to-do income levels, especially those of $15,000 and over. In those groups lie not only the greatest potential savings but also, we submit, a greater equity in the savings effected.

The second implication has to do with price as a means of promoting energy conservation. In the earlier part of this chapter we noted the potential strength of price as a reducer of energy demand. But if energy policy is to be equitable as well as effective, the attractiveness of allowing prices to rise "with the market" must be tempered by the awareness of the disproportionate burden that higher energy prices place on the poor. Unless this aspect is given sufficient consideration and the poor protected against further price increases, energy policy will continue to operate toward promoting, rather than reducing social inequality by asking the poor to pay more than their share of the human costs of the energy shortage.

❋ *Chapter Ten*

Focus on Families

Few national events have been studied in quite the manner set forth in this book. Most studies of such events or conditions concentrate on large economic and political systems and deal with macro-level data. Historically few studies have focused on the impact of these events on families and on the adjustments made by families to these events.[1] Hopefully such investigations in the future can, with increasing sophistication, study the effects on families of other types of national developments such as inflation, unemployment, disaster, as well as other environment-related shortages which are likely to occur in the years ahead.

We include in this emerging field of family-oriented studies the analysis of the effects of public policies on families. In the few short years since this study was planned, policy analysis from the perspective of the family has seen a surge of interest on the part of political leaders, administrators, and social scientists.[2] The concluding section of this chapter is devoted to this subject.

The systematic employment of an analytical model likewise marks the present study as a somewhat singular approach to the investigation of the interface between large-scale events and the family. This last chapter attempts first to assess the strengths and weaknesses of that model, which was developed with several purposes in mind.

Quite obviously we required for the present study a framework on which to base our analysis of the impact of the energy shortage on households. It was hoped that such a model would accommodate impacts both great and small, thus being applicable to situations hardly identifiable as "crises," but which nevertheless occasioned adjustive behavior on the part of households. At the same time, the model was to be applicable to different types of national events or conditions, not solely to the energy situation. Likewise, it was to facilitate comparisons of the impact of a given event on different types of families, distinguishable by income, ethnic background, size, and position in the life-cycle.

Further the model was to provide some sense of the sequence and continuity of the adjustive process and a method of characterizing different types of adjustments for analytical purposes. It was also to take cognizance of the family's "openness" as a social system, not only in receiving inputs from its environment but, as a result of its adjustive processes, providing outputs into the environment, thus in turn affecting other social units.

THE MODEL IN SUMMARY FORM

The family is viewed in the model as a social system with internal components and processes involving the family members and with significant relationships and transactions with the surrounding environment. Internally, the components are thought of as capacities and resources that are required for the performance of certain tasks. The family is dependent on its environment for a continual flow of certain resources (e.g., financial support) to replenish its capacities. Other capacities (e.g., the degree of integration among family members) are less dependent on sources outside the family and are to a greater degree based on the characteristics and resources of the family members themselves.

The family performs tasks both for its own members (e.g., providing emotional support) and for other systems (e.g., providing labor to employers). Some tasks are affective in nature, others are predominantly utilitarian. The performance of these tasks is dependent not only on a family's resources, but also on the demands that are made on the family by legal requirements, widely accepted norms, and the expectations of various groups to which a particular family belongs, such as its neighborhood or its ethnic or religious group.

The model directs attention to six elements that play important parts in the policy-family interaction. The six elements are: (1) The stressor event; (2) initial impacts on capacities and task performance; (3) cognitive processes, (4) adjustment, (5) the impact of successive adjustments on the family and on other systems, and (6) residual effects in terms of crisis readiness/proneness. These were presented in detail in Chapter Two.

Obviously, the lessons drawn from the application of the model to the energy situation must be limited by the fact that the energy shortage presented only one specialized type of mass impact. As indicated in our discussion of stressor events, the model includes several dimensions of such events. On these dimensions, the energy shortage forms a particular configuration.

As described in Chapters Two and Three, the Arab oil embargo can be characterized as a stressor event whose source was external to the family; moderately related to the family cycle; with extensive but highly diffuse long-run warning of eventual shortage, but little clear short-run warning of the oil embargo and its effects on the family. The "crisis" had a moderate impact, though affecting different families with different intensities and though moderate, almost exclusively harmful. A different kind of event—widespread unemployment, high inflation, national mobilization—would present a somewhat different configuration. The nature of the energy shortage as a specific stressor event thus emphasized certain aspects of the model, while other aspects were less relevant in this specific situation.

As stated above, the oil embargo, though it was perceived as a national crisis, actually did not produce a severe enough impact on most households to be thought of as a crisis. Nevertheless, it did have a modest and rather widespread impact and occasioned modest adjustments. It is reassuring that the analytical model is sufficiently sensitive and inclusive to "pick up" those adjustments and to accommodate them within a conceptual framework. In this respect, the model has served its purpose well.

It should be noted that the model also suggests types of data which this study did not gather. For example, more data might have been gathered with respect to the decision-making process than simply who made the decision to conserve energy. Much more data might have been obtained about stated motives for various behaviors. This is also true for data on the effects of the shortage on family integration. Was there more tension? Were household members drawn more closely together or further apart? How were the daily activities of children affected by less use of the car?

Putting this another way, the model lends itself to further utilization even within the specific stressor event of the energy shortage. The limitations on its use were due on the one hand to the ever-present necessity to keep questionnaires within feasible length, and on the other hand by the staff's inability to devise questions which would be sufficiently sensitive to pick up the least obvious impacts.

The question of validity looms like a spectre over all self-reported data. We knew that we could afford only such gross validation as we reported in Chapter Six. But in the selection and phrasing of questions, the validity issue was constantly before us, in some cases constituting an imposing constraint. But to repeat, some of the reason for not fully exploiting the analytical model had to do with the minimal nature of the impact of the energy shortage and the consequent difficulty of the respondent in sorting it out and reporting it validly. It is a combination of the above considerations that leaves us with little to report on the impact of the shortage on the health of household members or on the solidarity of the household or on interpersonal relations. In these matters, our filter questions indicated such low frequency of gross response that it seemed pointless to refine the nuances.

Again, the model directs attention to the interface between the family and other social systems. We have recorded and reported some aspects of this interface, especially those dealing with adjustments in consumption patterns and, to a lesser extent, in labor force participation. In both these aspects, we have pointed out that while the household is acted upon, as it adjusts to these impacts, its adjustments in turn constitute an impact on other systems. We have indicated briefly the nature of these ripple effects. Obviously, much more work needs to be done in acquiring an adequate understanding of these reciprocal processes and their effects. It is apparent to us that a simple linear cause-effect model is not adequate for such analysis, but that future work may well take the path of a modified system-subsystem model.

Another aspect in which the model suggests a promising avenue for future research is closely related to this question of reciprocal impacts. As the model suggests, and as our data show, some types of household adjustments have the effect of "absorbing" the impact, as it were, without passing on the effects of these adjustments to other systems.

As an example, a change may occur in intra-household relationships in the form of greater hostility, more frequent family discussions, or a closer feeling of unity, without any noticeable effect being perceived by other social systems such as employers, retail stores, service agencies, churches, and the like. On the other hand, reduced purchases, changes in shopping patterns, and less utilization of commercial recreation facilities constitute types of household adjustments which transfer impacts to other systems. The distinction points up exciting new paths for investigation which are only partly pursued in the present study.

THEORETICAL ISSUES TO BE RESOLVED

Thus far, we have been considering aspects of the analytical model which are not fully explored in the present study. To the extent that the model was utilized, the results seem reassuring. Nevertheless, the model in its present form leaves us less than fully satisfied. A number of theoretical issues suggest limitations which might be overcome in future efforts.

A primary objective of the analytical model was to assist investigations in going past a more or less global concept of "impact on households." It was designed to conceptualize and delineate the manner in which such impacts take place and to register the anticipated or actual impact of a stressor event, such as the energy shortage, on the family's capacities and on its task performance. In connection with both of these, we have proposed and utilized a number of categories that permit the investigator to become more specific as to (1) different types of impacts which the same stressor event may have on different families, and (2) the effects that different stressor events may have on the same family, as well as the corresponding adjustments in both instances. This characteristic of the model appears to be useful and we feel that this represents an important step forward in family research.

Nevertheless, the model still appears to be too static. It gets beyond the family as a "black box," but only by pointing out that the black box has certain compartments, which can be typologized. The model was developed inductively from two different sources—our study's data and the literature on family stress and crisis. It is significant that our study was based on survey-type data, primarily utilizing precoded questions. Hence, the data were already preformed into categories by the very nature of the research instrument. True, it might have been possible to solicit more data about intrafamily processes and about differential impacts within the household (e.g., differential effects on different household members). Yet most investigators would agree that process data, which would begin to give a fuller picture of the interaction taking place within the black box, would have required other modes of data-gathering. These might include more flexibly structured interviews, participant observation, and so on. These were not within the scope of the present study. Further investigation would help to illuminate intra-household processes and thus enable the model to be more dynamic, as well as more sensitive to differences among household members.

The reference to individual household members raises a somewhat different issue. The issue has to do with the alternative implications of focusing on the household or on the individual members as the unit of analysis. As mentioned above, individual household members may be affected differently and may react differently to stressor events on the household. Should not the analysis therefore be directed to the individual members rather than to the household as a unit? This is a distinct possibility and such a study would have merit on its own terms. But the present study, and the model which we have sought to develop, deliberately focus on the household.

Member interaction and differential impacts and adjustments on or by members are important as they affect the household group, its capacities as a social unit, and its performance of tasks as a family. Here is another area that, conceptually and empirically, needs much more development. In this study we did not, for example, trace through the process by which an impact on one member of the family is transmitted to the family as a whole or the reverse of that process. Nor did we attempt to distinguish among households of different size and composition. For instance in a household composed of all young adults the interaction processes are bound to differ from households with children or with three generations living together.

Our general emphasis on the collective unit rather than the individual arises from an initial interest in the manner in which various stressor events coming from the national or macro-level affect families, and how family adjustments feed back into the larger social processes. This field of investigation has important policy implications which are much broader than the energy shortage and to which we shall turn presently.

MORE IS INVOLVED THAN CONSUMPTION AND LABOR

An additional limitation of the model has to do with another aspect of the interface between households and other systems, alluded to earlier, namely the prevailing manner of conceptualizing that interface. It is reflected in the model's concentration on two avenues or channels of interaction between the family and other social systems, i.e., the process of consumption of goods and services and the process of participating in the labor market. The model does not elaborate the category called "other," which was designed to make room for a variety of additional types of interrelationships.

The two avenues are certainly basic, acknowledging the family's functions in the two important economic activities of production and consumption. We said above that this is the "prevailing" way of viewing the family in its relations with other social systems, though these two functions are seldom brought together as the two strands of family/society interaction in connection with a particular issue in the manner of the present study. Most economic studies of the relationship between families and other social systems concentrate on either the consumer behavior or the labor market behavior of families. The explanation is apparent: Economic theories, even highly divergent ones, view the family from these two perspectives to the virtual exclusion of other types of interface.

Thus, in their highly relevant work on *Economy and Society*, Parsons and Smelser confine their analysis of the interchange of the economy with the family or "household" to the topics of labor supply and household consumption.[3] Thus for the economy the family is accorded importance only for its activity in producing and consuming goods and services. This characteristic is not only shared by neo-Marxian economists, but emphasized by them. This stems from the analysis by Marx and Engels of the family as a unit from which the surplus value of labor is extracted by the ruling class, and as a means of disposing, for profit, of the goods so produced by the ruling class.[4] By way of illustration, Manuel Castells, in his outline for a neo-Marxist approach to the question of urbanism, analyzes the "urban" phenomenon as a spatial concentration of means of production and consumption necessary for the reproduction of the labor force.[5]

It is quite appropriate therefore to have emphasized these two important economic functions of households in the present study. But having done so, we must recognize that there are other important aspects of the family/society interface which are not treated in an economic model. From the many possible examples of such aspects, let us consider three.

The family is widely acknowledged to perform a function of socialization, the inculcation into the young of the values and behavior patterns of the larger society. One need not be a Parsonian to acknowledge the importance of this function of matching new members of a society, in their personal development, to the role structure of that society. Social scientists, notably Margaret Mead, have long since pointed out the problems which arise when there is a dissonance between the socialization process and the role structure of society and have quite appropriately centered on the family in examining the dislocations of this type which exist in American society.[6] The interchange with other societal components in this respect is both one of the family's receiving values, and their reinforcement, from the surrounding institutions of society and of transmitting these to the young in the socialization process.

To give another example, the adjustments which come out of the family's reaction to stress may be such as to violate the prevailing norms, to become problematic. Here, again, the family as a system receives impacts or various types of sustained "inputs" from the surrounding society, and in turn impacts that society with adjustments which may be characterized as dependency, immorality, crime, neglect, menaces to public health, and so on. Of course, by an intellectual tour de force, one might range such types of interchange under the economic rubric, coverting them into positive or negative units of productivity or of consumption of goods and services, or of a standard monetary value.

Still another sphere of family/society interaction concerns a broad range of activities that involve participation in political processes. In the present study we took note of the attitudes of families toward the energy crisis, as they were colored by attitudes toward the Nixon Administration. And we gave some description of the exploratory efforts of state and local governments to deal with the new energy situation. But we did not examine the impacts, if any, that families may have had on public bodies and their policy-making, though we did note that on a case-by-case basis some families appealed to the allocation authorities for special arrangements necessitated by health conditions within the family.

We see the need to expand the model to account for other types of interchange than those readily subsumable under consumer activity or labor market activity for which we have left a category in the model. We are convinced that an injustice is done to this important component of society by reducing its importance solely to production and consumption in a narrow economic sense.

A still different consideration concerns the model's potential usefulness for assessing not only events or conditions such as the energy shortage, but for an assessment of the impacts of different types of *public policies* on families.

PUBLIC POLICIES AND FAMILIES

There is rising concern about the effects of public policies on American families.[7] This stems in part from renewed interest in the family as a major institution that is experiencing rapid changes in function, size, composition, and life-style. In part, the concern springs from a general uneasiness about the adequacy of public policies in meeting the needs of the changing American family.

Difficult questions are beginning to command attention: Are existing policies that are explicitly concerned with the family having their desired outcomes? In the much larger arena of public policies that are not directly addressed to families—for instance, economic development, transportation, agriculture—what are the intended and unintended consequences of specific policies and programs for American families and households? Cutting across all policy areas, what are the contradictions, unwanted overlaps, and gaps from the family perspective?

Social scientists and policymakers concerned with these questions find a lack of conceptual clarity, a scarcity of analytical tools, and a dearth of empirical studies. This statement may seem overdrawn, in view of the vast literature analyzing various policies, presumably in terms of their effects on individuals and families. But actually, few of the policy analysis studies deal in any systematic way either with the nature of the impact of the policy on families or with the dynamic processes through which this impact occurs and adjustments are made.

Part of the thinking behind the present research was the conviction that what is ordinarily called "family policy" is the tip of the iceberg, and that most families are much more massively affected by the side effects of policies whose avowed purpose is not to affect the family at all, but rather to accomplish some other objective. There is some questioning in the current debate whether the United States has any family policy at all, anything which could be thought of as a deliberate, carefully thought-out series of postures vis-à-vis the family which is consistently applied in appropriate fashion to new legislative and administrative measures.

In the current debate family policy is thought of largely in terms of deliberate measures and programs designed to "help" families in some way or to influence the rate of population growth. When family policy comes up for discussion, it is usually in terms of social and health services, income transfer payments, social insurances, marriage and divorce laws, protective legislation, and the like. What we mean by the "tip of the iceberg" is that although such measures surely have important impacts on the family, another, possibly more massive set of impacts comes from policy areas in which families receive little or no explicit and sustained consideration—from labor policy, fiscal policy, military policy, foreign policy, agricultural policy.

In our view it seems more useful to study the various and sometimes contradictory ways in which families are affected by these major public policies than to assume that this country has a unified, coherent "family policy." In some quarters, indeed, there is grave concern as to whether it is an appropriate role for government to have one, since it suggests the possibility of an incursion on individual rights.

It is surprising that these broad public policies have received so little systematic attention. We believe that one reason why they are seldom assessed in terms of their impact on families of different types is that there is no conceptualization available on the basis of which the nexus between public policies and specific families or classes of families can be operationalized for research purposes. The closest thing to an exception to this statement is the utilization of economic analysis in pursuing the relationship between income maintenance programs and work incentives. This is a highly delimited, though important area. Further, it treats these two sets of variables globally rather than in dynamic, processual terms. More important, it is limited to a consideration of incentives to gainful employment—an admittedly important aspect of policy impact on families, but quite obviously only a fragmented aspect of the ways in which families are affected by public policies.

To repeat, although public policies have important effects on family structure and processes, the processes through which these impacts occur and the explicit nature of the adjustments made to them constitute an important gap in sociological knowledge and theory of the family and in research methodologies on the interface between families and social policies.

At the present time, largely through the impetus of Vice President (formerly Senator) Mondale, there is a growing interest in a broad approach to the question of assessing the impacts of a wide range of existing public policies on families. There is the additional objective—as yet relatively vaguely defined—of developing a procedure whereby future legislative proposals which may affect families in one way or another will be subjected to a "family impact statement" to correspond to the environmental impact statements that are now required for certain legislative and administrative proposals. It is not clear that the basic costs-benefits model as applied by economists is adequate for such assessments, chiefly for the reason given earlier that the concern for the family is, or should be, more than a concern for its labor market performance or for its consumption patterns.

Does the family adjustment model employed in the present research have potentiality for developing in the direction of a framework for such family impact assessments across a broad range of public policies? Quite frankly, the hope that this might be the case was part of the motivation of the authors of this volume in undertaking the energy impact study in the first place.

Our conclusion is that the model does indeed have potential, but is far from what is needed to do this task adequately. As favorable or promising omens, it should be noted that the energy shortage was not a "family program" as such. It has been treated by most analysts primarily in terms of alternative energy sources, import prices, industrial usages, substitute effects on production and price, and so on. Yet, as this study shows, the energy shortage had definite, measurable impacts on families, which this model helped to specify and assess, along with the families' adjustments and their repercussions. Second, this assessment was possible even though the intensity of the impact was not great and the duration of the shortage was relatively brief. This is important in that presumably the impact of most public policies on families may be only slightly discernible, remaining well below the level of what one might describe as a "crisis" for families.

What remains to be seen is whether the model is adaptable for more long-range impacts, which over time and in combination with other impacts may be great, but which at any given moment are difficult to sort out from the tangled web of environmental influences under which families function. The question can be answered definitively only after considerable effort has been devoted to developing and applying the model for public policy assessment purposes.

The model used in this research was developed to study the family as a micro-system. That is, it was developed for studying individual families and coming to general findings through the aggregation of data from the 1,440 families in the present study. An intriguing question, and also one which may be of importance for public policy analysis, is whether the model is adaptable to, or transmutable into a model for, analysis at the macro-level. By this we mean whether aggregate data, such as national employment rates, prices, level of economic activity, labor market participation, wage rates, interest rates, and so on can be plugged into aggregate family data, such as divorce rates, delinquency rates, birthrates, marriage rates, morbidity and death rates, and so on, so that aggregate analysis at the national system level can be made.

We are aware of the hangfire nature of the first big wave of efforts to develop policy-relevant social indicators—a matter with which this last mentioned point is closely intertwined. The results of this movement so far have not been fully reassuring. It is possible that one of the main points of difficulty with the development of meaningful policy-relevant social indicators has been the lack of a systematic model within which some of the more meaningful relationships among the indicators could be assessed and in which a clearer idea could be developed as to what indicators are really meaningful, and why.

We do not by any means presume to have the answer to this question on the basis of our experience in developing and utilizing the present model for aggregating micro-level data. We sense that even at the micro-level, the analysis needs to pay more attention to process, and to consider more aspects of family functioning than only consumption and labor market activity. Above all, we do not believe that there is any one single definitive method for developing meaningful and useful assessments of the impact of present and anticipated public policies on families. Our hope is that the present study and our model will be taken as a modest but useful step in directing the attention of social scientists and policymakers to the importance of studying the impact of public policies on families.

Appendixes

Appendix A
Survey Design and Implementation

1. *Selection of Household Respondents*

The study was designed to obtain certain data from the female head of household and other data from a "designated worker." (In some instances the female head of household would also be the designated worker.) Whenever the female head of household and/or the designated worker were not available for an interview, alternate respondents were selected by the procedures outlined below, on each successive call at the dwelling.

General Household Data	Call 1	Call 2	Call 3
The preferred respondent is:	Female head	Female head	Female head
If above person is not available, interview:	Male head	Male head	Male head
If second choice not available:	Call back	Call back	Interview the designated worker
If the third choice is not available:	Not applicable	Not applicable	Interview any adult

2. *Selection of the Designated Worker*

In order to select the "designated worker" all household members age sixteen or older were listed on a screening form. Those members who had worked on a full-time basis for at least six months since November 1, 1973 were listed independently of other family members. An equal "X'ing" pattern was used for selecting a designated worker. This "X'ing" pattern assured that all full-time workers were

208 Families in the Energy Crisis

given an equal opportunity of being included in the sample. While it was desired that the designated worker himself be interviewed about his working experience, a systematic selection procedure was developed so that someone other than the designated worker could be interviewed if he/she were not available. This procedure is described below.

Employment Data	Call		
	1	2	3
The preferred respondent is:	Designated worker	Designated worker	Designated worker
If above person is not available:	Call back	Male head	Male head
If second choice not available, interview:	Not applicable	Female head	Female head
If the third choice is not available:	Not applicable	Call back	Interview any adult

3. Characteristics of Designated Workers

Table A-1. Occupational Distribution, Brandeis Sample and National Data

	Brandeis Sample	National*
Clerical and Sales Workers	20.6%	23.3%
Craftsmen & Foremen	20.4	12.9
Professional and Technical	17.1	14.0
Manager, Officials & Proprietors	16.8	11.0
Operatives	9.1	16.4
Service Workers	7.9	13.5
Farm Workers	5.8	3.8
Nonfarm Laborers	2.1	5.0

*U.S. Statistical Abstract—1971 Employed Persons by Major Occupational Groups, Table 366, p. 230.

Table A-2. Non-Agricultural Employees, Brandeis Sample and National Data

	Brandeis Sample	National*
Manufacturing	23.3%	26.3%
Wholesale and Retail	13.4	21.5
Government	12.9	18.2
Services	17.6	16.9
Transportation and Public Utilities	9.3	6.3
Finance, Insurance, RE	7.8	5.4
Construction	—	4.6
Mining	—	0.8

*Full- and part-time workers who worked for pay in 1971, U.S. Statistical Abstract 1972, p. 225, Table 361.

4. *Selection of Establishments*

In order to investigate households in their roles as consumers and employees, it was decided also to survey a cross-section of retail, manufacturing and other businesses and public organizations. Since the interest of the study was in the interaction between these establishments and households, selected samples of both were chosen in the same communities.

The industrial sample in each of the three areas consisted of samples of establishments selected in a single-phase operation. The samples were stratified on the basis of type of industry and size of establishment as measured by the number of employees.

The description of the universes in each of the areas was obtained from *County Business Patterns 1972*, published by the Bureau of the Census, in which counts are given for the number of establishments by employee size and by Standard Industrial Code categories. This tabulation supplied a frame from which names of establishments could be selected. The extent to which the detailed information provided in the *County Business Patterns* could be used depended upon the extent to which frames for samplings were available. For example, in Hartford, an excellent *State Industrial Directory* was obtainable which listed names and sizes of all manufacturing plants. In addition, insurance companies are a major industry in Hartford and it was possible to obtain the names of the leading insurance companies in Hartford from various directories. The Yellow Pages constituted an additional source. In Mobile a list of all employers of 200 or more employees was obtained. In addition to this source, the Yellow Pages were used. In Salem, Oregon, the *State Industrial Directory of Manufacturers* and the Yellow Pages were used.

The selection of establishments was made with probabilities proportionate to the number of employees. The sample design used dictated that establishments sampled be weighted to insure representativeness of the data. The weighting procedure called for ratio estimating from the establishment sample to the universe of establishments studied. In order to develop these weights, establishments were grouped into four strata in Hartford, and three strata in Mobile and Salem. These subdivisions grouped establishments by number of employees. This substratification was necessary in order to give smaller weights to the larger companies who were relatively oversampled.

Interviewers were screened by telephone to determine the person within the establishment who was "most informed about how the energy situation affected their establishment." After determining who this person was an appointment was made to conduct a personal interview.

5. Collection and Processing of Data

Questionnaire Construction

The questionnaires used in this study were first drafted by the Brandeis Project staff and then revised in collaboration with Audits and Surveys, Inc., in order to clarify questions, eliminate inconsistencies and redundancies, and fill in content where further data were needed for analytical purposes. During this questionnaire construction period, representatives of both the project staff and Audits and Surveys, Inc., conducted informal pretest interviews.

The formal pretest was conducted in communities in northern New Jersey by Audits and Surveys, Inc., with approximately fifty households and forty establishments. The establishment pretest sample was taken from the Yellow Pages of the Passaic County telephone book. All major establishment categories were represented. Interviews were attempted with the ten largest companies in the Paterson area. The pretest findings were incorporated into the design of the final questionnaire.

Interviewing

Personal interviews were conducted between November 11 and November 30, 1974 in approximately 1,460 households and 600 establishments. Audits and Surveys, Inc., validated by telephone from New York 20 percent of each interviewer's work to insure that the reported interviews in fact took place. Households without telephones were validated in person by a local interviewer not assigned to the Brandeis project.

Data Processing

Coding and editing of the questionnaires were carried out as questionnaires were received from the field. Code building in open-end questions was accomplished through analysis of verbatim write-ups from 10 percent of the compiled questionnaires.

Tape preparation consisted of (1) the transfer of all data from questionnaires to punch cards; (2) a consistency check of all cards by electronic computer; and (3) reformatting the data into a 360 compatible tape.

Tests of Significance

Tests of Significance were computed in the printouts. They are presented in this volume only in connection with the results of the Validation Study in Chapter Seven. Elsewhere, small differences in the findings are treated as being roughly equivalent and no special inferences are drawn from them.

Collection of Data on the 1977 Energy Crisis
Information on the events of the winter of 1976-77 and their effects on families was collected in July and August, 1977 through personal interviews with knowledgeable informants in each of the three metropolitan areas, many of whom had been seen earlier in the study, and from newspapers.

In addition, data were obtained from a subsample of 11 percent of the original 1,440 households. The subsample was representative of the three areas and of the four income groups in this study. In addition, 21 percent of the subsample consisted of minority households in order to insure an adequate representation of that group. Telephone interviews were used as the means of collecting the data. Respondents were notified in advance by mail that a phone call would be made. Fifty interviews were completed in Hartford, 52 in Mobile, and 52 in Salem.

The data from the telephone interviews were compared with data from the same households obtained in 1974 and in 1975.

Appendix B
Follow-Up Mail Survey in September 1975

The data collected in the original survey provided three time periods for comparison: (1) the precrisis period; (2) the in-crisis period in 1973-74; and (3) the time of the interviews in the homes, November 1974. A follow-up questionnaire was developed to ascertain changes that had taken place after November 1974 in both behavior and attitudes.

The entire sample of 1,440 household respondents was mailed questionnaires at the end of August 1975. At the end of September a reminder was mailed. By October 15, 1975 a return rate of 57 percent was achieved, calculated as follows:

1,440 questionnaires mailed
856 total returns
99 noncodable returns
757 codable returns

1,440-99 = 1341 $\frac{757}{1341}$ = 56.5%

Selected characteristics of those who responded to the mail questionnaire are compared below with characteristics of the original sample of 1,440.

Table B-1. Characteristics of Mail Survey Respondents (in percent)

	Mail Survey (n=757)	Original Sample (n=1,440)
Income		
Under $5,000	13.0	17.8
$5,000-$9,999	21.4	22.7
$10,000-$14,999	31.5	29.1
$15,000-up	34.0	30.4
Age of Head		
16-24	2.8	4.3
25-44	36.6	38.2
45-64	40.4	37.2
65-+	20.2	20.3
Race		
White	93.4	87.4
Black	6.6	11.4
Household Size		
1 member	11.0	12.1
2-4	73.3	70.5
5-+	15.8	17.4
Work Status		
Full Time	74.0	73.7
Part Time	2.8	3.5
Retired	18.0	16.3
Unemployed	5.2	6.6
SMSA		
Hartford	53.7	49.0
Mobile	27.1	33.8
Salem	19.1	17.2
Single Family Dwelling		
Yes	90.0	87.4
No	10.0	12.6

Appendix C
The Validation Study[a]

Information on the amounts of electricity, natural gas, and fuel oil consumed by a subsample of the original 1,440 households was obtained in order (1) to test the validity of respondents' answers to a number of critical questions in the initial interviews and (2) to test the accuracy of the estimates generated by the Heating Energy Consumption Index, the In-House Energy Consumption Index, and the Air Conditioning Energy Consumption Index.

Those households who paid directly for their electricity and natural gas and who controlled their own heating were first identified. From this pool of 1,220 households a sample of 728 households was selected so as to insure an adequate number of households in each income class in each metropolitan area.

Forms were mailed to the selected households in May 1976 asking them to describe their use of various forms of energy and requesting them to sign an authorization for the Brandeis project to obtain data on their consumption directly from their suppliers of electricity, natural gas, and fuel oil. Households were contacted by telephone to encourage responses. There was a 30 percent response rate, producing 215 replies, as shown below.

The major gas and power companies had been contacted in advance and without exception had indicated their willingness to participate in this phase of the study, which often required considerable effort to search their records and, in some instances, to make special computer runs. The information consisted of the amount of

[a]Discussed in Chapter Seven, pp. 110-116.

216 Families in the Energy Crisis

energy used (i.e., cubit feet of natural gas, KWH of electricity, or gallons of fuel oil) and the dollar amount paid for the two twelve-month periods, November 1972 through October 1973 and November 1973 through October 1974. Smaller fuel oil distributors were contacted as they were named in the returned authorizations and almost 90 percent of these cooperated.

The record of authorizations mailed and returned is given below by income groups and by community.

Table C-1. Authorizations Sent and Returned in Validation Study

	Total		Under $5,000		$5,000-$9,999		$10,000-$14,999		$15,000+	
	Sent	Ret.	Sent	Ret.	Sent	Ret.	Sent	Ret.	Sent	Ret.
Hartford	260	89	44	14	65	21	73	28	78	26
Mobile	273	56	77	12	63	12	66	17	67	15
Salem	195	70	45	13	60	21	44	18	46	18
TOTAL	728	215	166	39	188	54	183	63	191	59

The project staff is very grateful to the following companies that cooperated in this study. Some of the utility companies were helpful in providing use and cost data in addition to their assisting in the validation study.

Major Utility Companies Cooperating in this Study

Northeast Utilities Company
Portland General Electric Company
Connecticut Natural Gas Corporation

Mobile Gas Service Corporation
Alabama Power Company
Salem Electric Company
Northwest Natural Gas Company

Fuel Oil and Other Suppliers Who Cooperated

Connecticut
Kasden Fuel Oil Co.
Automatic Comfort
Desmarais Oil Co.
Connecticut Refining Co.
Pattison Fuel Oil Co.
National Oil Company

The Valley Coal Co.
Viger Oil Co.
J.S. McCarthy Oil Co.
Miner Lumber Co.
H.C. Rohde Oil Co.
Mercury Oil Co.

Gask's Oil Service
Quinion Oil & Trucking Co.
Hall and Muska, Inc.
Bantly Oil Company
Mellen, White & Palshaw
Moriarty Brothers, Inc.
Suburban Propane
Doyker Brothers
Washburn Oil Co.

Alabama
Blossmas Gas, Inc.
City of Fairhope Utilities
Amoco Oil Company

Oregon
H.A. Simmons Fuel Oil Co.
Russ-Pratt Service Oil
Valley Oil Co.
Home Fuel Oil Co.
Comfort Heat
City-Wide Oil Service
Master Service Oil

Newgate Oil Co.
C&S Oil Co.
State Line Oil Co.
Tenneco-Laurel Oil Co.
Wyman Oil
Cabral Oil
Model Oil Co.
Keller Oil
Oilpower Group
Troiano Oil Company

Bay Minette Utility Board
Riviera Utilities

Mobile Oil Company Products
Ross Oil Co.
C.J. Hansen, Inc.
Pacific Power and Light
Cal-Gas Co.
Farmers Oil Co.
Hatter Oil Co.

Appendix D
Socioeconomic Differences among Families in Brandeis Sample

Table D-1. Income Distribution of Brandeis Sample by Metropolitan Area

	Total		Low Under $5,000		Low-Middle $5,000-$9,999		Middle $10,000-$14,999		Upper $15,000 or More	
	No.	%	No.	%	No.	%	No.	%	No.	%
Hartford	706	100.0	48	6.8	130	18.4	220	31.2	308	43.6
Mobile	487	100.0	153	31.4	126	25.9	131	26.9	77	15.8
Salem	247	99.0	55	22.2	71	28.8	68	26.5	53	21.5
TOTAL	1440	100.0	256	17.8	327	22.7	419	29.1	438	30.4

220 Families in the Energy Crisis

Table D-2. Salient Characteristics of Households in the Sample

	Brandeis Sample % of Households	U.S. Households
1. *Size of Household*		
1 person	12.1	18.5
2-4 persons	70.5	63.2
5 or more persons	17.4	18.3
2. *Work Status of Head of Household*		
Full-time work	73.7	
Retired	16.3	
Not employed	6.6	
Part-time work	3.5	
3. *Age of Head*		
16-24	4.3	8.0
25-44	38.2	37.1
45-64	37.2	35.2
65+	20.3	19.7
4. *Race*		
White	87.4	
Black	11.4	

Source: U.S. Bureau of the Census, Current Population Reports, Series P-60, No. 89, July 1973; "Household Money Income in 1972 and Selected Social and Economic Characteristics of Households."

Table D-3. Work Status by Age of Household Head in Brandeis Sample (n=1,389) (in percent)

					Total	
Age of Head	*Full-Time*	*Part-Time*	*Retired*	*Not Employed*	*No.*	*%*
16-24	86.4	5.1	1.7	6.8	58	100.0
25-44	94.4	2.3	0.6	2.8	531	100.1
45-54	91.3	2.8	2.1	3.8	289	100.0
55-64	70.6	4.3	17.7	7.4	231	100.0
65+	16.1	5.7	62.5	15.7	280	100.0

Table D-4. Household Income by Age of Household Head in Brandeis Sample (in percent)

Age of Head	Low	Low-Middle	Middle	Upper	Total No.	Total %
16-24	26.7	35.0	28.3	10.0	60	100.0
25-44	6.0	20.6	37.6	35.8	534	100.0
45-54	8.0	17.6	29.1	45.3	289	100.0
55-64	17.6	23.2	26.2	33.0	233	100.0
65+	46.5	28.9	15.8	8.8	284	100.0

Table D-5. Incomes of Brandeis Households by Race (in percent; n=1,440)

	Low	Low-Middle	Middle	Upper
White	14.3	21.2	31.2	33.2
Black	44.5	32.3	13.4	9.8

Table D-6. Responses by Income Groups to Selected Questions (in percent)

Item	Question	Low	Low-Middle	Middle	Upper
1	Changes in use of car:				
	Precrisis highway speed	58	60	62	63
	No. mph reduction in speed	−6	−7	−8	−9
	Cut driving to save gasoline	75	81	79	80
2	Reduced activities:				
	Shopping	68	71	67	64
	Driving children to school	37	40	36	35
	Time with family members	7	11	6	8
	Entertaining friends	10	17	11	14
	Visiting	40	48	52	47
	Sports & recreational trips	30	31	28	27
	Attending meetings	28	29	28	22
	Going to movies	41	43	35	31
	Eating out	39	42	37	33
	Vacation plans influenced	23	31	40	40
	Shortened time or distance	11	20	37	33
	Stayed home	80	70	54	53
3	Data from Matre study in Texas				
	Reduced work driving	7	11	5	12
	Reduced family driving	12	13	22	26
	Reduced pleasure driving	21	21	27	37

		\multicolumn{4}{c}{Income Groups}
Item	Question	Low	Low-Middle	Middle	Upper
4	Increased activities:				
	Time with family members	13	23	23	23
	Watching TV	11	14	25	18
	Entertaining	6	8	7	10
5	Substitutes for driving				
	Car pooling	22	32	33	41
	Bicycling	14	15	18	22
	Walking	46	27	31	21
6	Heating				
	Able to control temperature	81	91	96	98
	Lowered temperature	35	39	53	61
	Precrisis winter temperature	71	70	70	70
	No. degrees lowered	−1.1	−1.1	−1.5	−1.9
	Shut windows	14	13	18	20
	Closed off rooms	54	45	38	39
	Difference between ideal and changed temperature	−0.1	−1.1	−1.5	−0.9
	Used less hot water	47	50	51	56
7	Electricity reductions				
	Cut back in Hartford	64	84	81	74
	Cut back in Mobile	83	79	74	60
	Cut back in Salem	59	60	53	45
	Reduced use of:				
	Electric stove	23	32	32	27
	Lighting	76	79	85	84
	Dishwasher	—	52	42	45
	Clothes washer	41	36	31	30
	Clothes dryer	36	47	47	47
	TV	25	24	23	22
	Air-conditioning	62	70	66	72
8	Consumer behavior				
	Decided not to buy cars	20	34	40	59
	Decided not to buy appliances	29	23	19	14
	Changed type of clothing bought	13	15	22	20
	Could not afford	55	41	31	28
	Too costly to operate	22	24	26	10
	Gasoline too high or scarce	—	23	20	33
9	General effects of crisis				
	Affected "the ways things were going"	33	35	40	32
	Felt more inconvenience than others	5	12	9	9
	Felt less inconvenience than others	20	16	19	26

		\multicolumn{4}{c}{Income Groups}
Item	Question	Low	Low-Middle	Middle	Upper
10	Most important reason for reducing:				
	A. Use of cars				
	Price	51	46	39	28
	Availability	22	31	38	41
	Duty	24	21	23	27
	B. Heating				
	Price	39	52	41	33
	Duty	30	38	32	43
	C. Electricity (price only)	75	76	74	68
	D. Air-conditioning—				
	Price of electricity	80	64	73	52

Table D-7. Precrisis Typical Household Energy Expenditures[1]

	Hartford	Mobile	Salem	U.S.[2]
Automobile—cost of gasoline	$ 548	$ 430	$ 431	$ 345
Heat Only	292	94	154	195
Air-conditioning only	—[3]	96	—[3]	
In-the-home	179	140	157	194
TOTAL	$ 1,019	$ 760	$ 742	$ 734
1969 Median Income[4]	$12,314	$7,733	$8,992	$9,586[5]
% of Median Income	8.3	9.8	8.3	7.7

1. Based on data primarily from 1972-73.
2. The U.S. figures are from The Citizens Advisory Committee on Environmental Quality, *Citizen Action Guide to Energy Conservation*, p. 15, for mid-1973. Electricity covers major appliances, electric water heat, cooking, air-conditioning, lighting and others. Heating is a national average for natural gas, oil and electricity plus natural gas water heat and cooking with natural gas.
3. Air-conditioning for Hartford and Salem is included under In-the-home consumption.
4. U.S. Bureau of Census, *Census of Population & Housing*, 1970, Census Tracts, Final Report PHC (1): (87, Hartford), (133, Mobile), (182, Salem).
5. *1973 U.S. Statistical Abstract*, p. 332.

Table D-8. Selected Responses of Black and White Respondents (in percent)

Item	Question	Black	White
1	Used car year before crisis	78	94
	Homeowners	69	81
	Able to control heating temperature	77	95
2	Driving reductions		
	In general	80	79
	For shopping	71	67
	For recreation	71	67
	For ferrying children	89	80
	For visiting	73	64
	Substituted public transportation	14	8
	Substituted car pools	15	21
	Vacation plans affected	26	36
3	Other reductions in energy use		
	Lowered temperature in winter		
	Cut use of hot water	57	53
	Reduced use of electricity	87	71
	Reduced use of air-conditioning	76	69
4	Attitudes		
	Believed energy crisis real	25	37
	Blamed gov't in Washington	39	24
	Blamed oil and gas companies	20	35
	Felt *more* inconvenience than others	9	9
	Felt less inconvenience than others	9	22
5	Primary reason for cutting down		
	Price of gasoline	58	37
	Availability of gas	31	35
	Duty to save gas	12	25
	Cost of air-conditioning	76	63
	Duty to reduce air-conditioning	20	23

Notes

NOTES TO CHAPTER ONE
INTRODUCTION

1. An outstanding exception to this is Dorothy K. Newman and Dawn Day, *The American Energy Consumer: A Report to the Energy Policy Project of the Ford Foundation* (Cambridge, Mass.: Ballinger Publishing Company, 1975).

A comprehensive synthesis of recent studies, many of which bear on the family, appears in Marvin E. Olsen and Jill A. Goodnight, *Social Aspects of Energy Conservation* (Portland, Oregon: Pacific Northwest Regional Commission, Northwest Energy Policy Project, 1977).

2. Reuben Hill, *Families Under Stress: Adjustment to the Crises of War Separation and Reunion* (New York: Harper and Brothers, 1949), p. viii.

3. S. David Freeman, *Energy: The New Era* (New York: Walker and Company, 1974), p. 16.

4. Ivan Illich, *Energy and Society*, New York: Harper and Row, 1974, p. 1.

5. Connecticut Energy Agency, *Energy Emergency Plan for Connecticut*, January 14, 1975, p. 6.

6. See, for example, Richard La Piere, "Attitudes vs. Actions," *Social Forces* 13 (March 1934): 230-237; Irwin Deutscher, "Words and Deeds: Social Science and Social Policy," *Social Problems* 13, 3 (Winter 1966): 235-254.

7. *Playboy*, May 1976.

NOTES TO CHAPTER TWO
AN ANALYTICAL MODEL OF FAMILIES AND CRISES

1. United States Senate, Committee on Labor and Public Welfare, Subcommittee on Children and Youth, *American Families: Trends and Pressures, 1973* (Washington, D.C.: Government Printing Office, 1974), p. 2.

226 Families in the Energy Crisis

2. Statement by Jimmy Carter, 12:00 p.m., August 3, 1976, Manchester, New Hampshire.

3. John Dewey, *How We Think, A Restatement of the Relation of Reflective Thinking to the Educative Process* (Boston: D.C. Heath and Co., 1933).

4. Allen H. Barton, *Communities in Disaster: A Sociological Analysis of Collective Stress Situations* (Garden City, New York: Doubleday, 1969).

5. J.W. Powell, in J.W. Powell, J.E. Finesinger, and M.H. Greenhill, "An Introduction to the Natural History of Disaster," Vol. II, Final Contract Report, Disaster Research Project, Psychiatric Institute, University of Maryland, 1954. Cited in George H. Grosser, Henry Wechsler, and Milton Greenblatt, *The Threat of Impending Disaster: Contributions to the Psychology of Stress* (Cambridge, Mass.: MIT Press, 1964), p. 24.

6. Barton, *Communities in Disaster*, p. 38.

7. Erik H. Erikson, *Childhood and Society* (New York: Norton, 1950).

8. Rhona V. Rapoport, "Normal Crises, Family Structure and Mental Health," *Family Process* 2 (1963): 68-80; Gerald Caplan, *Principles of Preventive Psychiatry* (New York: Basic Books, Inc., 1964).

9. Reuben Hill, *Families Under Stress: Adjustment to the Crises of War Separation and Reunion* (New York: Harper & Brothers Pub., 1949).

10. Erich Lindemann, "Symptomatology and Management of Acute Grief," *American Journal of Psychiatry* 101 (September 1944): 141-148.

11. James A. Robinson, "Crisis," in David L. Sills (ed.), *International Encyclopedia of the Social Sciences*, Vol. 3 (New York: Macmillan & Co., 1968), pp. 510-514.

12. A.J. Wiener and H. Kahn, *Crisis and Arms Control* (Harmon-on-Hudson, New York: Hudson Institute, 1962).

13. Jean Lipman-Blumen, "A Crisis Framework Applied to Macrosociological Family Changes: Marriage, Divorce, and Occupational Trends Associated with World War II," *Journal of Marriage and the Family* 37, 4 (November 1975): 889-902.

14. Lipman-Blumen, "A Crisis Framework," p. 890.

15. Robert H. Neuhaus and Ruby Hart Neuhaus, *Family Crises* (Columbus, Ohio: Merrill Publishing Co., 1974).

16. Richard Lazarus, *Psychological Stress and the Coping Process* (New York: McGraw-Hill Book Co., 1966).

17. Joseph S. Roucek and Roland L. Warren, *Sociology: An Introduction* (Paterson, New Jersey: Littlefield, Adams & Co., 1951, 1957), p. 280.

18. Henry Pratt Fairchild (ed.), *Dictionary of Sociology* (Ames, Iowa: Littlefield, Adams & Co., 1955), p. 78.

19. John T. Zadrozny, *Dictionary of Social Science* (Washington: Public Affairs Press, 1959), p. 74.

20. Irving L. Janis, *Psychological Stress: Psychoanalytic and Behavioral Studies of Surgical Patients* (New York: John Wiley & Sons, Inc., 1958).

21. Reubin Hill, "Generic Features of Families Under Stress," in Howard Parad (ed.), *Crisis Intervention: Selected Readings* (New York: Family Service Association of America, 1965), p. 34.

22. Erik H. Erikson, *Identity, Youth and Crisis* (New York: W.W. Norton, 1968).
23. Edwin Schneidman, "Crisis Intervention: Some Thoughts and Perspectives," in Gerald A. Specter and William L. Claiborn (eds.), *Crisis Intervention*, Vol. 2 (New York: Behavioral Publications, 1973), pp. 9-16.
24. Julian R. Taplin, "Crisis Theory: Critique and Reformulation," *Community Mental Health Journal* 7, 1 (1971): 13-23.
25. Kurt Lang and Gladys Engel Lang, "Collective Responses to the Threat of Disaster," in Grosser et al., *Threat of Impending Disaster*, pp. 58-76.
26. Barton, *Communities in Disaster*.
27. Judith Lang, "Planned Short-Term Treatment in a Family Agency," *Social Casework* 55, 6 (June 1974): 369-374.
28. Howard Halpern, "Crisis Theory: A Definitional Study," *Community Mental Health Journal* 9, 4 (1973): 342-349.
29. Howard J. Parad and Gerald Caplan, "A Framework for Studying Families in Crisis," in Parad (ed.), *Crisis Intervention*, pp. 53-74.
30. Hill, *Families Under Stress*, p. 10.
31. Lipman-Blumen, "A Crisis Framework," p. 890.
32. James P. Spradley and Mark Phillips, "Culture and Stress: A Quantitative Analysis," *American Anthropologist* 74, 3 (June 1972): 518-529.
33. Hill, *Families Under Stress*, pp. 313-314.
34. *Ibid.*, p. 10.
35. Ernest W. Burgess, "The Family and Sociological Research," *Social Forces* 14 (October 1937): 1-6.
36. Talcott Parsons and Neil J. Smelser, *Economy and Society* (New York: The Free Press, 1956, 1965), p. 16ff.
37. Hill, "Generic Features of Families Under Stress," p. 34.
38. *Ibid.*, pp. 41-42.
39. Talcott Parsons, *The Social System* (Glencoe: The Free Press, 1951, 1964), p. 60.
40. Hill, "Generic Features of Families Under Stress"; Robert C. Angell, *The Family Encounters the Depression* (New York: Chas. Scribner's Sons, 1936).
41. Donald Hiroto and Martin Seligman, "Generality of Learned Helplessness in Man," *Journal of Personality and Social Psychology* 31, 2 (1975): 311-327.
42. Ruth A. Brandwein, Carol A. Brown, Elizabeth Maury Fox, "Women and Children Last: The Social Situation of Divorced Mothers and their Families," *Journal of Marriage and the Family* 36 (August 1974): 489-514.
43. Betty E. Cogswell and Marvin B. Sussman, "Changing Family and Marriage Forms: Complications for Human Service Systems," in Marvin B. Sussman (ed.), *Non-Traditional Family Forms in the 1970's* (Minneapolis: National Council on Family Relations, 1972), p. 141.
44. W.I. Thomas, *The Unadjusted Girl* (Boston: Little, Brown and Co., 1923), p. 42.
45. Earl Lomon Koos, *Families in Trouble* (New York: King's Crown Press, 1946).
46. Hill, "Generic Features of Families Under Stress."
47. Lazarus, *Psychological Stress*.

48. Taplin, "Crisis Theory," p. 17.
49. Hill, "Generic Features of Families Under Stress," p. 43.
50. *Ibid.*
51. Parsons, *The Social System*, p. 7.
52. Peter Wright, "The Harassed Decision Maker: Time Pressures, Distractions, and the Use of Evidence," *Journal of Applied Psychology* 59, 5 (October 1974): 555-561.
53. Beverly Olson and J.E. Lubach, "Innovation in the Nursing Role in a Psychiatric Program," *American Journal of Nursing* 66 (1966): 314-318. Cited in Taplin, "Crisis Theory."
54. Kurt Lewin, *Field Theory in Social Science: Selected Theoretical Papers* (New York: Harper & Brothers, 1951), p. 231.
55. *Ibid.*, Chapter 9.
56. Lydia Rapoport, "The State of Crisis: Some Theoretical Considerations," in Parad, *Crisis Intervention, op. cit.*, p. 29.
57. James G. Miller, "A Theoretical Review of Individual and Group Psychological Reactions to Stress," in Grosser et al., *Threat of Impending Disaster*, pp. 11-33.
58. Ruth Cavan and Katherine Ranck, *The Family and the Depression* (Chicago: University of Chicago Press, 1938).
59. *New York Times*, April 22, 1976, p. 4.
60. Hiroto and Seligman, "Generality of Learned Helplessness."
61. Hill, *Families Under Stress*, pp. 15-16.
62. Lipman-Blumen, "A Crisis Framework," p. 891.

NOTES TO CHAPTER THREE
THE ENERGY CRISIS UNFOLDS IN HARTFORD, MOBILE, AND SALEM

1. John F. Early, "Effect of the Energy Crisis on Employment," *Monthly Labor Review*, August 1974, pp. 8-16.
2. *Time*, "The Icy Grip Tightens," February 14, 1977.

NOTES TO CHAPTER FOUR
1,440 FAMILIES REACT

1. Gordon E. Moss, *Illness, Immunity and Social Interaction: The Dynamics of Biosocial Resonation* (New York: John Wiley & Sons, 1973).
2. These have recently been summarized in a composite report, Olsen and Goodnight, *Social Aspects of Energy Conservation*.
3. In this chapter we have drawn on the following sources: James R. Murray, Michael J. Minor, Robert F. Cotterman, and Norman M. Bradburn, "The Impact of the 1973-1974 Oil Embargo on The American Household," National Opinion Research Center, University of Chicago, December 1974 (NORC); Donald L.

Warren and David L. Clifford, "Local Neighborhood Social Structure and Responses to the Energy Crisis of 1973-1974," University of Michigan, January 2, 1975; *Gallup Poll Index*, 1974. (No. 103); *Harper's and The Atlantic*, "The State of the Nation," April 1974; David Gottlieb and Marc Matre, "Conceptions of Energy Shortages and Energy Conserving Behavior," unpublished paper, American Sociological Association, August 1975; William P. Kuvlesky, "Youths' Perceptions of Impacts of the Energy Crisis on Family Life: Ethnic Differences among Teen-Agers in Galveston, Texas," Prairie View A&M University, September 25, 1975; Ted Bartell, "The Effects of the Energy Crisis on Attitudes and Life Styles of Los Angeles Residents," University of California, Los Angeles, American Sociological Association, August 1974; Decision Research Corporation poll conducted for and published by *The Boston Globe*, December 9, 1973; Louis Harris and Associates, Inc., and the Center for the Study of Man in Contemporary Society, University of Notre Dame, "Gasoline Shortage and the Public Response," March 27, 1974. This study was proposed by the University of Notre Dame and sponsored as a public service by Shell Oil Company.

4. The Massachusetts poll conducted by Decision Research Corporation, reported 26% felt there was a real energy crisis; the Warren and Clifford survey in the Detroit area reported 21% believers, and Gottleib and Matre reported 28% in Texas.

However, in their summary of similar studies, Olsen and Goodnight state "roughly half the people in the United States appear to believe that this country faces a serious long-term energy problem (this figure has ranged between 38% and 64% in various studies)." They go on to identify four approximately equal groups in the U.S. population: (1) those who view the energy situation as an immediate and long-term problem; (2) those who do not consider it a problem now but expect it to become a serious crisis within the next 25 years; (3) those who reject the idea that energy availability is now or ever will be a problem for this country; and (4) those who do not think there is an energy crisis but have no precise opinion on the issue. Olsen and Goodnight, *Social Aspects*, pp. 7-8.

5. *New York Times*, December 23, 1973.
6. Gottlieb and Matre, "Concepts of Energy Shortages."
7. Bartell, "Effects of the Energy Crisis."
8. *Gallup Opinion Index*, February 1974.
9. Warren and Clifford, "Local Neighborhood Social Structure."
10. *Ibid*. Warren and Clifford also reported from Detroit that "the extent to which people believed the energy crisis was real had little effect on how much they conserved."
11. NORC.
12. Bartell, "Effects of the Energy Crisis."
13. Bonnie Maas Morrison and Peter Michael Gladhart, "Energy and Families: The Crisis and the Response," *Journal of Home Economics*, January 1976, pp. 15-18.
14. Robert Blood and Donald Wolfe, *Husbands and Wives* (Free Press, New York, 1960), p. 21.
15. Reuben Hill and David Klein, "Family Decision Making and Economic Behavior," in Eleanor Bernert Sheldon (ed.), *Family Economic Behavior* (Philadelphia: J.B. Lippincott Company, 1973). p. 27.

NOTES TO CHAPTER FIVE
FAMILY ADJUSTMENTS

1. Agnes M. Hooley, "A Survey: The Energy 'Crunch' and its Effect on People," The Anderson Center for Personal Development, Bowling Green State University, Bowling Green, Ohio, May 1974.

2. James R. Murray et al., "The Impact of the 1973-74 Oil Embargo on the American Household," *National Opinion Research Center*, University of Chicago, December 1974 (NORC), p. 38, state that 45 percent had cut back on this kind of driving.

3. The same finding was made in *Harper's and the Atlantic*, "The State of the Nation," April 1974, p. 33, where it was reported that 36 percent of their respondents had altered their vacation plans because of the energy problem.

4. NORC, pp. 148-152.

5. The comparable figure reported in the NORC surveys was 66 percent. NORC, p. 54.

6. Donald L. Warren and David L. Clifford, "Local Neighborhood Social Structure and Responses to the Energy Crisis of 1973-74," University of Michigan, January 2, 1975, p. 5, report that 9 percent of their sample in and around Detroit said they had installed more home insulation. NORC found that 5 percent of homeowners changed their heating equipment.

7. NORC reported that 84 percent of the households said they had been trying to cut back on the use of electricity, NORC, p. 62. Gallup found that 62 percent said they were using less electricity, (The Gallup Opinion Index, No. 103, January 1974).

8. NORC reported 64 percent, p. 38.

9. Survey Research Center, University of Michigan, "Panel Study of Income Dynamics," *ISR Newsletter*, Winter 1975, p. 3.

10. The findings from this study conform in general to the summary of parallel studies written by Olsen and Goodnight, who comment: "During periods of immediate crisis—such as the 1973-74 petroleum embargo—most people will attempt to conserve energy in small ways. At that time, at least three-quarters of the public apparently reduced their levels of home lighting and heating somewhat.... About two-thirds of the population also reported that they drove less (amount not specified) for recreation and shopping.... In general, these conservation actions required minimal effort and expense, and did not significantly alter people's usual lifestyle." Marvin E. Olsen and Jill A. Goodnight, *Social Aspects of Energy Conservation*, (Portland, Oregon: Pacific Northwest Regional Commission, Northwest Energy Policy Project, 1977), p. 9.

NOTES TO CHAPTER SIX
ATTRITION, REPERCUSSIONS, AND ENERGY CONSERVATION

1. James R. Murray et al., "The Impact of the 1973-74 Oil Embargo on The American Household," *National Opinion Research Center*, University of Chicago, December 1974 (NORC), p. 290.

2. A national survey conducted in the summer of 1975 by Response Analysis showed that 40 percent of adults questioned said their "household was using less electricity than a year ago; only 11 percent said they were using more." The most often mentioned method was turning off lights, which is not likely to have much effect on total consumption. However, significant numbers of consumers were reducing their use of television and air conditioning, which can affect demand for electricity. *The Sampler*, Response Analysis, Princeton, N.J., Winter 1976.

3. *Energy Reporter*, December 1975.

4. Marvin E. Olsen and Jill A. Goodnight, *Social Aspects of Energy Conservation* (Portland, Oregon: Pacific Northwest Regional Commission, Northwest Energy Policy Project, 1977), p. 9, report that data collected after the immediate crisis of 1973-74 indicated that the "conservation practices are still being done, but by a smaller proportion of the population."

5. John J. Donovan and Walter P. Fischer, "Factors Affecting Residential Heating Energy Consumption," Technical Report, MIT-NEEMIS-76-002 TR, July 16, 1976.

NOTES TO CHAPTER SEVEN
DIFFERENT FAMILIES, DIFFERENT BURDENS

1. Dorothy K. Newman and Dawn Day, *The American Energy Consumer: A Report to the Energy Policy Project of the Ford Foundation* (Cambridge, Mass.: Ballinger Publishing Company, 1975), pp. xxiii-xxiv.

2. James R. Murray et al., "The Impact of the 1973-74 Oil Embargo on The American Household," *National Opinion Research Center*, University of Chicago, December 1974 (NORC), p. 84.

3. See Robert Perlman, "Vacations—for Whom?" *Social Policy*, July-August 1973, pp. 50-55.

4. Donald L. Warren and David L. Clifford, "Local Neighborhood Social Structure and Responses to the Energy Crisis of 1973-74," University of Michigan, January 2, 1975, p. 6, found the same for car pooling.

5. NORC, p. 86.

6. Mary D. Stearns, *The Social Impacts of the Energy Shortage: Behavioral and Attitude Shifts*, prepared for the U.S. Department of Transportation, September 1975, pp. 1-5.

7. Eight percent of the households did not have anyone who had driven a car for every day use for a year preceding the interviews. This rather stringent definition meant that the proportion of carless households was smaller than other studies indicate. The percentage was 11 percent in Mobile, 8 percent in Salem, and 5 percent in Hartford. Newman's study reported 15 percent of the households without a car. Census data put the figure at 17 percent (*U.S. Statistical Abstract 1973*, p. xix) and *Auto-Facts and Figures* (January 1973) set the number at 21 percent.

8. The National Opinion Research Center reported with respect to car usage "very weak indications of a positive association of conservation behavior with income" and "unsystematic shifts by income class, with the bulk of reductions in car use occurring in the lower to middle income groups." NORC, p. 80.

9. NORC, p. 109.

10. Above $6,000 about 85 percent of the households cut back on electricity and below that income it was 80 percent for the most part. (NORC, p. 112.) In Detroit "reports of turning off lights increased from 79 percent for persons with incomes under $5,000 to 93 percent for those with family incomes of $25,000 or more." (Warren and Clifford, "Local Neighborhood Social Structure," p. 6.)

11. Marvin E. Olsen and Jill A. Goodnight, *Social Aspects of Energy Conservation* (Portland, Oregon: Pacific Northwest Regional Commission, Northwest Energy Policy Project, 1977), p. 9.

12. Warren and Clifford, "Local Neighborhood Social Structure," p. 6.

13. Stearns, *Social Impacts of the Energy Shortage*, p. 3-2.

14. Dorothy K. Newman, *Let Them Freeze in the Dark*, report prepared for the Office of Economic Opportunity, February 1974, Table 1.

15. For a thorough discussion of the income-related differences in energy consumption, see Newman and Day, *The American Energy Consumer*, Chapter 5, "The Energy Gap—Poor to Well Off."

16. See Foster Associates, *Energy Prices 1960-73*, A Report to the Energy Policy Project of the Ford Foundation (Cambridge, Mass.: Ballinger Publishing Company, 1974).

17. Newman and Day, *The American Energy Consumer*, pp. 112-113.

18. *New York Times*, January 15, 1975, p. 1.

19. Dorothy K. Newman, *Let Them Freeze in the Dark*, p. 7.

20. Technical Analysis Paper No. 3, *The Impact of Rising Residential Energy Prices on the Low Income Population*, Office of Income Security Policy, Office of the Assistant Secretary of Planning & Evaluation, Department of Health, Education, and Welfare, March 1975.

21. "A Study of the Effects of Rising Energy Prices on the Low and Moderate Income Elderly," prepared for the Federal Energy Administration, March 1975, pp. 4.2-4.5.

22. "The Impact of Rising Energy Costs on Older Americans," Hearings before the Special Committee on Aging, U.S. Senate, Ninety-Third Congress, Second Session, Sept. 24-25, 1974 and Nov. 7, 1975. The excerpts are from the November 1975 report, pp. 1-6.

23. Vernon E. Jordan, Jr., "The Energy Crisis for Blacks, A Disproportionate Burden," *New York Times*, Op-Ed Page, February 9, 1974.

24. Newman and Day, *The American Energy Consumer*, p. 171.

25. *Ibid.*, p. 184.

26. William P. Kuvlesky, "Youths' Perceptions of Impacts of the Energy Crisis on Family Life: Ethnic Differences among Teen-agers in Galveston, Texas," Rural Sociology Department of the Texas Agricultural Experiment Station at Texas A&M Univ. and the College of Agriculture of Prairie View A&M University, September 1975.

27. T.P. Schwartz and Donna Schwartz-Barcott, "The Short End of the Shortage: On the Self-Reported Impact of the Energy Shortage on the Socially Disadvantaged," University of Delaware, 1974, pp. 12-15.

28. *Ibid.*, pp. 14-15.

29. See Robert Cochran, "The Great Energy Crisis of 1973-74: The Response

of OEO and Community Action," prepared for the Office of Economic Opportunity, undated.

30. Newman and Day, *The American Energy Consumer*, pp. 114-115.

31. In their summary, Olsen and Goodnight observe that "as a general principle, the higher one's socioeconomic status the more likely one is to adopt energy conserving practices and to support energy policies." This tendency, they indicate, "does not appear to differ between men and women, generally decreases with age, and may be slightly more prevalent among whites than blacks." Olsen and Goodnight, *Social Aspects of Energy Conservation*, pp. 11-12.

32. Newman and Day, *The American Energy Consumer*, p. 121.

33. James N. Morgan, "Gasoline Price Inflation: Its Impact on Families of Different Income Levels," *Economic Outlook USA*, Survey Research Center, Spring 1974, p. 8.

34. The Survey Research Center's Panel Study of Income Dynamics at the Univ. of Michigan found that "one-fourth of the car owners in the lowest income decile spent over one-fifth of their total income on gasoline." *IRS Newsletter*, Winter 1975, p. 3.

35. Stearns, *Social Impacts of the Energy Shortage*, pp. 3-5.

NOTES TO CHAPTER EIGHT
THREE YEARS LATER—CRISIS II

1. The 1977 study used several questions as originally worded in the 1977 Gallup polls in order to compare responses. These and other surveys referred to in this chapter are: *The Public's Behavior and Attitudes During the February 1977 Energy Crisis* (Princeton, N.J.: The Gallup Organization, Inc., Conducted for the Federal Energy Administration, February 1977 and March 1977); Gallup Poll of April 1977 cited in the *Boston Sunday Globe*, April 17, 1977; Gallup Poll of July 1977, cited in *The New York Times*, August 13, 1977; Louis Harris, *Americans Concerned About Energy*, February 14, 1977; Kenneth Schwartz, *The Public Opinion Challenge to American Business* (Princeton, N.J.: Opinion Research Council, ORC Public Opinion Index, June 1977).

2. The Gallup February 1977 survey found that 51 percent of their respondents' thermostats were set at 65° or higher *during the day* while 49 percent set theirs at 65° or less; 60 percent of the Gallup group reported that their settings were lower than the year before. The average setting nationwide in the March 1977 Gallup survey was 66°.

3. This was a higher proportion than the 41 percent of the respondents in a Gallup survey in March 1977 who said they had done something since Thanksgiving to reduce gasoline consumption.

4. We found 34 percent in agreement with extra taxes on big cars; the March 1977 Gallup survey found 37 percent.

5. A Harris poll in February 1977 noted that 70 percent think that a 25 cent a gallon rise in the price of gasoline would be effective. Only 51 percent believed that a 10 cent rise would be effective, and 44 percent felt it would not curb gasoline consumption.

234 Families in the Energy Crisis

6. A greater proportion (88 percent) indicated disapproval with these measures in the March 1977 Gallup survey. The opposition numbered 71 percent in the ORC June 1977 study.

7. The comparable figure in the March 1977 Gallup survey was 55 percent. In the ORC poll it was 41 percent who opposed the gas-guzzler tax.

8. The Gallup survey in February 1977 reported a nearly identical figure of 68 percent who disapproved of the idea of unlimited energy use.

9. The ORC survey in April 1977 found that 40 percent of their respondents reacted favorably to the Carter proposals, 41 percent "half and half," and 15 percent unfavorably.

10. The Gallup survey in February 1977 found 50 percent who favored government assistance for installation of extra insulation or storm windows. By March 1977 the Gallup figure climbed to 59 percent who favored incentives for insulating homes. The April 1977 ORC study found that 83 percent approved the use of incentives to encourage more insulation of homes.

11. In our study, 14 percent favored taxes to discourage consumption; the February 1977 Gallup survey reported 18 percent.

12. In March 1977, the Gallup organization reported nearly identical data; 45 percent agree and 42 percent disagree with the oil companies' rights to drill off shore.

13. The February 1977 Gallup poll showed that 59 percent believed the fuel shortage was real. The Harris poll for the same month showed that 82 percent felt that the energy situation was serious. In March, the figure from Gallup was 46 percent who believed the shortage was real. The *Boston Globe* reported an April Gallup survey that found 45 percent who believed that the energy situation was "very serious" and 51 percent who believed it only "fairly" serious or "not serious" at all. As the winter of Crisis II faded, more attrition in these attitudes was evident. *The New York Times* cited a July 1977 Gallup study that pointed to only 15 percent of the sample who thought that the energy crisis was the "most important problem facing the nation."

14. David Montgomery and Dorothy Leonard-Barton, *Toward Strategies for Marketing Home Energy Conservation*, Research Paper No. 372, Stanford University, Graduate School of Business, July 1977, p. 9.

NOTES TO CHAPTER NINE
ENERGY CONSERVATION AND PUBLIC POLICY

1. Executive Office of the President, *The National Energy Plan*, April 29, 1977, p. vii.

2. Marvin E. Olsen and Jill A. Goodnight, *Social Aspects of Energy Conservation* (Portland, Oregon: Pacific Northwest Regional Commission, Northwest Energy Policy Project, 1977), p. 28.

3. In this connection it is interesting to note that an experiment in feeding back to homeowners information on their consumption of electricity produced noticeable savings. The researchers report that "giving homeowners daily feedback on their rate of electricity usage reduced their consumption about 10.5%. Interviews revealed that homeowners had, indeed, used feedback infor-

mation to modify energy usage, largely by being more systematic about thermostat control of their air conditioners." Clive Seligman, John M. Darley, and Lawrence J. Becker, "Psychological Strategies to Reduce Energy Consumption: First Annual Progress Report," Princeton University, The Center for Environmental Studies, November 1976.

4. Six serious limitations of pricing as a regulatory strategy are discussed in Olsen and Goodnight, *Social Aspects of Energy Conservation*, pp. 45-61.

5. FEA *Energy Reporter*, March 1975.

6. M. Janice Hogan, "Energy Conservation: Family Values, Household Practices, and Contextual Variables," Ph.D. dissertation, East Lansing, Michigan State University, 1976. Cited in Bonnie Maas Morrison and Peter Michael Gladhart, "Energy and Families: The Crisis and the Response," *Journal of Home Economics*, January 1976, p. 17.

7. Dorothy K. Newman and Dawn Day, *The American Energy Consumer: A Report to the Energy Policy Project of the Ford Foundation* (Cambridge, Mass.: Ballinger Publishing Company, 1975), Chapter 5, especially pages 87, 88, 107, 121.

8. See, for example, Newman and Day, *The American Energy Consumer*, p. 179.

9. Newman and Day, *The American Energy Consumer*, p. 107.

10. A nonfarm family of four would be at the poverty level if its income was $5,038 or less in 1974. (*Statistical Abstract of the United States 1975*, p. 399.) An urban family of four in 1973 would need $8,181 to live at the lowest of three standards of living, though above the subsistence level. (*Monthly Labor Review*, August 1974.)

NOTES TO CHAPTER TEN
FOCUS ON FAMILIES

1. Actually the energy crisis of 1973-74 stimulated a number of studies focused on the family. These have been referred to throughout this book and are brought together in summary form in Marvin E. Olsen and Jill A. Goodnight, *Social Aspects of Energy Conservation* (Portland, Oregon: Pacific Northwest Regional Commission, Northwest Energy Policy Project, 1977).

2. Sheila Kamerman and Alfred J. Kahn, "Explorations in Family Policy," *Social Work*, May 1976, and Janet Z. Giele, "Family Policy," in J.Z. Giele, *Women and the Future* (New York: Free Press, forthcoming).

3. Talcott Parsons and Neil J. Smelser, *Economy and Society: A Study in the Integration of Economic and Social Theory* (New York: The Free Press, 1956, 1965). It is significant that in this work which examines the interchange between the economy and other parts of the society, neither "family" nor "household" appears in the index as a key term of reference. Nevertheless, the household is brought into the analysis, specifically in terms of its consumption and labor market behavior. See pp. 68, 71, 119, and 160.

4. The definitive Marxian treatment of the impact of the organization of production on family forms is in Frederick Engels, *The Origin of the Family*,

Private Property and the State (New York: International Publishers, 1942). The work originally appeared in 1884.

5. Manuel Castells, *La question urbaine* (Paris, Francois Maspero 1973), p. 442.

6. Margaret Mead, *Sex and Temperament in Three Primitive Societies* (New York: Dell Publishing Company, 1967); Ruth Benedict, "Continuities and Discontinuities in Cultural Conditioning," *Psychiatry*, May 1938; Mirra Komarovsky, "Cultural Contradictions and Sex Roles," *American Sociological Review*, October 1942.

7. See, for example, *Toward a National Policy for Children and Families* (Washington, D.C.: National Academy of Sciences, 1976), and *American Families: Trends and Pressures 1973*, Hearings before the Sub-Committee on Children and Youth of the Committee on Labor and Public Welfare, United States Senate, September 24-26, 1973.

About the Authors

Robert Perlman is a teacher and researcher in social welfare and social policy, with a primary interest in the relationships between public policies and American families. He is the author of *Consumers and Social Services* and co-author of *Community Organization and Social Planning*. For 15 years he was a practitioner and planner in social service and community development agencies. He is Professor of Social Welfare at the Heller School of Brandeis University.

Roland L. Warren is Professor of Community Theory at The Florence Heller Graduate School for Advanced Studies in Social Welfare, Brandeis University. He is a widely known authority in the field of community, and the author of *Studying Your Community*, *The Community in America*, *Truth, Love, and Social Change*, *The Structure of Urban Reform* (with Stephen M. Rose and Ann F. Burgunder) and *Social Change and Human Purpose*, and articles in numerous professional journals. Dr. Warren is the past chairman of the Committee on Community Research and Development of the Society for the Study of Social Problems, and past chairman (1972-74) of the Community Section of the American Sociological Association. He is a former Guggenheim Fellow and the recipient of a research scientist award from the National Institute of Mental Health.